CLARA COLLET 1860–1948
An Educated Working Woman

CLARA COLLET
1860–1948
An Educated Working Woman

Deborah McDonald

WOBURN PRESS
LONDON • PORTLAND, OR

First published in 2004 in Great Britain by
WOBURN PRESS
Chase House, 47 Chase Side, Southgate
London N14 5BP

and in the United States of America by
WOBURN PRESS
c/o ISBS Inc, 920 NE 58th Avenue, #300
Portland, Oregon 97213-3786

Website: www.woburnpress.com

British Library Cataloguing in Publication Data

McDonald, Deborah
   Clara Collet 1860–1984: an educated working woman
   1. Collet, Clara 2. Women social reformers – England Biography 3. Social
   reformers – England – Biography 4. Women in the civil service – England –
   Biography 5. Civil service – England – Biography
   I. Title
   303.4′84′092

                    ISBN 0-7130-0241-7 (cloth)
                         0-7130-4060-2 (paper)
                         ISSN 1462-2076

Library of Congress Cataloging-in-Publication Data

McDonald, Deborah, 1952
   Clara Collet 1860–1984: an educated working woman / Deborah McDonald.
      p. cm
   ISBN 0-7130-0241-7 (cloth) – ISBN 0-7130-4060-2 (paper)
    1. Collet, Clara E. (Clara Elizabeth), 1860–1948. 2. Women social reformers –
   Great Britain – Biography. 3. Women – Employment – Great Britain – History.
   4. Women – Education – Great Britain – History. 5. Women – Great Britain –
   Social conditions. 6. Great Britain – History – Victoria, 1837–1901. 7. Great
   Britain – History – Edward VII, 1901–1910. I. Title.

   HQ1595.C65M33 2003
   305.4′092–dc21
   [B]

                                                          2003056397

Typeset in 11/12.5pt Palatino by FiSH Books, London
Printed in Great Britain by MPG Books Ltd, Victoria Square, Bodmin, Cornwall

Contents

List of Illustrations

Foreword

By any definition Clara Collet was a feminist – yet I doubt she would have accepted the description. Throughout the latter part of the nineteenth century and the early twentieth, she advocated for the rights of women. Her own life was a powerful example. But she was not a political activist in the classic sense. Her contribution to the advancement of women was rooted in an unusual discipline – statistics.

Clare Collet's ability to earn a living and live an independent life stemmed from her education. Her Unitarian father was Director of Music at the South Place Chapel – a meeting place for radical thinkers. Annie Besant, William Morris, George Bernard Shaw and Sidney Webb debated there. Mr Collet also edited a foreign policy review and Karl Marx's contribution to this paper led to an important friendship between Clara Collet and Eleanor Marx.

Thus Clara grew up in an environment of intellectual discipline in which people were encouraged to think for themselves and question conventions. At the age of twelve she was sent to the North London Collegiate School, a new and radical institution for the education of young women.

Clara Collet was strongly influenced by her women teachers. According to Clara, the Headmistress Miss Buss gave them 'unrivalled opportunities of seeing and listening to every man and woman who was doing anything for the advancement of women's education'. One significant advance was the admission of women to London University in 1878. It was perfect timing for Clara. With help from Miss Buss she was able to secure a teaching post in Leicester, a salary and permission to study for a BA degree. Clara was not yet eighteen but she made the transition to a new city and (without training) to a full-time job as a teacher.

Clara obtained her BA in 1850 and went on to gain the newly instituted London University's teacher's diploma. But despite her success she tired of teaching. Her detailed diary from this period records her need to be admired, periods of self doubt and an interest in men. At a time when marriages of convenience were common, Clara was determined to marry only for love and probably only then, if she could have a career as well. After seven years in Leicester she had decided against marriage for financial security, and teaching as a career. She gambled on seeking a new career in London and taking a master's degree.

Clara's retum coincided with shocking revelations of conditions in the East End of London. She joined the Charity Organisation Society. Her philanthropic work with the COS set the pattem for her subsequent career as a leading economist and statistician of women's employment. Within a year she became the first woman to gain an MA in political economy. She joined innumerable societies which brought her to the attention of many of the eminent men of her generation. In 1888 Charles Booth asked her to join his team of investigators into poverty in the East End. She went to live there for three months, documenting the working conditions of women. Her experiences led her to support trade union membership and advocate a minimum wage – both ground-breaking concepts in the late nineteenth century.

Clara's gamble paid off. In 1892 she was employed as an Assistant Commissioner compiling evidence for the Royal Commission of Labour on the Employment of Women. This led directly to her appointment as a Labour Correspondent in the newly created Labour Department of the Board of Trade. Clara thus became the first woman to hold a significant post. in the civil service.

Clara Collet was now confident and financially secure with a large circle of friends and varied interests. The latter led her to the novels of George Gissing, who became the most important person in her life. It is likely she may have hoped for romance, but he was married and when he did become free he fell in love with someone else. Nonetheless Clara devoted herself to him and his work, undertook responsibility for his two children after his death and maintained a life-long friendship with the woman he loved.

Her career in the civil service went from strength to strength. She employed bright women and was at pains to ensure that women's interests were always on the agenda. She must have been a considerable influence for change, working with Churchill, Ramsey MacDonald and William Beveridge.

Clara Collet left a diary and letters that she knew would be read, but destroyed much that might have given us a further insight into her feelings. This well-researched book is based on her own records and other primary sources written by fnends and colleagues. Many important papers have been discovered by the author and are now indexed into the extensive bibliography and available for students of the history of this period.

Joan Ruddock MP
House of Commmons
September 2003

Acknowledgements

I would like to thank everyone who helped to make this book possible. Firstly the teaching staff at the Charles Booth Centre, Milton Keynes, for introducing me to Clara Collet and her contribution to the work of Booth.

Staff at the various libraries where I carried out my research have also been very helpful. I would like especially to thank all the librarians at my local library at Beckenham, Kent for willingly obtaining obscure interlibrary loans. Also to staff at Toynbee Hall library; staff at the University of Warwick, Modern Records Centre; staff at University College, London, Manuscripts and Rare Books section; staff at the University of London Library, Senate House; the Marshall Library of Economics, University of Cambridge; and the Archivist at the Royal Holloway Library (now housing the Bedford College archives); library staff at the North London Collegiate School; staff at Regent College (formerly Wyggeston Girls' School); archival staff at the London School of Economics; and finally the Local Studies Librarian, Leicestershire Record Office.

I wish especially to thank Professor Pierre Coustillas and his wife Hélène for all their help in providing information, support and for spending hours of their precious time in helping with the early stages of editing. They may not always have agreed with my conclusions but have nonetheless encouraged me in my work.

Other academics who have helped me in this venture include Professor Peter Morton for adding a note about my work on his Gissing website, and Professor Jacob Korg who took the trouble to read the manuscript and write some cover blurb. On my travels to Sidmouth, I received help from the Sidmouth District council (John was especially helpful) in helping to locate Clara's final home; and for information from Potburys Undertakers.

From my request letter for information on Clara, written some years ago now, for the *Sidmouth Herald*, I would like to thank Connie Barrett and Gerald Counter who knew Clara during her last years in Sidmouth, and who took the trouble to contact me with their personal recollections.

David Doughan MBE, formerly of the Women's Library, London Guildhall University, I would like to thank for not only reading the manuscript and agreeing to write cover blurb, but also for suggesting I contact Frank Cass Publishers.

I must also thank Dr Clive Hill with whom I collaborated over the bibliography and Mary Greensted (née Comino), Keeper of Visitor Services, Cheltenham Art Gallery and Museum, for providing me with a letter written by Ernest Gimson and for supplying other information about him.

More than anyone else I must thank my husband David McDonald. I know every author adds their spouse in the acknow-ledgements, but in his case, he not only provided a chauffeur service around London and to Sidmouth, and accompanied me to the Gissing Conference in Amsterdam, he also helped me with my research. Thus his input was more than just tolerating my obsession, although he did that as well.

I hope not to have left out anyone pivotal to this book, although I fear I may have done so, as so many people were helpful. If that is the case may I add my thanks now? I must also add that despite all the wonderful help received, any errors are my own.

Finally, I must thank Clara Collet, who enthused me to write the story of her life. I hope I have done her justice and at last placed her amongst those inspirational women who have helped to change the course of history and that my work will encourage others both to use her own vast bibliography to study Victorian/Edwardian women's work and to write further versions of her life.

'But...', the girl hesitated... 'don't you approve of any one marrying?'

'Oh, I'm not so severe! But do you know that there are half a million more women than men in this happy country of ours?'

'Half a million!'

Her naive alarm again excited Rhoda to laughter.

'Something like that, they say. So many odd women – no making a pair with them. The pessimists call them useless, lost, futile lives. I naturally – being one of them myself – take another view. I look upon them as a great reserve. When one woman vanishes in matrimony, the reserve offers a substitute for the world's work. True, they are not all trained yet – far from it. I want to help in that – to train the reserve.'

The Odd Women, George Gissing (1893).

Are girls worth educating? Apparently not, as their parents do not think them worth paying for. The expectation that marriage will in a few years after the girl leaves school solve all difficulties and provide for her is at the root of all the confusion...If only the relatives of these girls could realise that at least one-half of them will never be married...that there is no means of predicting which of them will be married, and that any of them may have to support... them-selves all their lives.

'The Prospects of Marriage for Women', in
Educated Working Women, Clara E. Collet (1902).

Introduction

For any historian studying women's work and the 'sweated trades' during the late Victorian and early Edwardian era, Clara Collet's work provides much interesting and relevant background information.

Almost an exact contemporary of Beatrice Webb (née Potter), about whom an inordinate amount has been written, Clara's life has largely been ignored. Partly as a result of Beatrice's husband, the MP Sidney Webb, partly because of the publication of her voluminous diary, and partly as a result of the legacy of coming from a wealthy and famous family, Beatrice Webb became and has remained well-known.

Clara Collet's success was of her own making. She made no famous marriage; indeed she did not marry. She too wrote a diary, less detailed than Webb's, but fascinating nonetheless. It remains unpublished. She was born into a middle-class family with a comfortable but far from grand income. There was always an expectation that she would have to earn her own living, or marry, as her father was not able to provide financially for the future of his five children.

Yet Clara was no less a success as a social investigator and reformer than her more famous acquaintance. Her peers considered her work superior to Webb's as do present-day researchers. The influence she had on social and economic policy was as great if not greater than Beatrice Webb's. As a Civil Servant she was responsible for advising Cabinet Ministers on matters concerning women's work and in the process influenced them to introduce reforms for the benefit of women and the poor.

Her life was as interesting as Beatrice's, and although her diary is shorter and less complete than that of her acquaintance, it is as full of famous names and interesting anecdotes. No full-length biography of Clara has previously been attempted. This book aims to fill that gap.

Using her diary, her ten years' correspondence with the author George Gissing, his diary, the numerous published articles penned by her and the letters sent to her by other correspondents, it is possible to reconstruct the fascinating life of a middle class, working woman, reflecting on the problems women still had to overcome at the turn of the century and on the improvements already made.

Clara Collet's working life began in 1878 as a school mistress, the most common occupation for a single, educated woman in Victorian Britain, but she was not content with this profession. After completing seven years as a teacher, she left to take an MA degree at University College, London, one of the few universities to offer degrees to women at the time. On the successful completion of her studies, and after a period spent working for Charles Booth, collecting statistics for his project on the extent of poverty in London, Clara made a mid-career move and commenced work in the Civil Service. Despite this institution still being a bastion of male domination, within a few years she was promoted to Senior Investigator in the Labour Department and worked with Lloyd George, Winston Churchill, William Beveridge and James Ramsay MacDonald. Clara's area of expertise in the Board of Trade was all aspects of women's work, education and training. By the time she reached retirement age she was 'the principal authority on women's occupations'[1] in Britain, influencing policy and decision-making within parliament.

Acquaintances and friends outside her work included Karl Marx and Eleanor, his daughter, whom she had befriended during their childhood; Charles Booth with whom she had collaborated, collecting statistics for his great explorative work *The Life and Labour of the People of London*; Beatrice Webb during their mutual work with Booth and later sitting on various committees; and lastly, but most importantly, the man with whom she enjoyed the closest of friendships, the Victorian novelist George Gissing. After Gissing's early death she had a 'war of words' with H.G. Wells, fighting to uphold Gissing's reputation.

In England at the end of the nineteenth century there was a surplus of women over men. These 'Odd Women', to use the title Gissing gave to a novel he had written on the subject prior to meeting Clara, were generally not given much opportunity to develop their skills in order to become gainfully employed even in the few areas in which women were traditionally allowed to participate. The limitations that this imposed resulted in hardship and problems for the women involved. Clara broke with convention to make a career for herself in the traditionally male sphere of the Civil Service. She possessed a sharp intellect and a strong personality, and these attributes, along with the cultural changes taking place at the end of the nineteenth century allowed her to overcome many of the obstacles facing women at this time and achieve the position she did. Despite the demands of work she found the time and energy to pursue a varied and full social life, and participated actively in the numerous societies of which she was a member.

This is the story of Clara Collet, illuminating the changing times in which she lived, highlighting the 'Woman Question' and illustrating the situation faced by a middle-class woman worried about making a living, yet at the same time showing how a woman with courage and intelligence was able to succeed in the public sphere, hitherto rarely open to women.

NOTE

1.   A.L. Bowley, 'Obituary: Clara E. Collet (September 10, 1860–August 3, 1948)', *Economic Journal*, Vol. 60 (June 1950), p. 408.

Part I

Childhood 1860–78

1

Of Humble Origins

It was hardly into a life of poverty that Clara Collet was born on 10 September 1860, yet nor was it into a life of luxury. The family home was at Sunny Bank, Maryleville Road, Hornsey Lane, Islington; a road of mixed character with poor families living intermingled with more middle-class families like the Collet family. Women worked at the 'numerous laundries round about'[1] and Collet Dobson Collet, Clara's father, was considering purchasing a small laundry himself to supplement his income as a teacher of singing and editor of the non-profit-making journal, the *Free Press*. The neighbours were of widely differing occupations varying from labourers to stockbrokers, and from farm workers to bank clerks.[2] Despite the obvious poverty of some of the occupants, the road was in a pleasant elevated location with views overlooking the surrounding environs and, on a clear day, central London. Yet it was far enough away from the city to ensure the avoidance of the worst of the fogs, the stench of the sewage-filled Thames and the moral and physical dangers of the street people populating all but the better areas of the capital. It was close enough to enable easy access to the Crouch End railway station on the Great Northern Railway line which was less than five minutes walk away. The other advantage was that Hornsey Lane, being close to Highgate provided a useful source of middle- and upper-class clients able and willing to pay for Mr Collet's singing lessons.

Clara Elizabeth Collet was the fourth child to be born to the Collets; her siblings were Caroline Mary, known as Carrie, who was 5 years old; Wilfred aged 3, and little Harold who at 2 was himself still a toddler. When Clara was 2 years old the final member of the family, Edith Sophia, was born.

Collet Dobson Collet had started life as Collet Dobson but along with Sophia, one of his sisters, he decided to reclaim the old family name of Collet which had been lost due to matrilineal descent some generations earlier. Mr Collet was 'a musician of distinction' and 'an acknowledged authority on musical matters'.[3] In addition to teaching singing he was the choir director at Finsbury Chapel and later the musical director of the South Place

Chapel. Not only was the South Place Chapel a centre for nonconformist worship, it was also a meeting place for radical thinkers to share ideas and ideologies. Those who made contributions at debates held at the Chapel included Annie Besant, T.H. Huxley, William Morris, George Bernard Shaw, Bertrand Russell, Leslie Stephen, Graham Wallas, Sidney Webb, Rebecca West and later Mr Collet's daughter, Clara. George Gissing sometimes attended these debates.

Collet Dobson Collet had, four years before Clara's birth, taken over the editorship of the radical monthly journal known as the *Free Press*. This journal had originated several years earlier as the *Sheffield Free Press*, a mouthpiece for the views of David Urquhart, the founder of the Working Men's Foreign Affairs Committee. In 1856 the journal moved to London when Collet began his long association as editor and manager. He did not like the title so renamed the paper, *The Free Press: A Diplomatic Review*. The *Free Press* had been known as a journal without principles and with no predetermined views. In its new form its ideology was to remain the same and the editorial commented that,

> *The Free Press* then is the reverse of all other journals. It deals with each case on its own merits. It has neither opinions on 'politics' nor predilections for men. Its only maxim is that 'The State can be monitored only by the highest justice.' ... We have added to our title a second and an explanatory one. *Free Press* is not only unmeaning, but absurd...*Diplomatic Review* is a term which defines a large portion of our contents, without excluding the remainder.[4]

and so in 1866 the *Diplomatic Review* was born.

The journal was a repository for comment on foreign policy. Although designed originally to be read by working men to correspond with Mr Urquhart's ideology, it was actually subscribed to mainly by 'the diplomatic and political classes'. The circulation was small and it ran at a loss. Mr Collet can hardly have made much of a living from this area of work and from time to time had to invest money of his own into the journal to keep it running. He continued his singing lessons and did open the small laundry business, which he ran, with the help of his wife, Jane, to supplement their income. Laundries were rate-aided in order to make them inexpensive enough to enable the poor to be able to take advantage of their services. This subsidy was an attempt by the government to clean up London in order to reduce diseases such as cholera, the last serious outbreak of which had been in 1866–67 when Clara was aged 7.

By the time Mr Collet made the application for his daughter's secondary schooling in 1872, he stated that he was 'formerly' editor of the *Diplomatic Review*, yet his name continued to appear until 1877, after which time the journal ceased altogether. In 1876 the editorial column mentioned the paper's financial difficulties. One measure considered necessary was an increase in the price, although the promise was made that it would still be sold cheaply to working men belonging to committees. In addition the journal's offices had moved to cheaper premises. Clara wrote that her father 'resigned the salary of editorship, retaining the responsibilities',[5] so presumably he was trying to prevent the paper from folding by drawing no salary. He was to continue with his singing lessons and running the laundry for his future income.

The ancestral family had been wealthy. Clara Collet's interest in genealogy during her retirement years resulted in records being made and books written which documented the family history back to the sixteenth century.

The family background was one of unorthodox religion, merchant pursuits and adventurous characters. By the time Clara was born, the family, although of respectable middle-class origins, was by no means wealthy. Her father, with his radical Unitarian beliefs, was keen to provide an education for his daughters and there was an expectation that all the family would work for a living.

During his association with the *Diplomatic Review*, Mr Collet met many eminent people, who subsequently became known to his children. Frederic Le Play, the French political economist, John Stuart Mill and Karl Marx all contributed to the journal and it was as a result of this latter collaboration that the young Clara made her first close friend.

Karl Marx' youngest and favourite daughter, Eleanor, nicknamed Tussy (to rhyme with Pussy), was five years older than Clara. Both girls came from unorthodox family backgrounds. Marx had been living in virtual poverty whilst compiling his great works on communism and class. Had it not been for his friend Friedrich Engels' financial assistance he would certainly have become destitute. Engels had accumulated considerable wealth from his manufacturing pursuits in Manchester.

Tussy's early childhood was spent in two rooms in Dean Street, Soho shared with up to eight other family members. A description of the accommodation given by a visitor paints a very bleak picture, 'There is not one clean or decent piece of furniture in either room, but everything is tattered and torn, with thick dust over everything and the greatest untidiness everywhere.'⁶ It was under these conditions that Marx had to write, on the large table covered with his children's toys, sewing, old crockery, his own pipes, tobacco and ashtrays whilst sharing with seven other family members and the housekeeper who had been with the family for many years. It is a miracle that Marx managed to work at all and it must have required great determination. It is no wonder that from 1857, Marx chose to escape the chaos of home, to work at the newly constructed circular reading-room at the British Museum [Library] whenever he was able.

The Marx family had to endure these poor living conditions for eight years but Tussy was only born towards the end of this period. In 1855, the year of her birth, the family inherited some money from Mrs Marx' uncle in Germany and the following year from her mother also. This enabled the family to move to 9, Grafton Terrace, Kentish Town, a better area and more spacious accommodation. The family lived there for seven and a half years but the inheritance was soon spent and the family were once again living in poverty, albeit in several rooms rather than only two. Mrs Marx found the hardship difficult to withstand and she became frail and unwell. Marx spent his days immersed in work but the continued reliance on Engels for financial assistance was becoming an embarrassment. It is probable that Marx hid the requests for money from the children and especially from Eleanor, the youngest.

Mrs Marx was pleased when Tussy's elder sister, Laura, became engaged to Paul Lafargue. Lafargue's family was of the bourgeois class which Marx condemned, being owners of plantations and property in Santiago and Bordeaux, the proceeds of which were expected to pass to him. However, their son was interested in the new revolutionary politics which gave him something in common with his prospective father-in-law.

> [When] the daughter of an 'eminent and aristocratic family of their acquaintance', the Cunninghams, did Jenny and Laura the honour of inviting them to be the sole bridesmaids at her wedding, Mrs Marx was so overcome by this honour that it was all she could do to collect her wits and what little money that could be scraped together to buy the girls, 'bonnets, cloaks and heaven knows what else', for the occasion.⁷

Nothing was denied the girls despite their poverty. Mrs Marx did not try to shield her girls from the bourgeoisie so disliked by her husband.

In 1864 another double legacy came the way of the family saving them once again from their financial reliance upon Engels. This enabled the Marx family to move to 1, Modena Villas (renamed 1, Maitland Park Road in 1868), in Maitland Park, another improvement in both the size and location of their house. The family lived here for 11 years and it was here, when Tussy was 13 years old and Clara 8, that the two girls first met although the date of this meeting is uncertain. Clara later claimed that it was in the summer of 1869[8] that the meeting took place, but Eleanor spent from May to October of that year with Friedrich Engels in Manchester. She had been writing from memory in 1944 when recounting this occasion and may have been mistaken as to the exact date. It could have been early autumn as, 'At last, on 12 October (1869) Eleanor came back to London in time for a brief family reunion.'[9] It is unlikely to have been the previous year as Eleanor was ill with scarlet fever in June and left to convalesce in Ramsgate for most of August, although they may have met just before she left or after she returned. However, the following year seems more likely. Caroline and Wilfred had been sent to Calais to learn French in 1870 but they had been forced to return in July due to the civil war in France. Apart from a brief trip to Ramsgate in August, Eleanor was in London for most of the summer, in which case she would have been 14 and Clara 9 when they first met, and the year 1870.

Clara had not endured anything like the financial hardship of her friend during her childhood, but her family were not wealthy. Both she and Tussy had fathers who mixed with radicals. Their unorthodox connections set them apart from other more socially conventional families. The Collets' nonconformist faith and the Marx' foreignness further increased this gap between the two families and their contemporaries. It was their families' differences from others which drew the girls together.

Unlike Eleanor, who had a good relationship with her parents, at least during her childhood, Clara commented years later, 'I wonder if I should have been worse if I had been happy and understood when I was a child; probably not better.'[10] The girls were both highly intelligent and helped their fathers with their work. In the autumn of 1869 Eleanor first began to help Marx – helping him in clearing out his study. Throughout her life Eleanor supported both her father's work and ideals. In 1873–75 Clara earned her pocket money of 6d by helping her father, 'pasting or inserting into guard books and indexing the letters received by [him] in connection with the editorship of the monthly *Diplomatic*

Review'.[11] She did this work in her father's study, thus enabling father and daughter to spend time together as they worked.

With their families' unorthodox lifestyles the girls had much in common and few other friends. The friendship grew. On Clara's side there may have been an element of hero worship as Tussy was her senior. She was in awe of Eleanor's appearance and describes her at the time of their first meeting as wearing a 'frock of blue merino trimmed with white swan's down' and says that she 'won her heart'.[12] The occasion was a Shakespeare reading session at the Collet family home in Hornsey Lane, which involved her family, Mrs Marx, Eleanor, Laura and Jenny Marx, and an actress friend of the Collets named Theresa Furtado. Karl Marx was not present at this event. Whilst the older members of the entourage were engaged in the serious business of reading the play, Eleanor spent her time upstairs with the children, including Clara, and the friendship began. From Clara's description, the youngsters had no qualms about which rooms they used. They went up to the 'fair sized landing opening into surrounding rooms, into all of which we gave ourselves admission'.[13]

She may have been in awe of Tussy's beauty but Clara was not unattractive herself. She was petite, with dainty features with slightly hooded eyelids, full lips and a high forehead. In a photograph taken of her, aged 30, her hair was pulled severely back from her forehead and fixed at the neck in a sensible plaited bun. Conversely Eleanor had what every Victorian girl wished for; thick naturally curly hair which she wore loosely around her face and caught gently at the back allowing it to tumble down over her shoulders. She had a large nose about which she once jokingly wrote, 'I, unfortunately only inherited my father's nose – (I used to tell him I could sue him for damages as his nose had distinctly entailed a loss on me), and not his genius.'[14] Her eyes were not symmetrical. Clara, like others, did not notice her new friend's faults. Eleanor's ebullient personality made up for her lack of natural beauty giving the impression to the younger girl that the elder was perfect in every way. A description of the young Eleanor given by a contemporary noted that she was, 'Not really beautiful, but she somehow gave the impression of beauty by reason of her sparkling eyes, her bright colouring, her dark locky masses of hair.'[15]

Although her diary does not begin until her sixteenth year, Clara made mention of her early years in articles she wrote later. In addition much can be conjectured. Her mother does not feature largely in her life at any time and with her comment on her unhappy childhood and later derogatory remarks in her diary it seems unlikely that a close relationship existed between any of the children and their mother. Mrs Collet had been married previously as on her daughter's birth certificate it states that her mother's name was 'Jane Collet, late Marshall, formerly Sloan'. Presumably her first husband, Mr Marshall, had died young. There is no evidence of any offspring from this marriage.

Clara had a closer relationship with her brothers and sisters than with her mother. She remained close to them to the end of their lives. With her father she shared an interest in the theatre which brought them together for a period but although there is no indication of any problem between the two there is little evidence that they were particularly close, although she did respect him, his work and his views.

In 1935, when she was 75, she wrote an article entitled, 'The Present Position of Women in Industry' which was published in the *Journal of the Royal Statistical Society*. In this she says that one of her earliest recollections was with the family at a performance at Drury Lane Theatre when she was only 5 years of age and, 'my first memory of the separate existence of my brothers is my surprise at their enjoyment of the clowning which came like a douche of cold water on my ecstasy after the ballet and transformation scene'.[16] In a Unitarian family such as hers, all the children were treated in a similar way and thus it was not until this time that she first realised that she was different from her brothers. That this apparently insignificant incident remained in her memory all those years later shows its strong impact on her. Clara was, even as a child, not swayed by her brothers' opinions. She did nothing to modify her own attitude but was sure that she was right and her brothers wrong – this ability to stick to her own judgements was a trait which helped her in her adult life. Her brothers were wrong to find the clowns more enjoyable than the ballet which she believed to be better. Even at the age of 5 Clara knew her own mind.

In the same article she recollects an episode which occurred when she was 11 years old. She was taken by her nursemaid for a walk to a nearby field and became drawn into conversation with a 'field labourer, on the other side [of a hedge], who explained to me how the rich ground down the poor and handed me a baked potato from his lunch'. From this incident she became aware of the differences between rich and poor and listened carefully to what the young man said, did not pass comment and earned the reward of part of his lunch. Her diplomacy skills and ability to communicate with people from all backgrounds were already being formed.

She came from a highly unorthodox background. Most of her ancestors had been religious dissenters; there had been writers of radical newspapers and heretical religious tracts; adventurers travelling far and wide across the globe to India, South America, Australia and New Zealand when these journeys posed serious risks; and there had been wealth passed down from the great Joseph Collet which had been lost.[17]

That many of her predecessors had been followers of the Unitarian faith may account for their adventurous outlook, their fairness in business and their questioning of convention. All of these traits can be seen in Clara. It cannot be an accident that Barbara Leigh Smith (Bodichon), Florence Nightingale, Octavia Hill, Harriet Martineau, Charles Booth, Joseph Chamberlain, Mary Wollstonecraft and Beatrice Potter, all radical thinkers fighting for social justice and equality, were either Unitarians or heavily influenced by their ideals.

What was it about this religion which encouraged its adherents to challenge the social mores and push for change? Unitarianism grew from roots laid down during the Reformation and Renaissance when people throughout Europe were questioning the dogmas of the Catholic faith including corruption by its clerics. All aspects of the faith were challenged including the Trinity, or the worship of God the Father, God the Son and God the Holy Ghost. Although Jesus is believed by the Unitarians to have been a wonderful man whose teachings should be followed, it is not felt that there is evidence for his actual worship as the Son of God. The religion began in Eastern Europe where it was tolerated but only became accepted in Britain after the Religious Toleration Act of 1689. It has developed into a religion without a creed where its members are encouraged to think for themselves and to exhibit toleration for others. Unitarians do not believe in the doctrine of original sin or everlasting punishment. They have never adopted an active role in converting people to their religion. The application of reason rather than faith has been instrumental in Unitarians possessing a regard for education. Clara described Unitarianism as 'a progressive faith, not a Church, and its very implications, when once they have become commonplaces of thought, move the third and fourth generations to go out to discover their grounds of sympathy with other religious bodies'.[18]

Due to their being excluded from mainstream education it was deemed necessary for Unitarians to open institutions primarily for fellow dissenters. Universities such as University College, London, known as the 'Godless institution in Gower Street', and the

Universities of Manchester, Birmingham and Sheffield[19] were all established in order to provide education for Unitarian men and other dissenters, 'They were indeed nurseries for revolutionaries, turning out students trained to approach all subjects with a critical rather than a reverent eye.'[20] Oxford and Cambridge Universities did not open their doors to dissenting men until 1871.

1. South Place Ethical Society as it is today. Clara and her father used to lecture at the original site. (David McDonald.)

The Unitarians encouraged women, even as far back as the eighteenth century, to obtain an education in order that they might be able to educate their sons in the absence of available schools, and so a tradition of learning amongst Unitarian women became established. This was formalised with the introduction of colleges such as Bedford College, known as the Ladies' College in London, founded by Elizabeth Reid in 1849. As a result of a campaign by women including Barbara Leigh Smith (Bodichon), and Emily Davies, Girton College, Cambridge was opened to women in 1869, including those of dissenting religions, but they were not allowed to receive a degree, merely a certificate of attendance.

Clara then, was born into a household which encouraged free thought. Her father's editorship of the *Diplomatic Review* resulted in their mixing with many radical visitors and friends. The children were all expected to 'ask questions about anything which roused [their] curiosity'. Although she said that, 'nothing tempted me to read a line of the *Free Press*'. It was a serious publication even by Victorian standards. It is not surprising that a young girl would have had no desire to read its dry content.

Every Sunday the Collet family visited the South Place Chapel in Finsbury where a sermon was preached. These sermons were unlike those preached in Anglican churches. In Unitarian chapels although the Bible is used as a basis for the sermons, the minister regularly reads from writing from other faiths or a secular article from a publication such as *The Guardian* which had been founded by Unitarians in 1821. The sermon often took the form of a discussion in which the whole congregation would be invited to participate, encouraging its members, including the young Clara, to think for themselves and question conventions.

Mr Collet put his Unitarian principles into practice and arranged for Clara and her sisters to attend a school which was as good as that to which he sent his sons. This was the North London Collegiate School in Camden, a new and radical school for the education of young women.

NOTES

1. Charles Booth, 'Appendix: Streets and Population Classified', in Charles Booth, *Life and Labour of the People in London*, Vol. 2 (London: Macmillan, 1892), p. 24.
2. 1851 Census.
3. Clara Elizabeth Collet and Henry Haines Collett, 'The History of the Collett Family: The Family of Collett', Vol. 2 (Unpublished MS, in the British Library (1935)). Henry Haines Collett was from a different branch of the family, hence the variation in spelling of his name.
4. 'Editorial', *Free Press: The Diplomatic Review*, Vol. 14, No. 4 (April 1866).
5. Letter to Dr Sraffa from Collet, Collet 1/2, p. 3. Papers held at the Marshall Library of Economics, University of Cambridge. By permission of the Faculty of Economics and Politics, University of Cambridge.
6. Boris Nicolaievsky and Otto Maenchen-Helfen, *Karl Marx* (London, 1936), pp. 241–2.
7. Yvonne Kapp, *Eleanor Marx, Family Life: 1855–1883*, Vol. 1 (London: Virago, 1979 (repr. 1986), p. 75.
8. Collet 1/2, p. 1. Marshall Library of Economics, University of Cambridge. By permission of the Faculty of Economics and Politics, University of Cambridge.

9. Kapp, *Eleanor Marx*, p. 117.

10. Clara Collet, MSS diary, copy at Warwick University, MSS 29/8/1/1–146, 1 February 1885.

11. Collet 1/2, p. 2, Marshall Library, Cambridge.

12. Ibid., p. 1.

13. Ibid.

14. Letter from Eleanor Marx to Karl Kautsky, 1912, quoted in Chushichi Tsuzuki, *The Life of Eleanor Marx, 1855–1898 – A Socialist Tragedy* (Oxford: Clarendon Press, 1967). Reprinted by permission of Oxford University Press.

15. Marian Comyn (née Skinner), 'My Recollections of Karl Marx', *The Nineteenth Century and After*, Vol. 91 (January 1922), pp. 161–9.

16. Clara E. Collet, 'The Present Position of Women in Industry', *Journal of the Royal Statistical Society*, Part II (1942), pp. 122–4.

17. See Appendix 1 for a fuller account of Collet's ancestors.

18. From Charles Booth archives held at the University of London Library, I/2395. This paragraph is from an article published in *Social Services Review* (1927), University of Chicago, entitled 'Some Recollections of Charles Booth', by Clara Collet. MS 797, p. 4.

19. Jeremy Goring and Rosemary Goring, *The Unitarians* (Exeter: Religious and Moral Education Press, 1984), p. 32.

20. Claire Tomalin, *The Life and Death of Mary Wollstonecraft* (London: Penguin, 1974 (repr. 1985)), pp. 44–63.

2

Education and Revolution
1873–78

Not only was it a part of their father's religious principles to give his daughters as good an education as his sons, but it was also pragmatic and prudent. He knew that he would be unable to afford to support them should they not marry. A more traditional father would have made the assumption that his daughters would marry and thus no longer depend on him, rather than educating them in such a way that they could, if they wished, become financially independent. Perhaps Mr Collet had the good sense not to rely on marriage for his daughters realising that women formed the majority of the population at that time, a statistic of which he, being a journalist, was probably more aware than other middle-class fathers. Whatever the reason, Clara had him to thank for her good education. She had attended a primary school close to home at 2, Victoria Terrace, Hornsey Road, Hornsey, until she was 11 when she was sent to Calais for a year to learn French.

In 1869 the family had gone on holiday to Calais and her eldest sister Caroline had been left behind at the 'Dames de la Sainte Union' which was managed by nuns whilst Wilfred was sent to a school run by 'secular priests' in the same locality.[1]

Caroline and Wilfred's trip abroad was truncated by the Franco-Prussian War which began on 15 July 1870. The French Emperor Napoleon III surrendered at Sedan, thus ending the Second Empire, but Paris held out against the Prussians in a siege which lasted until the following January. Many revolutionary Parisians believed that Napoleon III should have fought for longer. The newly appointed Third Republic was to be headed by Adolphe Thiers, a man still loathed for his oppression of the people during the 1848 Revolution. With the large number of weapons they had amassed during the siege, the popular uprising took control and proclaimed itself the Commune of Paris. 'It came to be seen as the embodiment of social revolution.'[2] Many of the members were followers of Louis Auguste Blanqui and others of Pierre Proudhon who belonged to the Working Men's Association of which Karl Marx was secretary.

During this revolutionary upsurge in France, Eleanor Marx travelled to Bordeaux with her eldest sister Jenny to visit their sister Laura who was now married to Paul Lafargue. He had been heavily involved in the Paris uprising. The timing of Eleanor's arrival in France coincided with the bloody overthrow of the Commune in Paris, by Thiers and the Republican army. Eleanor and her sisters were in danger as a result of their association with Paul Lafargue and their father who had openly supported the Commune. Lafargue escaped over the border into Spain expecting to be followed shortly by his wife Laura, Jenny and Eleanor, who had been forced to remain behind to nurse Laura's baby during a terminal illness.

2.   Eleanor Marx became Clara's friend as a result of the friendship between their fathers. (Bundesarchiv, Koblenz.)

3. Karl Marx would sit in and watch performances of the
    'Dogberry Club' and laugh until the tears ran down his face.
    (Bundesarchiv, Koblenz.)

After the infant died the girls left but were arrested at the
Spanish border. Eleanor protested her British citizenship but to no
avail. The three sisters were taken back to the house in which they
had earlier been staying by 24 gendarmes. The house was
searched. Even the mattress was taken apart in the search for
bombs and evidence against them. The gendarmes became
suspicious of the special lamp that had been used to warm the milk
for Laura's deceased baby, which the Republicans thought was full
of petrol to be used as a bomb. Jenny was interrogated for two
hours but divulged nothing. Eleanor was cross-examined next
using the method of tricking her into contradicting her sister. Her
questioning did not begin until midnight and went on until 2 a.m.;
a gruelling and frightening ordeal for a 16-year-old girl who had
been up since 5 o'clock the previous morning. Despite the
questioning the police did not find sufficient evidence to condemn
the girls who were then taken to a 'gendarmerie' where they were
locked up for the rest of the night and the following day. They were
finally allowed to leave the police station although their passports
were not returned for ten tense days. This must have been

especially nerve-racking as Jenny had been carrying an incriminating letter from the recently executed Gustave Flourens, which she had slipped into an old book in the police station at an unguarded moment. Had it been found the girls would most likely have been detained.

On her return to England, Eleanor delighted in the telling of her revolutionary stories. One can imagine the two girls together, with the elder recounting the exciting and dangerous tales of her adventures. To the young Collet already full of admiration for her older friend, these stories added to Eleanor's appeal, although they never converted her to the idea of revolutionary methods as a means to impart social change.

In 1872, with the ending of the political turmoil in France, Clara and Harold were sent to Calais to study French at the same institutions as their siblings. During her year in Calais the nuns were successful in instilling an excellent basic knowledge of the French language into their pupil for later Clara became fluent and was able to read challenging French literature with ease as well as to converse with her many French friends in their native language. She continued to receive instruction in other subjects during her time abroad. Later at her secondary school she was considered so far in advance of her fellow students in decimals as a result of her year in France[3] that she was promoted to a higher class. Why her parents chose to send the girls to a convent school in France is unclear. It seems a surprising choice for a Unitarian child to be sent to a Catholic institution.

At the age of 11, in all probability during the summer break from her French school, which she spent back in England, Clara became friendly with the daughter of the family's charwoman who was the same age as she was and also extremely bright. She had learnt to do 'vulgar fractions', a feat which Clara had also accomplished and which she recognised as being a difficult and unusual achievement for children of their age. 'We shelled peas together one day, and I mentally paid homage to a superior. Katie Dobbin was to become a pupil teacher at a board school... with every prospect of becoming a fully-qualified teacher.' This was at the beginning of compulsory education for all when it was necessary to pick the best of the children to 'be trained to teach what they were taught until such a time as there was a supply of competent young women to teach what they knew'.[4]

The poor had long since had opportunities for education in the various ragged schools. The rich had 'select academies, boarding schools and governesses but for girls of [the middle classes] there seemed to be little or no chance of an education at all compared to that becoming available for their brothers'.[5] Frances Mary Buss proceeded to provide that service in London with the aim of supplying well-educated women teachers. In 1864 a Royal Commission had been set up to investigate boys' education and as an afterthought agreed to look at that of girls. Miss Buss was asked to give evidence. Lord Taunton, the Chairman, questioned her as to whether, 'As far as you are able to judge, do you think the class of school mistresses is as good as it ought to be?' She replied, 'The class of teachers generally is not.'[6]

Frances Buss was born in 1827 to middle-class parents. Her father was a successful artist whose work had been exhibited in the Royal Academy and who supplemented his income producing etchings for books. Her mother had been devoted to her children when they were young and when they were older she founded a preparatory school in Kentish Town.

The education Miss Buss had acquired was typical of its age. She had been sent to a small school in Mornington Crescent, London, which provided only a basic education. Despite this, the area, being an artistic and literary centre, gave Buss the opportunity of being able to mix with actors and artists. This encouraged an early interest in the performing arts which remained with Buss throughout her life. Her secondary school was run by Miss Wyand in Hampstead Road around the corner from where George Cruickshank the caricaturist lived. She studied there from the age of 10.

By the time she was 14, Miss Buss began teaching, initially as an assistant at the school she had just attended, a common way for a girl to commence in that profession, and by the age of 16 she was regularly left in sole charge of the small school. This provided her with the experience and confidence necessary to enable her to make a useful contribution when her mother opened her own school.

By 1844, as a result of campaigning by Emily Davies, Queen's College had allowed the entry of women. Reverend Llewellyn Davies, Emily's brother, became its first head teacher. Queen's College and Bedford College, which opened in 1849, offered girls a form of secondary education. Miss Buss was able to attend evening classes at Queen's College which offered a wide range of academic subjects and at the age of 23 she was awarded the Queen's College Diploma, the highest qualification available to a woman at the time.

In 1850 Frances Mary Buss opened the North London

Collegiate School with the aim of introducing educational opportunities to middle-class girls who had no alternative means of obtaining an education. She managed to keep the fees relatively low which was helpful to her poorer pupils but resulted in the constant worry of her finding enough funds to keep the premises running. The school was situated in Camden. By 1871 it moved to larger premises at 202, Camden Road. The education was liberal and 'All the pupils who enter are considered as upon the same equality. The same high tone of feeling is expected from all, the same attention to instruction, the same advantages offered to every pupil.'[7]

From 1865 Cambridge Local Examinations were extended to girls' schools. These tests correspond to the present day GCSEs and Advanced level examinations and had been offered to boys some years previously. The North London Collegiate School was involved in the pilot scheme set up two years before and Buss was pleased to be able to report back to the parents in 1868 that, 'The fears entertained by some persons that these advantages may be too dearly brought by the injury to health and to the moral tone consequent upon over-excitement are not justified by experience.'[8]

On 26 December 1872, Collet Dobson Collet enrolled his daughter at the North London Collegiate School. In May 1873 she sat the entrance examination. Halfway through the examination she was called out by Miss Buss who wished personally to give her a few encouraging words as she was a friend of Clara's great aunt, Mary Barker. Miss Buss would not have had to show any favouritism in accepting Clara who had always shone academically. The NLCS was the obvious choice for the Collet girls to attend, being of liberal orientation, promoting the advancement of women's education and being located close enough to home to be reached by a short train journey. The railway line to Crouch End had been opened in 1867 and we know that she used the train to travel to school from a diary entry made on 15 September 1876 when she was 16 years of age:

> Man in the train today who begged leave to open the carriage window in order to wave goodbye to his wife who was not up when he went away, who lives in a house facing the line. Lady remarked he was very attentive and he told her she was not the first person who had said that; that people should always be attentive to their wives and not trample upon their tenderest feelings...I thought I should have laughed out right. Wonder how attentive he will be in two years hence.[9]

Her cynicism was well-developed for one of her age.

From 1884, many years after she had left school, Clara had two routes by which to enter London from Crouch End where her parents lived until their deaths and where she stayed periodically. This was the year that the first cable tramway in Europe was built to climb Highgate Hill to the south-west end of Hornsey Lane, by the 'Steep Grade Tramway Company'. It was also able to tow heavy goods carts, with their horses being led up behind. On occasion the journey proved dangerous and after a series of mechanical failures and accidents the line went out of operation from 1892–97. There was another major accident in 1899, upon enquiry of which it was discovered that both driver and conductor were drunk.[10]

Clara's first diary entries were mostly about her school days and illustrate that her years at the North London Collegiate School were happy ones. She was more than able to cope with the work and was often scathing about those less capable than herself:

> A nice idea introduced; printed forms given us to fill up every day about how long we take over our lessons. Some of the girls say they take 6 hours at homework instead of 3. Must they not be duffers. I don't much care myself; I am generally under time, never over.[11]

Despite having a generally good attitude towards her studies she nonetheless once commented in her diary that she would rather do nothing at all, which she claimed was 'the pleasantest occupation I know of'.

She had many school friends, such as Sarah Mason, who holidayed in Scotland; Hilda Miall who had been to Denmark; Nelly, Mary and Annie Groom with whom she went to tea on several occasions. She preferred Mary who was 'the brightest of the three and has ten times more fun and daring in her than the others. I don't know whether she is nice or not yet.'[12]

Whilst she was young Clara regularly discussed her perception of people's opinions of her in her diary, exhibiting doubts about her ability to make friends. It is possible that if she had problems with her peer group it may have been due to her overconfidence and outspokenness. On the first occasion when invited to tea with the Groom sisters she met their brothers about whom she made instant character judgements, deciding she did not like the look of Arthur who was 'dull and bad tempered and conceited. Harry not bad, not clever but looks hard working and seems almost modest for a man.'[13] On the same evening, having just met the rest of the family she asked for their photograph album and spent some time telling the characters of the people whose photographs were contained therein. The girls told her that she was right in all except one but Clara was convinced that they were wrong about that although she had the common sense to confine that comment to her diary!

She enjoyed sport. The North London Collegiate School was proud of its musical gymnastics classes which were introduced in 1866 as a remedy for the 'mental strain of examinations'.[14] Callisthenics were also part of the curriculum. The parents generally believed that their girls' health had improved as a result of these exercise classes. This was a remarkable change of attitude from when the school had first been opened when 'The mildest form of gymnastics (such as jumping over a stick held a few inches above the ground) was deemed so unladylike that some girls were withdrawn from the...classes.'[15] Clara played shuttlecock and went to the gymnasium to climb the ladders. She continued to exercise long after she started work in order to keep fit and later showed off that, 'I rowed for the first time for three hours and was not a bit stiff.'[16]

Miss Buss was a strict headmistress, yet the girls held her in high regard as she aimed to be fair. She lent Clara her own books to read, recognising her pupil's ability, and enjoyed playing an active role in her studies. In turn Clara respected Miss Buss, remarking that she gave pupils 'unrivalled opportunities of seeing and listening to every man and woman who was doing anything for the advancement of women's education'.[17] These attitudes had the effect of instilling an interest in women's issues upon the impressionable mind of her pupil. The two remained in contact long after Clara had left school. They even spent a few days holiday together. A girl who had left the school some years after Clara remembered that Miss Buss 'never cared to enjoy any pleasure alone; someone must always share her drives, join her in her cottage in the country and on her holidays both at home and abroad, often at her expense'.[18]

Another 'old girl' recollected that 'Many people only saw the aggressive side of her', yet this pupil 'greatly enjoyed [her] three years in Form VI',[19] and remembered Miss Buss recounting a story about a journey she had made to London by train where she had befriended some boys who were returning to their school. They enjoyed the company of the austere, prim woman and informed her of all the practical jokes they planned to play in the coming months at their school, oblivious to the fact that they were addressing a headmistress. She found this episode highly amusing and regularly told it to her older students at the NLCS.[20]

In 1875 Miss Buss employed a new young teacher on a part-time basis to teach mathematics and German. She was Mrs Bryant. Lessons were highly enjoyable with the newly widowed mistress and Clara remained in contact with her for many years after she left school. She attended her annual garden parties, congratulated her on her appointment in 1895 as Miss Buss' successor and partici-pated in meetings with her at the Economic Club, which Mrs Bryant had joined as representative of the London University Senate.

In the Prize List of 1870–80 Clara can be seen as having won the prize for General Diligence presented by the Countess of Hardwicke. She was one of only three girls who had passed the Leaving Certificate. She gained passes in Latin, mathematics (elementary), Natural Philosophy (mechanical division), English and she gained a distinction in both French and German. She thanked her year in France for her good result in French; for her distinction in German she thanked the Marx family. Eleanor had been helping her a little with her German as she was not as good as the other girls in her class. Miss Oswald, her German teacher, had been giving the girls lectures in which they were not allowed to take detailed notes. Clara had been attentive enough to catch a name – Scipio Africanus – although she had understood little else of the lesson. She asked Karl Marx for assistance and he suggested that she should check the *History of the Punic Wars* by Schlosser in order to locate the information. Marx took her up to his study, where he located the book and the chapter to which Miss Oswald had been referring. She was thus able to complete the assignment for which, by these somewhat devious means, she obtained a distinction.[21]

When Carrie had left school five years before Clara, there had been no tertiary education available to women other than Girton, Cambridge, which allowed women to follow a degree-level course but did not confer upon them a title. Carrie became a teacher without qualifications. In May 1878, the year Clara finished her secondary education, Emily Davies succeeded in her campaign to persuade London University to include women in their degree programme. 'On the occasion of the presentation of degrees at the University of London, the Chancellor, Lord Granville made the great announcement that henceforth women should be eligible for all the degrees and honours of the university.'[22] Miss Buss was delighted and for Clara the timing could not have been better. She would be able to go ahead with a teaching job, whilst at the same time studying for an external degree.

Miss Buss regularly took her pupils to plays in London performed by actors such as Ellen Terry and Henry Irving. Perhaps her enthusiasm was transmitted to Clara, for a love of the theatre became one of her lifelong passions. It also provided the common interest which as we shall see was to cement the friendship that had already spawned between Clara and the older Eleanor Marx.

NOTES

1. 'Secular priests' are what Clara calls her brother's teachers in her description of her association with Karl Marx written in 1944 – it is possible that this term is incorrect. The originals of her recollections of Marx are in the Marshall Library, Cambridge.
2. J.M. Roberts, *A History of Europe* (Oxford: Helicon Publishing, 1976).
3. See the entry by Collet for the planned North London Collegiate School's (NLCS) centennial book. The entry was not used but has been kept at the NLCS. It was written on 4 June 1948 when Collet was 87, two months before her death.
4. Collet, 'The Present Position of Women in Industry', pp. 122–4.
5. R.M. Scrimgeour, *The North London Collegiate School – 1850–1950: A Hundred Years of Girls' Education* (hereafter *NLCS*) (Oxford: Oxford University Press, 1950), p. 28–9.
6. Annie E. Ridley, *Frances Mary Buss and Her Work for Education* (London: Longmans, Green, 1895).
7. Scrimgeour, *NLCS*, p. 30.
8. Ibid., p. 35.
9. MSS diary, 15 September 1876.
10. Old Ordnance Survey Maps, London Sheet 19, Highgate 1894, Pamela Taylor. The Godfrey Edition, published by Alan Godfrey Maps, Newcastle-upon-Tyne.
11. MSS diary, 15 September 1876.
12. Ibid., 26 September, 2 October and 6 October 1876.
13. Ibid., 6 October 1876.
14. Scrimgeour, *NLCS*, p. 46.
15. Ridley, *Frances Mary Buss*, p. 55.
16. MSS diary, 9 July 1882.
17. See letter to Mr Sraffa from Collet, 22 September 1944, Collet 1/2 p. 4. Marshall Library, Cambridge.
18. Scrimgeour, *NLCS*, p. 55.
19. Ibid., p. 56.
20. Ibid., p. 57.
21. Collet 1/2, p. 3. Marshall Library, Cambridge.
22. Ridley, *Frances Mary Buss*, p. 271.

3

Dogberrys and Marxs 1873–78

'Since August 1877 the Dogberry Club has been established. The first meeting took place...and the club was formed',[1] Clara noted in her diary. From 1869 when they had first met, Clara and Eleanor's friendship had developed. After their initial meeting Clara visited the Marx household regularly with her father. Her memory of these occasions was of a 'room full of people all talking French at the top of their voices'.[2] The only person she could later identify was M. Longuet, who had married Eleanor's elder sister. The rest of the company remained anonymous, although most were political refugees following the Paris Commune. While she was away for her study year in Calais her mother and sister remembered an occasion whilst visiting the Marx household when one 'Frenchman proudly told [her] mother that everyone in the room was under sentence of death',[3] for their bourgeois connections.

Marx and Engels were themselves not entirely sympathetic with many of these refugees. Engels wrote that:

> All these people want to live without any real work, their heads full of alleged inventions that are supposed to make millions if someone will put them in a way to promote these inventions, for which only a few pounds are needed. But should anyone be obliging enough to comply, he is not merely done out of his money but decried as a bourgeois into the bargain...The disordered life during the war, the Commune and exile have hideously demoralised these people and only sheer hard necessity can bring a disorganised Frenchman to his senses.[4]

From 1875 Clara began visiting the Marxs alone or with her brother Wilfred. From the age of 15 she was considered old enough to be allowed to undertake the journey alone. The distance from Crouch End to Highgate was under two miles. By the following September, she complained, 'I wish Tussy would come back from Carlsbad, it's as dull as ditchwater without her.'[5] The age difference now that both girls were almost adults seemed less than at their earlier meetings. Eleanor had been visiting Carlsbad in Germany, to take the waters at 'The Queen of Bohemian Watering Places'. She had been there before, on the recommendation of her doctor, Elizabeth Garrett-Anderson, who believed it might help to relieve the 'hysteria' or what we would now call stress, from which she had recently been suffering. Her nervous condition had been brought on as a result of her engagement to Hyppolite Prosper Olivier Lissagaray, of whom her parents disapproved. Lissagaray, as he was known to his friends, was twice Eleanor's age. He was one of the refugees from the Paris Commune and had written a book on the subject, which Eleanor had translated. He had a poor reputation with women, which, along with her parents' antagonism towards her engagement, and the trauma of the death of Jenny's first child, proved too much for Eleanor's delicate constitution, resulting in insomnia and an inability to eat.

Carlsbad, although still a fashionable spa, was by the 1870s frequented by less eminent people than had once been the case. Visitors had included the King of Bohemia; the Holy Roman Emperor, Charles IV; Napoleon's Empress, Marie-Louise; Leibniz; Bach and Goethe. By the time Eleanor visited with her father it had become commercialised and far less exclusive. Nonetheless Eleanor found it charming and enjoyed the rural surroundings as much as the town itself.

In common with Marx, Clara also disliked Eleanor's choice of boyfriend. She would have 'Lissa fight a fifth or sixth duel (I don't know which) and get done for; he is not half good enough for her.'[6] She was jealous of anyone competing for her friend's affection but Eleanor proved in later life to consistently make poor decisions where men were concerned. Clara and the Marx family may have been justified in their condemnation of Lissagaray.

In 1876, on Eleanor's return, Clara found her friend 'prettier than ever; I wish Lissa would commit forgery and suicide. It would be such a relief.'[7] The Lissagaray problem lingered on from 1872 until 1881 when Eleanor finally gave in to the pressure and broke off the engagement.

Both Clara and Eleanor had become interested in Shakespeare readings as they grew up. Clara studied his plays at school. Eleanor was considering a career in acting and as a preliminary move had joined Frederick James Furnivall's 'New Shakespeare Society' on its formation in 1873. The aim of this society was to promote the study of Shakespeare's plays.

The girls regularly met to read Shakespeare together. On 14 October 1876, Clara's brother, Wilfred, invited guests around for a reading party.

We chose *As You Like It*. Tussy was Rosalind to Mr Hill's Orlando.
They both read very well. Mr Hill awfully tall and thin as a lamp
post, horribly small feet but he is clever and very nice...Carrie was
Celia...Danced afterwards. Grooms and Flo came as well.[8]

The Marxs would often visit Sadlers Wells Theatre where they
would watch the play from the pit, being unable to afford the more
expensive seats.

As a result of this common interest, the more formal 'Dogberry
Club' was established in 1877. The Marx and Collet families were
the principal members. The name was taken from the play *Much
Ado About Nothing*, in which Mr Dogberry is a pompous, egotistical
constable. Dogberryism is 'an utterance worthy of Dogberry,
wordy, i.e. consequential blundering and malapropism'.[9]

The meetings were to be held twice monthly, 'at different
members' houses, but as a matter of fact they were held more
frequently at the Marxs' than anywhere else'.[10] Collet was only able
to attend for the first year of the Club's existence as after this she
left to teach in Leicester but during that time she gave the Club her
full support. 'In November *Merchant of Venice* was read at the
Marxs'. Harry especially good as Shylock...Dolly and Clara
Maitland were there for the first time...Very jolly.'[11] 'In
December...*Twelfth Night*...Da good as Orsino. Mr Ambrose very
good as Sir Toby; he made a very favourable impression and was
elected a member. The evening was very nice and Miss Carlotta
very amiable.'[12] 'In January *Two Gentlemen of Verona* was read at
Coleridge Road. No-one was very good...Mr Ambrose sang
abominably and did not stand examination so well as the time
before. Dancing.'[13] 'February 16th 1878 – *Richard III* read at the
Marxs'. Da good as Richard. Tussy perfect as Lady Annie...Mr
Ambrose sang abominably again; he is immensely vulgar, drops
his H's and is very conceited. The next meeting will be here in
March.'[14]

Marx usually sat and watched the proceedings although he
'never read a part which, for the sake of the play, was perhaps quite
as well, for he had a guttural voice and a decided German accent'.[15]
His 'black eyes, though small were keen, piercing, sarcastic, with
glints of humour in them',[16] and,

> As an audience he was delightful, never criticising, always entering
> into the spirit of any fun that was going, laughing when anything
> struck him as particularly comic, until the tears ran down his cheeks
> – the oldest in years, but in spirits as young as any of us. And his
> friend, the faithful Frederic Engels, was equally spontaneous.[17]

Engels had moved from Manchester to London in 1870 and was involved in the reading of the plays at the Dogberry Club as well as spectating. At the end of the reading they 'finished up the evening with games and such pastimes as charades and dumb-crambo, chiefly – as it would seem from his extreme enjoyment of them – for the delectation of Dr Marx'.[18]

Clara saw a great deal of Marx during the years of her friend-ship with his daughter, yet they rarely discussed politics. One exception was during a theatrical debate. In March 1878 whilst she was studying *Julius Caesar* at school, one of her fellow pupils began a debating society. The first topic for discussion was 'Brutus versus Cassius'. She believed that evidence in the play showed Brutus as self-complacent, incapable of ruling and that once he became leader he rejected the advice of Cassius and became arrogant. Victorian critics generally perceived Brutus as the absolute hero of the play and he was exalted as such. The failings in his personality seemed to her to have been ignored. Caesar is aware of the danger from Cassius whom he sees as desirous of power,

> Such men as he be never at heart's ease
> Whiles they behold a greater than themselves,
> And therefore are they very dangerous. (I.ii. 207–10)

Of Brutus, Caesar had no such fears and is shocked at his betrayal when he recognises him as one of his assassins,

> Et tu, Brute! Then fall Caesar! (III.i.77)

Today Brutus is studied together with his failings. After Caesar's death he assumed leadership, thus getting what he desired by force. He took no notice of advice given him by experienced men. Yet in the Victorian age his actions were viewed as acceptable. Clara was not afraid to take the stance that Brutus was entirely at fault. She went to Marx to discuss her opinions with him, 'as the most natural thing in the world'. She stated that,

> My point of view was that Brutus' self-complacency was only surpassed by his incapacity and that in every single instance after he assumed leadership in which he rejected the advice of Cassius he was in the wrong. Every now and then KM nodded his head at quotations in support of my side.[19]

She was shocked by a comment Marx made at the end of their discussion. She had said that, 'I had accepted entirely the view that

Brutus was disinterested and noble in character – but his leadership was none the better for that. KM remarked that in historical fact Brutus himself was accused of having an itching palm'.[20] Yet in the play the opposite had been the case with the accusation made by Brutus of Cassius,

> Let me tell you, Cassius, you yourself
> Are much condemned to have an itching palm[21] (IV.iii.9–10)

Marx, therefore, supported Clara in her unorthodox reading of Shakespeare. She went on to comment that to Marx, Shakespeare's English idea of, 'revolution by assassination...must have been of absorbing interest'. During the years she had known Marx from 1869 until his death in 1883, he, 'for the first time in his life had... the opportunity of watching the gradual emancipation of the Demos by constitutional means and of comparing the English working man in his exercise of his new legal rights with insurgents in other countries'.[22] She was sure that he must have learnt something during this period in England as he could see reforms being implemented by the government without resort to revolution. During those years he witnessed laws being made to benefit ordinary people. In 1870 the Civil Service opened its exams to all and the Forster Education Act was introduced; in 1871 the purchase of commissions in the army was abolished; trade unions were legalised and protected; and Oxford and Cambridge opened to nonconformists; in 1872 the Ballot Act was passed; in 1875 the Housing Act, the Public Health Act and a further Trade Union Act legalising picketing were introduced; in 1876 Primary Education was made compulsory; in 1882 the Married Women's Property Act was introduced and the Democratic Federation (later the SDF), a Marxist political party, was founded. The 1867 Reform Act had given the vote to a great many middle-class voters who felt a responsibility for the poor. Clara had faith in the system to instigate reform into the constitution. She never became a follower of Marxism, and although many of her later ideas can be seen as supporting the working man and woman, she was a moderate who for most of her life supported the Liberals and who abhorred the idea of violent revolution. In 1945, along with many other Liberals, she voted for the Labour Party.

Whilst not agreeing with Marx's politics, Clara nonetheless viewed him as 'a kindly old man always friendly to me',[23] and never passed an adverse comment about him as a person.

The Dogberry Club had been established for the purpose of

entertainment but for Eleanor Marx, acting became more serious. By 1881 she began lessons with Mrs Vezin, an American actress, and was determined to make acting her career. Ellen Terry was the figure upon whom Eleanor modelled herself, as did most aspiring actresses of the time. After she had broken off the futile engagement to Lissagaray she consoled herself by directing all her energy into her theatre studies. A year later Mrs Vezin informed Eleanor that her skills were not good enough to enable her to make more than a mediocre career on the stage. By the end of the year she began her affair with Edward Aveling, ended her attempt at acting and her career in politics began.

Clara, meanwhile, pursued her own interest in the theatre in a more modest fashion. Her diary makes frequent references to the numerous plays she attended. The Dogberry Club used its members' fees to pay for trips to shows. She often went with the Marxs to see Henry Irving. In 1878 when they saw him at the Lyceum she thought he was, 'perfect and for the first time I appreciated the fact that his face is a beautiful one'.[24]

It was sometime during Clara's school years that the family moved house. This was prior to 1876 as she does not mention the move in the diary which she commenced in that year. The family was in the new house before January 1878 as she discusses a play reading which took place there at that time.

The area immediately north of Crouch End village was being developed and it was to one of these newly built houses, 7, Coleridge Road, that they relocated. This substantial Victorian semi-detached house, with intricate plaster adornments and of an attractive design, was a good enough size to take the growing family. The Crouch Hall Park development was part of a wider building scheme in the Hornsey area. Many of the older residents believed that it would herald the end of the local village atmosphere:

> It is clear that the doom of Hornsey is settled. Not much longer will it remain the quiet and secluded village of which everyone has so often heard. It bids to become a populous and thriving commercial centre... Occupiers of country-like cottages or the more self-satisfied tenants of the modern villa may protest against the place being spoilt, but the protestations come too late now. Hornsey is to be given over to the builders and when they get the place into their own hands, proposals to introduce tramways and similar schemes will receive a kindlier welcome than they did a few months since.[25]

The Collets did not share this negative view of the area as their new house was only about half a mile from their old one.

4. 7, Coleridge Road, Crouch End – the home of Clara's family
    from 1878 until the early twentieth century.
    (David McDonald.)

In 1878 Clara completed her secondary education. Her school
career had been successful and Miss Buss had no difficulty in
recommending her pupil to a friend of hers, Miss Leicester, who
was in the process of opening a new school. Her future appeared
to be decided. The conventional path for an educated middle-class
girl beckoned as it did so many other girls in a similar position.
There was little alternative. Few careers were open to middle-class
girls for whom it was still considered unsavoury to have to work
at all. Philanthropic occupations provided an outlet for the
ambitions of many an educated middle-class girl, but this work

rarely came with a salary. A career on the stage such as Eleanor would have liked to pursue was not acceptable for an educated or upper-middle-class society woman. Clara was to begin her working life in the conventional way.

After an abortive trip to the Marxs' to bid them goodbye – they were not at home – she left for Leicester. Her teaching post was to commence but she had misgivings. She was not sure whether she would like living away from home and was worried as to whether teaching was the career she wanted to pursue, but she was nonetheless convinced that it would be an improvement on life at home as she had not been happy there. Miss Oswald (her German teacher at the NLCS) and the Marxs were the only people she expected to miss.

Yet by February 1882 an irreparable rift occurred between herself and Eleanor Marx. Shortly after her move to Leicester, Clara became acquainted with a woman named Polly Blackwell who reminded her of Eleanor. She was attractive and intelligent with many mannerisms in common with her but, 'as much strength of will and originality. I like her very much but the remembrance of TM makes me doubt our always doing so.'[26] Something had caused an estrangement between the two girls. Years later after her return to London she met Eleanor outside the British Museum. In her diary she wrote:

> Today I spoke to Tussy and we made friends; she asked me to go and see her and I explained why I could not; she flushed a little but she knew that I was not blaming her and that I cared for her as much as ever. She promised that if ever I could help her she would ask me. I hope she will if she needs help and that no cowardice of mind will ever prevent me from giving help when she asks for it herself.[27]

What had occurred to cause this rift in their relationship? Clara's diary is infuriatingly silent on this issue. Therefore, only speculation is possible.

The most likely explanation is that, if she had a dislike for Lissagaray, Eleanor's new partner would prove even more difficult for Clara to like. It is hard to find a flattering description of Edward Aveling. 'Ugly, egotistical, and mean' is how H.M. Hyndman described him in his *Further Reminiscences*, and continued to say that he:

> did not like the man from the first. 'Nobody can be so bad as Aveling looks' was a remark which translated itself into action in my case. In spite of the most unpleasant rumours about his personal character,

alike in regard to money and sexual relations, I put compulsion on myself and forced myself to believe that . . . his forbidding face could not in truth be an index to his real character.[28]

Yet Hyndman went on to say that Aveling was one of those men who whilst being repulsively ugly nonetheless charmed women when often the most handsome failed. It must have been this appeal which attracted Eleanor. By the time he met Eleanor, Aveling had become an outspoken secularist despised by many. Aveling's views on religion, which may have caused a problem for many Victorian women, would not have been the sole cause of the rift between Eleanor and Clara. The unorthodox Clara was unlikely to have found these views particularly abhorrent – many of her future friends were to have equally secularist beliefs. She had commented, 'sometimes when I feel blissfully happy or dreadfully miserable, I believe in Him myself but I don't feel any real faith or trust'.[29]

After a stunningly successful academic life acquiring numerous scholarships and prizes at both University College, London and Cambridge University, Aveling settled down to teach science part-time at the North London Collegiate School from 1872–76, before leaving to take his D.Sc. and commencing lecturing in science at King's College. During his period of teaching at the NLCS Clara was on the receiving end of his statistics lessons. If his dry, laconic personality permeated his teaching in the way it did his writing it is quite likely that she had already formulated a poor opinion of the man before he had begun his relationship with her friend. However, despite his written word being 'pompous, florid, empty and so much hot air',[30] when delivering speeches he was a clever orator who captivated his audience. Clara was not taken in by the pomp.

The more likely cause of the rift between the two young women would have been Aveling's marital status; for when Eleanor first met and set up home with this unattractive, difficult man, he was already married. His marriage, to Isabel Frank, had taken place about the time he had begun his work for the NLCS. Miss Frank was the daughter of a wealthy Leadenhall poulterer. She was the same age as Edward, attractive and considered by Mr and Mrs Aveling as a suitable match. Aveling married her for her money. The union was not a happy one and within two years the couple had separated. Engels claimed that Aveling's wife had not been able to cope with Edward's atheistic and socialist attitudes and had run off with a clergyman with whom she had more in common.

Aveling did not wish to divorce his estranged wife as he harboured hopes that on her death he would inherit at least some of what he believed would be a fortune. His wife did not die until 20 years later, alone, after falling into a diabetic coma, and left Aveling the relatively small sum of £126 15s 4d.

Eleanor and Edward began their relationship in the early part of 1882, which coincides with Clara's diary entry, implying the rift in their friendship. However, the affair did not become public knowledge until 18 months later. Perhaps because Clara lived some distance away Eleanor took her into her confidence early. It was not until 1884, the year before Eleanor and Clara met up outside the British Museum, that Aveling and she announced their decision to live together. Marx had died the previous year and Eleanor's mother some years earlier, so there would have been no opposition from them as there had been over Lissagaray. Eleanor was nervous about the reactions of her sisters and friends. She sent them letters to explain the situation. To her sister Laura, she wrote:

> You must have known, I fancy, for some time that I am very fond of Edward Aveling – and he says he is fond of me – so we are going to 'set up' together...I need not say that this resolution has been no easy one for me to arrive at...Do not misjudge us...I shall await a line from you and Paul very anxiously.[31]

To Dollie Radford (née Maitland), a friend from the Dogberry days, she wrote:

> I had half intended to tell you this morning what my 'plans' I spoke of are – but somehow it is easier to write...Well then this is it – I am going to live with Edward Aveling as his wife. You know that he is married, and that I cannot be his wife legally, but it will be a true marriage to me...I shall quite understand if you think the position one you cannot accept, and I shall think of you both [i.e. her and her husband, another Dogberry member, Ernest] with no less affection if we do not any longer count you among our immediate friends. Always, my dear old friend, yours lovingly, Tussy.[32]

It is probable that Clara received a similar letter whilst away in Leicester and that, already finding the relationship between Eleanor and Edward hard to cope with, she was unable to come to terms with the idea of her friend living openly with Aveling.

She may also have disapproved of her friend's political activities. Eleanor had become openly radical, socialist and revo--lutionary in her beliefs. As a school teacher, whilst sympathetic towards some socialist ideas, her opposition to revolutionary ideas continued. In an article entitled 'Socialism' written for the school magazine, she asks the reader to consider, 'the line of argument of those who least of all command our sympathies, the Revolutionary Socialists'.[33] She continued by reasoning that whereas followers of these ideas believe that land and businesses should be taken into state control, it was more important to share out talents than wealth:

> All Socialists if they are consistent [i.e. in believing in the sharing out of possessions], are logically bound to regard themselves as trustees holding any talents they may possess, for the good of those less gifted, and under a moral obligation to exert those talents that they may be used to the fullest advantage. [Only by] socialising the individual ... can we hope to modify the tendencies which send the weakest to the wall, and that the law of the survival of the fittest ... may be subordinated to a higher law ... and that the general welfare may be promoted.[34]

Clara wanted to change society. She could see, as much as any socialist, that society warranted change, but her methods were for the individual to take responsibility for the problems of the poor as a moral obligation. Many socialist societies were being set up in London around the end of the 1870s to early 1880s spurred on by the writings of Marx and William Morris amongst others. Clara was not convinced by their ideas. She called Henry Mayers Hyndman, a follower of Marx and the founder of the Marxist Democratic Federation, a 'shallow wind-bag'.[35] As she points out in her diary she was also finding that her own ideas were becoming inconsistent with those of a conventional teacher.[36]

Clara's attitude towards conventional parliamentary politics was not complemintary. In her diary she wrote that her father wanted Gladstone's impeachment at the time that Bright resigned. She agreed that Gladstone,

> Has made rather a muddle of things. It does not seem possible to feel any enthusiasm for any party whatsoever. They all seem untrue ... Parliament is the biggest sham imaginable. Local Government is grand in comparison ... I don't think we are going to ruin as Da does, because the Parliament is the very worst organisation in the country and there is a good deal of solid worth outside it.[37]

Change, in her view, needed to come through slow evolutionary processes rather than violent revolutionary ones.

Although her views would have been at odds with Eleanor's, her tolerant attitudes would have made it unlikely that on its own this would have been sufficient for the termination of their friendship.

Some aspects of the lifestyles of modern women such as smoking was another area in which Clara was more conventional than some of her friends. This habit was beginning to spread amongst women as a way of proving their independence. We know that Eleanor smoked from a letter she sent to a man named Hirsch on 30 December 1876 in which she thanked him for the present of a packet of cigarettes he had sent her for her twenty-first birthday. We also know that her old friend disapproved of this habit. Some years later she wrote that she, 'Met Miss Trump in the smoking room. Sophy and Miss C.P. Sanger both smoked cigarettes. I wish nice people like these two did not do it; but the habit is spreading and it is useless to fight against it.'[38] Another of her female acquaintances to smoke was Beatrice Potter. Beatrice recognised its evils and by 1902 she was not only trying to give up smoking but also meat, fish, tea, eggs, coffee, and alcohol, all of which she thought were doing her harm.

Beatrice Potter was not very taken with Eleanor. She described her as

> Comely, dressed in a slovenly picturesque way with curly black hair flying about in all directions. Fine eyes full of life and sympathy, otherwise ugly features and expression, and complexion showing the signs of an unhealthy excited life, kept up with stimulants and tempered by narcotics.[39]

If this description was true Clara might have found her friend's habits in discord with her own, but Marx had died just two months prior to the meeting between Beatrice and Eleanor. The latter's problematic nervous health rendered it likely that the upset would have made her unwell. Any narcotic medication may have been prescribed by the doctor to help her through the crisis, in which case Beatrice's observation may have been correct though unfair.

Eleanor mixed with Engels and his family who on occasion enjoyed a drink. In 1869 Eleanor wrote a letter to her sister from Manchester, where she was staying with Engels, in which she said that Engels had come home to find, 'Auntie, Sarah, me and Ellen ... all lying out full length on the floor with no stays, no boots and one petticoat and a cotton dress on and that was all'.[40] They were all drunk. On another occasion whilst on holiday in Paris, Eleanor commented that they went 'bockomanning' which was her

5. 'The Den', 7, Jew's Walk, Sydenham, London. The home of
   Eleanor Marx and Edward Aveling and the place where
   Eleanor committed suicide. (David McDonald.)

invented name for sightseeing interspersed with glasses of beer drunk at regular intervals.

By the time she was an adult Clara may have viewed Eleanor differently from how she saw her as an idolising schoolgirl. Eleanor's smoking, drinking escapades and narcotic use may have proved too much for the more sensible Clara who later collected evidence for the proposed Temperance Bill. Whatever the reason for the split in friendship, Eleanor was never again mentioned in Clara's diary or correspondence.

During their last meeting, despite her request that Eleanor should ask for help should she ever need it, she did not contact her old friend when she was in trouble. Thirteen years later, in 1898, and after a career actively promoting the socialist cause, Eleanor, unable to reconcile herself to Aveling's consistently difficult behaviour, committed suicide whilst living in Jew's Walk, Sydenham. This occurred after an argument brought on by the double pressures of Aveling's announcement of his marriage to another woman and his recent serious illness during which he had not allowed Eleanor to nurse him. The morning Eleanor sent her maid to the chemist to purchase the lethal Prussic Acid, Aveling had intended, against Eleanor's advice given in view of his continuing poor health, to take a trip to London. Aveling had repeatedly given her cause for jealous concern and on several occasions Eleanor had written to friends that life was difficult and death would be welcomed.

Death from Prussic Acid poisoning is quick but excruciating. The symptoms, which appear within seconds, are difficulty with breathing and convulsions, followed by muscular paralysis and death. A smell of bitter almonds exudes from the body for several hours after the death. It is a drug not often chosen for suicide on account of the agony it causes. What Clara's reaction must have been to the news of Eleanor's death we do not know. Did she remember her last conversation with her friend and her promise to be there if Eleanor ever needed her? She must have felt some regret for not having kept in touch with her oldest friend. Her diary entries for the early part of 1898 are missing so we are only able to speculate as to her thoughts at this time.

However, that is to jump ahead in time.

NOTES

1. MSS diary, 27 February 1878.

2. Collet 1/2, p. 3. Marshall Library, Cambridge.
3. Ibid.
4. Written by Engels, September 1874, quoted in Kapp, *Eleanor Marx*, Vol. 1, p. 136.
5. MSS diary, 15 September 1876.
6. Ibid.
7. MSS diary, 6 October 1876.
8. Ibid., 14 October 1876.
9. *Chambers Dictionary* (Edinburgh: Harrap, 1993).
10. Comyn, 'My Recollections of Karl Marx', pp. 161–9. Marian Comyn was acquainted later in the Club's life, after Collet had moved. The first meetings alternated between the Marxs' and the Collets'.
11. MSS diary, 27 February 1878.
12. Ibid.
13. Ibid.
14. Ibid.
15. Comyn, 'My Recollections of Karl Marx', pp. 161–9.
16. Ibid., p. 161.
17. Ibid., p. 162.
18. Ibid.
19. Collet 1/2, p. 6. Marshall Library, Cambridge.
20. Ibid.
21. An itching palm was an expression meaning a hand ready to accept a bribe.
22. Collet 1/2, p. 6. Marshall Library, Cambridge.
23. Ibid., p. 5.
24. MSS diary, 16 February 1878.
25. *Hornsey and Finsbury Park Journal* of around 1885. Quoted in the Old Ordnance Survey Maps, London Sheet 12, 1912, David Mander. The Godfrey Edition, published by Alan Godfrey Maps, Newcastle-upon-Tyne.
26. MSS diary, 28 February 1882.
27. Ibid., 27 October 1885.
28. Quoted in Tsuzuki, *The Life of Eleanor Marx*, pp. 91–2. Reprinted by permission of Oxford University Press.
29. MSS diary, 29 March 1882.
30. Kapp, *Eleanor Marx*, p. 270.
31. Letter from Eleanor Marx to her sister Laura Lafargue in France, 18 June 1884. Institute of Marxism/Leninism, Moscow. Quoted in Ibid., p. 15.
32. Eleanor Marx to Dollie Radford, 30 June 1884, Radford family papers. Archive of California R126M3.
33. Clara E. Collet, 'Socialism', *Wyggeston Girls' Gazette*, April 1887.
34. Ibid.
35. Ibid.
36. MSS diary, 11 November 1883.
37. MSS 29/8/2/1 Warwick University, Modern Records' Office, typed diary, 'Diary of a Young Assistant Mistress 1878–85', 16 July 1882.
38. MSS diary, 4 December 1904.
39. Beatrice Webb, *The Diary of Beatrice Webb; Volume One – 1873–1892 – Glitter Around and Darkness Within* (London: Virago, 1982), pp. 87–8, 24 May 1883.
40. Letter from Eleanor Marx to her sister Jenny, 19 July 1869, Bottigelli Archives, quoted in Kapp, *Eleanor Marx*, p. 115.

Part II

Life in Leicester 1878–85

1

The School Mistress – A Pleasant Life

Miss Buss sent for me…She told me she had recommended me for a post in the new Wyggeston Girls' Grammar School to be opened Whitsun week. I should only have £80 a year to begin with but Miss Ellen Leicester, the Headmistress, would give me every facility for preparing myself for the intermediate arts examination in July 1879 and the Final BA in Oct 1880.[1]

Clara was lucky. It had only been in 1878 that London University agreed to the admission of women to take degree courses. That was the year she left the NLCS. Simultaneously a new school was being opened in Leicester by Miss Buss' friend. Miss Leicester came to the NLCS to ascertain whether she could recruit some new staff members amongst Miss Buss' pupils. She took an immediate liking to Clara and in addition to offering her employment was keen that she should continue her studies as an external student at London University and study for her BA degree, which in those days was taken in two parts, the First and Second BA. Two masters from the nearby Wyggeston Boys' School were prepared to give her lessons in Greek and applied mathematics and it was agreed that she should be able to manage Latin and English herself.

Despite having reservations about leaving home to live in Leicester, Clara's first impressions of her new employment and her move were positive. On 20 July 1878 she wrote, 'I came here five weeks ago today hardly expecting to enjoy myself. It has been delightful.'[2]

The next seven years are the most highly documented period of her life. Her diary entries were more reflective and introspective than at any other time and the articles she contributed to the *Wyggeston Girls' Gazette* the most informative as to her developing social conscience. Later her diary became more of a chronicle of events and her writings more an analysis of her statistical findings rather than elucidating much about her own beliefs and personality.

Clara was aware of the problems of diary keeping, 'when anything happens you have no time to write about it, when you have time nothing happens'.[3] She was also not quite sure for whom she was writing her diary – whether it was for herself or for others after her death.

> I have come to the conclusion that if I ever wish to write anything worth writing I ought to make a note of my own thoughts and opinions more than I have done; it will give me ease of writing, and providing I do it truthfully will be amusing to compare changing opinions. The most difficult thing in a diary is to write totally for yourself; try as hard as one will there is always the arrière pensée about what people would think if they read it. It has been particularly so with me as almost my only idea is whether people will admire me; the consequences have not been beneficial to the truth of the record.[4]

She went on to say that, although she was not keen on friends reading any sentiment she may have written about herself, she did not mind the idea of strangers reading it some time in the future. Her ideas of fame were already formulating by the age of 18 when about to embark upon her first job. In her diary she wrote that she must try to curb her habit of exaggeration and would henceforth try to stick to the truth.

By the following June (1879), a year after starting out as a teacher, life was so good that Clara was beginning to feel guilty that she was experiencing more than her share of happiness. This resulted in an irrational fear that something terrible might happen which would upset her status quo. Why should she be so happy? She hoped that people who suffered from hardship in their lives might feel pain and unhappiness less than those whose lives, like hers, had been blessed with good fortune; because otherwise she believed this would be unfair. She surmised that maybe, 'afterwards we shall be judged by the amount of pain we might have removed and they have the suffering they have undergone taken into account'. This was an altruistic concept and one that sums up her caring nature.

For some time her good fortune did continue and her diary entries dwindled aacordingly. Luckily there are other testimonials relating to her first years at the Wyggeston Girls' School.[5] The class containing the eldest girls was Class One. This was where she started her career as a school mistress, aiding Miss Leicester by taking charge of the 'most promising pupils'.[6] There were four other teachers plus a music teacher at the school in its inaugural term. The opening ceremony had taken place on Monday 17 June 1878. The *Leicester Chronicle* ran an article listing the subjects to be taught. These included English, mathematics, classics, geography, French, German, Latin, natural science, domestic economy, laws of health, needlework, drawing, singing and callisthenics. Religious instruction was included but any girl could be exempted from this class if their parents wished. The wide range of academic subjects offered, coupled with the possibility of exemption from religious education, highlights Miss Leicester's advanced outlook as to the education of women. It had much in common with that of her friend, Miss Buss. This suited the liberal-minded Clara.

The fees were reasonable; £1 per year for the entrance fee and payment of £2 per term for tuition fees. There were ten school rules, most of which are similar to those at any school today such as the time at which pupils must be in school. Just two would now strike us as somewhat harsh. First no speaking was allowed at any time after school commenced for the day at 8.50 a.m., anywhere in the school unless with permission from a mistress. The only exception was during lunch break. Secondly no story books were allowed on the premises.

The school building had been purpose built and, 'During the first half-term the school was in a very unfinished state, especially the lower rooms, and we were constantly meeting the workmen in our journeys up and down',[7] which must have proved rather tiresome for a new assistant mistress struggling to come to terms with the transition from being a schoolgirl herself and living at home, to being a school mistress and living away.

At some time during her first 18 months Caroline, her elder sister, joined her at Wyggeston which must have proved mutually beneficial for the girls. They went on holiday together for a week to Folkestone that summer and spent their social lives together.

Her new life as a teacher; planning lessons, taking classes and continuing her education soon became second nature. She studied mental and moral science for her Second BA with Mr Basset Hopkins as her tutor and took two lessons a week, on top of her normal work, from Mr Nelson and Mr Atkins, demonstrating her commitment to furnish herself with the necessary academic qualifications to enable her to be considered well-qualified.

Although she often mentions men in her diary she had already decided that she had no wish to depend on marriage for financial security. At this time her salary of £80 per annum was not a good one and it is possible that her father may have had to subsidise her, a common practice amongst middle-class working women at the start of their careers. This was a practice against which she wrote most vehemently in later life as she believed it prevented a living salary from being set for the middle classes, requiring young women to depend upon others.[8] Clara found Mr Nelson, the tutor, attractive and when he left wondered how she would be able to 'survive the loss'. She did so by being, 'busy enjoying myself ever since from the very day I knew I had passed [the examination] that I wonder how I ever managed to find time to do what I did'.[9]

'At last we have a BA! Clara Collet has just passed successfully the Second BA examination.'[10] This announcement was made in the December 1880 edition of her old school magazine followed by an announcement that her sister Edith had passed the Cambridge examinations (like 'A' levels) coming third out of all who had taken them and thereby qualifying for a scholarship of £15 a year for two years. Edith remained at the NLCS for the whole of her career becoming a well-respected and successful mistress. Her sister Clara, not content with her academic achievement thus far, decided to continue her studies.

In 1882 London University instituted a new examination for a 'Teachers' Diploma' and by March the following year Clara was preparing herself for the examination. This examination imposed a strain upon her with which she found difficult to cope. In a diary entry on 2 March, she wrote:

> I have been indulging in a fit of hysterical crying tonight. I feel so perfectly wretched and miserable and hopeless and worthless and tired. Instead of working for my exam I have been studying physical geography. The worry of school and the feeling of incompetence make me feel miserable. I do wish I could go to Girton or University College, or give up teaching or emigrate.[11]

In a note added later in a typed-up portion of her diary she commented that, 'Literature of Educational Theorists was responsible for this inspissated gloom'.[12] Despite the worry she passed the examination. Only five of the eight women who took the examination that year passed. Despite being one of the most highly qualified teachers in the country her doubts as to her future career as a school mistress increased from this period. She began to believe that her inability to make lifelong friends was due to her 'faculty of offending nearly everyone',[13] and this coupled with the feeling that her views were becoming increasingly unorthodox meant that she was not always a good teacher. She began to make plans to change her career. A very brave, one could almost say foolhardy, thing to do considering the security she had as a teacher, (she was earning £150 a year by 1885), and the lack of choice there was in the field of employment for an educated middle-class woman. Nevertheless, her mind was made up; teaching was to be abandoned and she would study for a Masters degree although she had no idea as to her future career.

NOTES

1. Typed diary, 1878 MS 29/8/2/1.
2. MSS diary, 20 July 1878.
3. Ibid., 16 February 1878.
4. Ibid.
5. This school is now Regent College.
6. Hilary Whitbread and Kathryn Zanker (eds), *Wyggeston Girls' School Centenary* (Rushden: Regent College, 1978), p. 16.
7. Ibid., p. 13.
8. Clara E. Collet, 'Prospects of Marriage for Women', in Collet, *Educated Working Women: Essays on the Economic Position of Women Workers in the Middle-Classes* (London: P.S. King, 1902), p. 62.
9. Typed diary, 25 February 1882.
10. *NLCS Magazine*, December 1880.
11. Typed diary, 2 March 1883.
12. Ibid.
13. MSS diary, 11 November 1883.

2

Relationships, Traumas and Celebrities

Despite eventually deciding that teaching was not the career she wished to pursue for the whole of her life, Clara did relish her time at Wyggeston, both professionally and socially. Within the first few weeks she had settled down and began enjoying life immensely. She went to socials and made friends with local people, the most important of whom were the Gimson family. Through them she became acquainted with the Leicester Secular Society to which they belonged. Mr Josiah Gimson owned a machinery manufacturing business which he had inherited from his father. Despite being fairly rich, he had a well-developed social conscience, desiring to extend co-operative activities, improve conditions in the town of Leicester, and to 'establish equality without revolution and equalise fortunes without dynamite',[1] a view with which Clara had much in common. From his first marriage Josiah had five children and from his second a further five. All the family followed Josiah in his unorthodox beliefs. The elder boys were groomed to take over the family business on their father's retirement. When Clara first became acquainted with the family around 1882, Mentor was 31 years of age, Arthur 29, Sydney[2] 22 and Ernest 18; she was the same age as Sydney and initially she was drawn closer to him than the others. At the various socials she attended she hoped to dance with either Sydney or his friend whom she names only as AH and who was two years his junior.[3] Sometimes she was asked to dance: 'We had a quadrille, AH sat next [to] me but did not ask me to dance until SG went and asked Polly, when he graciously offered his arm',[4] and sometimes she was not: 'This time no-one asked me to dance',[5] but not being one to worry unduly she invited some young boys to dance with her and had an enjoyable evening nonetheless. On most occasions Sydney accompanied her home afterwards.

She continued to enjoy the company of the two young men. Her preference was for Sydney whom she found to be a sensible young man whose religious or rather secularist views interested her. She enjoyed a provocative argument with him over his beliefs although she may have had less belief in God than Sydney himself. Yet whilst he called himself an agnostic Clara never labelled herself thus as the people she admired most believed in Him and, 'because some of their best qualities seem founded upon or at least anyway coincident with that belief. Sometimes when I am blissfully happy or dreadfully miserable I believe in Him myself but I don't feel any real faith or trust.'[6] AH was good company as well but in a more sisterly way than Sydney, so when at the next social evening, Sydney seemed to have lost interest in her and spent the entire evening with Polly Blackwell, she was upset. This change persisted and a couple of weeks later she commented in her diary that her evening walks with Sydney had ended. She was not unduly aggrieved at the passing of their intimacy although she reflected how sad it was that friendships pass. In her diary entry for 11 April 1882 (less than one month from the supposed trauma) she remarked that 'This year has been the happiest I ever shall spend I think or ever have.' She was still afraid that the excess of happiness she had felt over the previous year must result in some future unhappiness and wrote that she must not take her present happiness for granted as she appreciated every glorious day she was experiencing despite her 'constant terror of something miserable happening'.[7] Apart from the upset over the examinations the following year everything continued to be pleasant and exciting although she no longer harboured hope for a future with Sydney.

Being an educated middle-class woman earning her own living made her something of a misfit amongst society outside the school environment and that of the Leicester Secular Society. When she received a Valentine card which depicted Cupid breaking his bow at the sight of a woman graduate and with the words, 'Love Gives Place to Learning', it upset her. It must often have been difficult for a Victorian woman to be an academic as it went so much against convention. She showed the card to Mr Hopps, who commented that the sender obviously did not know her. It was lucky she had sympathetic and enlightened friends who could provide support at times like these and prevent her from doubting her course of action.

Because of his connections with the Leicester Secular Society, Sydney managed to procure tickets for Clara to see Arnold Toynbee, a lecturer on Political Economy at Balliol College, Oxford, give a talk in March 1882 entitled 'Are Socialists Radicals?' Toynbee, a young man of 30, of delicate constitution, was recently married. He was considered to be the, 'leader of the younger

Oxford generation, who were inspired by his social ideals'.[8] With charm, good looks and a magnetic personality he was extremely charismatic. He was a political economist whose interest lay in solving the problem of the working classes and who had great empathy with any suffering. Toynbee had made the acquaintance of the Reverend Samuel Barnett, himself an Oxford man, who had been working in the East End amongst the poor of Whitechapel since 1873. The transcript of the lecture Toynbee delivered in Leicester appears not to be extant. In a lecture delivered shortly thereafter, he spoke of the need to help the poor but not by revolutionary means. He did not believe revolution was the wish of the majority of the people. For him the middle classes had failed the poor and it was now their duty to help them. He promised the working classes that,

> We will serve you, we will devote our lives to your service and we cannot do more...But we students, we would help you if we could. We are willing to give up the life we care for, the life with books and with those we love.[9]

Toynbee practised what he preached and during his summer holiday in 1875 he rented a room in Whitechapel where he visited the schools and helped the Charity Organisation Society in their relief work. He made himself a part of the community in order to be able to influence it for the good.

Clara was inspired by Toynbee's speech at Leicester. This may have provided the embryo for her own developing social conscience. Toynbee's belief in the responsibility of the middle classes to help the poor was a view she made her own in later years.[10] In her diary she wrote that she and her sister Carrie attended the lecture. Her entry commented favourably on Toynbee's attractive physical appearance and that he

> had a very sweet voice and good delivery. He gave a capital lecture although it does not seem so good to me now as it did at the time. He might be the aesthetic young man of *Punch* but Political Economy and aestheticism would hardly flourish together.[11]

Toynbee died a year later. There is a very brief entry in Clara's diary recording the event: 'March 13 1883: Arnold Toynbee is dead.' No further comment was made.

In the same year the sensational pamphlet, *The Bitter Cry of Outcast London*[12] was published, highlighting life in the London slums and alerting the middle classes to the dangers therein if the social problems were not tackled. This was one of the first widely publicised detailed descriptions given of the conditions in the East End; the area that Gentlemen and Ladies avoided so that they had hitherto been almost unaware of its existence.

As a result of this and other publicity, an attempt was begun to help the poor in the East End. Canon Barnett and his wife set up a venture named after their charismatic friend resulting in the building of 'Toynbee Hall'. This was the first University Settlement. It had the aim of educating and helping the poor to help themselves by sending a number of university students to live amongst them. The students would, in turn, benefit from the experience. *The Bitter Cry* influenced the young Clara by introducing the notion of philanthropy which over the next few years developed into a need to do something practical herself to help alleviate the suffering of her fellow human beings.

Such serious considerations were not to occupy all her time in 1882, for having stopped seeing so much of Sydney Gimson and his friend AH, by November she was involved in the latest Christmas play rehearsal at which Sydney's younger brother, Ernest began to court Clara. Ernest was 18 years old and articled to an architect. Although she was four years his senior, he had been working for Barradale's, a Leicester architect firm for a year, and considered himself quite mature enough to see a young lady. Barradale was the most advanced architect in the area and provided a solid training for Ernest. Simultaneously he enrolled at the Leicester School of Art in order to fulfil the academic requirements.

During the rehearsals for the Christmas play, Clara recorded that, 'Ernest Gimson had summoned up courage to put his arm round my waist and I nerved myself to corresponding deeds of heroism'.[13] Despite liking Ernest, Clara was not in love with him and by the following February, was ruefully proclaiming that she had met a Mr Bromberger to whom she was strongly attracted. Unfortunately he was with his wife. She spent a couple of days with them and she 'liked him immensely, he had been married a week and a half before – such is life'.

Although not in love with Ernest it is possible that he was in love with her. From her diary entries we can see that she had been seeing him regularly. They were both involved in the acting club, together with Sydney. Whilst living in Leicester she indulged her interest in drama in this club and by attending numerous theatrical performances both locally and back in London.

At this time Clara began to write some fiction and poetry. Her earliest example appears in the *Wyggeston Girls' Gazette* in which, as part of ideas for 'Amusements for Evenings at Home', in the number for December 1885 the editor provided a series of words required to be incorporated into a poem. Clara's contribution was the best published. The words given were:- Cliff, eyes, green, fate, sea, rock, sleep, bell. Her typically Victorian melodramatic offering was as follows:

> With awestruck glance, I gazed upon the cliff,
> Then on that figure lying with closed eyes,
> With visage pale and features cold and stiff;
> Upon that form that never more could rise;
> And I had done the deed, her awful fate
> My hand had dealt. I gazed upon the green
> And ever flowing deep; there seemed to be the gate
> By which I might rejoin her and be free;
> Free from the anguish of the awful shock,
> Free from the troubles of life's stormy sea,
> Free from the haunting thought of that dark rock.
> There on those foaming waters I could sleep,
> Buried without the aid of book or bell,
> Hushed by the murmurs of the mighty deep
> With only dashing waves to sound my knell.

This dark frame of mind may have been caused by the EW affair. On Sunday 25 May 1884 an entry in her diary was remarkable for the matter of fact way in which she recorded a proposal of marriage. The entry begins by making the announcement that Sydney had become engaged on 3 May to Miss Lovibond. No further comment is made other than this bare fact. A detailed description of a trip she had made to the House of Commons, Ladies' Gallery follows. At this she had been a spectator to an amendment being proposed to the 1884 Franchise Bill. Gladstone had made his speech on the subject several nights before but she listened to the other members' contributions to the bill, including Stansfield, Lawson, Colonel King and General Alexander who all spoke in favour. She heard Sir Stafford Northcote give what she considered to be a very poor speech also in favour. John Morley spoke against as did Labouchere who, she commented, was coarse and vulgar. She thought that Gladstone looked 'so clean' and although Randolph Churchill did not speak she 'conceived rather a sneaking affection for that worthless young man'.[14] Finally, almost as an addendum, in her manuscript diary Collet added that EW asked her to marry him and she had refused him twice.

Her next diary entry was not made for nine months when she stated that, 'Last term I was so miserable and limp, chiefly in consequence of the EW affair, that except school work I hardly did anything.'[15] EW had made an impact on the young woman. Her social life changed at this point. Previously she had gone out almost every night and been enjoying life. For a while she became confused and introspective in her diary. The question that remains unanswered is the identity of EW, who had managed to throw the apparently unruffable Clara into a state of upset and worry. He may have been a master from the nearby boys' school, or he may have been another acquaintance made via the Secular Society connection. In her diary Clara had a way of abbreviating names to ensure anonymity for anyone whom she wished not to identify. She commented early on in her diary that she did 'not like to put the full names for fear of accidents',[16] and this she maintained for most of the entries. She referred to Sydney and Ernest Gimson mainly by their first names, probably because she would not have minded their knowing what she wrote about them. It is possible that EW was Ernest William Gimson who at this point in their relationship she felt necessary to disguise for the sake of propriety in case of the aforementioned accidents now that her friendship had taken on a new tone. She may have decided to just use his first two initials as a code so that she alone would know whom she was talking about, but any future reader would only be able to guess at the identity. Her friendship with Ernest appears to have been developing prior to this time and no other person seems to have entered her life to usurp his position. One would have expected her to have commented on a rift in their friendship if she had begun a new relationship. Someone whom she had allowed to put his arm around her waist must have been a person with whom she felt comfortable and who was special. A respectable middle-class woman did not allow men to make such advances unless they were serious.

Although upset by the whole episode Clara believed initially that she had made the right decision in turning down EW. She commented that he hero-worshipped her, which provides evidence that EW could have indeed been Ernest who was younger than she was. Although she liked EW very much she did not love him. She began to doubt whether she would ever be able to care for anyone but herself, which made her realise that she would inevitably miss out on marriage and child bearing. By the next entry she shows that she was having second thoughts about her decision to reject EW. If it was Ernest, he had a good, affluent family background with excellent prospects for the future in his chosen architectural career. Had Clara married him, or whoever EW was, it would have relieved her of the necessity of worrying about depending on her own resources to make a living. She could settle down and raise a family in the Victorian tradition, never again needing to concern herself about examinations as she had recently been doing, nor whether she would be able to find work other than teaching. Being given the option of no longer needing to earn a living must have been attractive indeed. Ernest was a kindly man who would be able to provide for her every need; but did Clara want to give up work as she would have been forced to do on marriage? Was family life really what this working woman aspired to? Or did she harbour ambitions which marriage would not satisfy? She had already articulated her desire to leave teaching in order to take an MA. If she were to marry this would no longer be an option. Had she been desperately in love with this man, she would have gone for the safe and conventional option, but in view of her lack of serious emotions for him, the decision was made easier. She turned him down and had few qualms about having done so.

By May 1885 she had put the whole episode behind her. In her diary she commented that 'The little momentary weakness I had for him was the result of much thinking and has died out completely...He said he wouldn't ask me again.' Clara was afraid that if she made a decision to marry without love she might eventually meet someone else with whom she would fall in love which would only serve to make her dislike and resent EW, something she had no wish to do. 'It is much better to live an old maid and get a little "honey" from the short real friendships I can have with men for whom I really care myself than to be bound for life to a man just because he thinks he cares for me.'[17]

In the same entry she was already commenting about other men. Her friend Gertie's brother, Jack Spencer, was given a special mention. She described him as very tall and rather plain but she rather took to him and said she 'liked him very much in fact; he seems to have plenty of character and we got quite friendly'.[18] Nothing came of this friendship but it shows that by this time she had put EW behind her. Whoever the mysterious EW was we will never be sure but whether or not it was Ernest Gimson, however, she did remain in touch with him for very many years as we shall see.

In January 1884 William Morris visited Leicester at the invitation of the Leicester Secular Society to deliver a lecture entitled, *Art and Socialism*. He described the lecture as 'really Art under Plutocracy'.[19] Sydney and Ernest Gimson organised the visit and Clara greatly enjoyed the occasion.

There must have been many discussions about his ideas in the months following his visit. Morris was an ardent socialist and in 1884, the year of his visit to Leicester, he was involved, along with Edward Aveling and Eleanor Marx, in the formation of the Socialist League. His views can hardly have failed to leave a mark on Clara. Morris and Toynbee opened her eyes to the conditions of the poor in London and inspired in her a philanthropic wish to do something about such atrocities. Sydney left a description of Morris' visit in his book about the Leicester Secular Society:

> The bigger event to us was the coming of William Morris. His reputation as a poet and decorative craftsman (the Kelmscott Press had not then been started) was so high that we were definitely very nervous of meeting the great man. Ernest and I went to the station, and, two minutes after his train had come in, we were at home with him and captured by his personality. His was a delightfully breezy, virile personality. In his conversations, if they touched on subjects which he felt deeply, came little bursts of temper which subsided as quickly as they arose and left no bad feeling behind them. He was not a good lecturer. His lectures were always read, and not too well read, but they were wonderful in substance and full of arresting thoughts and apt illustrations. In their phrasing and general form they were beautiful.[20]

William Morris was invited back to the Gimson household for dinner after the lecture. Ernest and Sydney ended the evening up in the smoking room.

> When Mr Hopps had left, Morris, my sister Sarah, Ernest and I went up there and had a delightful talk which I can never forget. Sarah left us after about an hour but the other three of us sat talking until nearly 2 o'clock.
>
> I am sure that one reason for this long sitting was that Morris was particularly interested in Ernest, then 19 years old and articled to the Leicester architect, Isaac Barradale, and saw something of the possibilities in him. At any rate when Ernest was anxious to have some experience in a London architect's office, some two years later, he after much hesitation for fear of intrusion, wrote to ask Morris's advice and perhaps a letter of introduction to a suitable architect. At once Morris sent him three letters of introduction. Delighted and excited, Ernest took the three letters up to London, but he only had to present one, to J.D. Sedding, who at once took him into his office where he stayed for two years.

Whilst in London he joined several societies and committees with which Morris was actively associated, and came continuously under his influence, learnt a great deal from him and was imbued with those ideals which governed the rest of his life. Between his first visit to us in 1884 and Ernest's going to London in 1886, Morris paid us several visits and had, no doubt, become sure that Ernest would grow to something worthwhile under the right influence. Ernest went far and was recognised as one of the great craftsmen of his generation. I know he always felt he owed his great opportunity to the visits of William Morris to Leicester.[21]

Shortly after his arrival in London, Ernest wrote to his brother Sydney. He had already made contact with Clara and leaves us with a good description of life at 7, Coleridge Road:

I started after tea…smelling strongly of fish and beer. Clara came to the door and took me into the front room. Edith and Miss Richards were reclining on the sofa and Harold was amusing himself at the small billiard table in the middle of the room. This room is divided from the one at the back by folding doors which were open, disclosing a larger pleasant room, and a pretty piece of garden at the back. I had several games of billiards with Clara, and after cocoa (a substitute for supper) we played whist…I saw Mr Collet for about 10 minutes. He is a small quaint man, who might make an exceedingly good 'Lord Chancellor' you could imagine…I thought perhaps you would be interested to know what their home was like, as we have heard such queer descriptions, I was very agreeably surprised to find such a pleasant house. I am going to have a game of tennis with Clara at Mornington Crescent some evening. She wanted a bad player, so she asked me.[22]

During her years at Wyggeston, Clara became involved for the first time in campaigning for women's suffrage. In April 1882 on one of the school social evenings, an entertainment was devised whereby everyone had to write down a subject for debate. The papers were mixed up and redistributed. A woman by the name of Annie was handed the first paper to debate. It was Clara's contribution, as she proudly exclaimed in her diary and the subject that she had chosen for debate was 'Women's Rights'. In November of the same year she took part in a women's suffrage demonstration. This was probably a local Leicestershire event as she mentions that Sydney and AH had attended as well.

By 1885 she felt that the time was right for her to fulfil her plans of returning to full-time education:

The whole school united in sorrow at parting from two of our teachers, who had been in the school since it opened, more than seven years ago. Miss Clara Collet, BA, who is now studying in London was [a] teacher of the first class during the whole of that time...On Saturday, the 1st of August, thirty of Miss Clara Collet's girls drove with her to Longcliffe where they had tea.[23]

On the day that her departure was announced in the school assembly she was unable to contain her tears and was full of trepidation that she was leavi ng the 'pleasantest part of my life behind'.[24] Her career as a schoolmistress had thus ended. She was giving up job security and a good salary. During the seven years she worked at the school her income had doubled from £80 to the respectable sum of £160.

A tie was maintained with Wyggeston school by means of her sister Caroline who remained there teaching for several more years. The exact date Carrie left Leicester is not clear but she later suffered from several periods of illness from which she convalesced in Sidmouth – the beginning of many years of association the family had with the Devon seaside town. By 1898 Carrie was back living at 7, Coleridge Road, Crouch End, London, the Collet family home. Clara continued to make contributions to the *Wyggeston Gazette* from 1887–90 consisting of articles on the perils of revolutionary socialism; laissez-faire versus government intervention with regard to solving the problem of poverty (her solution was that people with intelligence and money had a moral obligation to help those less fortunate than themselves) and pro women's trade unions of which she wholeheartedly approved.

In 1890 Clara attended an Old Pupils' Association Meeting to give what was described as a rather racy talk on an author named Thomas Day whose 'life and love affairs proved very entertaining'.[25]

Her other continuing link with Wyggeston was her membership of the newly formed Association of Assistant Mistresses. She went to the inaugural meeting in January 1884 at the Grey Coat Hospital in Westminster and became a member of the Leicestershire branch. It is possible that Clara's interest in this association was spawned as a result of discussions with her old headmistress, Miss Buss, who was in favour of the setting up of such an association for school mistresses. Buss was the President of the Head Mistresses' Association. Mrs Bryant and Miss Sara Burstall, teachers from the NLCS, were also inaugural members of the Association of Assistant Mistresses. Bryant went on to become the second President of the Association. Sara Burstall had been in the same class as Clara at the NLCS and continued as a teacher at the school after attending Girton College. Mrs Millicent Fawcett was Acting Chairwoman. The aims of the Association were:

a) To further the interests of the profession;
b) To render their work of the highest efficiency;
c) To afford mutual help.[26]

Clara joined as a life member for the Midland Counties Branch of the Association. By 1887 she was an unattached member and remained so until at least 1888.

In 1885, when she returned to London, her future was unsure. She was making a jump into the great abyss of uncertainty – a brave step for a woman with no financial backing living in a world which allowed middle-class women into the workplace only very grudgingly.

NOTES

1. F. J. Gould, *History of the Leicester Secular Society* (Leicester: Leicester Secular Society, 1900).
2. Throughout her diary Clara refers to Sydney Gimson as Sidney. The correct spelling will be used here.
3. Mary Comino, author of *Gimson and the Barnsleys: Wonderful Furniture of a Commonplace Kind* (London: Evans Brothers, 1980), has suggested that AH may have been Alfred Hopps, a friend from the Leicester Secular Society. Clara does refer later to Mr Hopps by his full name rather than initials.
4. MSS diary, 28 February 1882.
5. Ibid., 7 March 1882.
6. Ibid., 28 March 1882.
7. Ibid., 11 April 1882.
8. Dr Werner Picht, *Toynbee Hall and the English Settlement Movement* (trans. Lilian A. Cowell) (London: G. Bell & Sons, 1914), p. 11.
9. Picht, *Toynbee Hall*, p. 22.
10. See Collet, 'Socialism'.
11. Typed diary, 30 March 1882.
12. Andrew Mearns, *The Bitter Cry of Outcast London* (London: James Clarke, 1883).
13. MSS diary, 19 November 1882.
14. Typed diary, 25 May 1884.
15. MSS diary, 1 February 1885.
16. Ibid., 16 February 1878.
17. Ibid., 10 May 1885.
18. Ibid., May 1885.

19. Clara E. Collet, 'Obituary: Charles Booth, The Denison Club and H. Llewellyn Smith', *Journal of the Royal Statistical Society*, Parts III–IV (1945), p. 482.
20. Sydney Gimson, 'Part 1', *Random Recollections of the Leicester Secular Society* (Leicester: Leicestershire Records Office, 1932), p. 22.
21. Ibid., p. 23.
22. Letter from Ernest Gimson to his brother Sydney (Syd as he calls him), 20 May 1886. The Arts and Crafts Archives at Cheltenham Art Gallery and Museum. Thanks to Mary Greensted.
23. *Wyggeston Girls' Gazette*, July 1885.
24. MSS diary, 10 May 1885.
25. *Wyggeston Girls' Gazette*, July 1890.
26. G.A. Richards, 'The History and Aims of the Association', MRC, Warwick University, unpublished MSS 59/4/7/14.

Part III

The East End, Poverty and Investigation 1885–93

1

Poverty in the East End and the Charity Organisation Society

Two millions of people, or thereabout, live in the East End of London. That seems a good sized population for an utterly unknown town. They have no institutions of their own to speak of, no public buildings of any importance, no municipality, no gentry, no carriages, no soldiers, no picture galleries, no theatres, no opera – they have nothing. It is the fashion to believe that they are all paupers, which is a foolish and mischievous belief, as we shall presently see. Probably there is no spectacle in the whole world as that of this immense, neglected, forgotten great city of East London. It is even neglected by its own citizens, who have never yet perceived their abandoned condition. They are Londoners, it is true, but they have no part or share of London; its wealth, its splendours, its honours exist not for them. They see nothing of any splendours; even the Lord Mayor's show goeth westward: the city lies between them and the greatness of England. They are beyond the wards, and cannot become aldermen; the rich London merchants go north and south and west; but they go not east. Nobody goes east. Books on London pass it over; it has little or no history; great men are not buried in its churchyards, which are not even ancient, and crowded by citizens as obscure as those who now breathe the upper airs about them. If anything happens in the east, people at the other end have to stop and think before they can remember where the place may be.

So wrote Walter Besant in 1882 in *All Sorts and Conditions of Men – An Impossible Story*,[1] a novel of social realism set in the East End of London in which he wished to illustrate to his readers the extent of poverty in the area. This theme was taken up by the sensationalist journalist George Sims and the Reverend Andrew Mearns. Mearns, as a vicar, was motivated to write his tract because of low attendance by the poor at Church services, a situation which seriously concerned him. His descriptions of the living conditions of the poor caused a ripple of horror among those living elsewhere in London. If not actually saddened to think that people could be living in such a way they were at least frightened to discover that potential revolution might be stirring just a few miles from their own dwellings. Mearns aimed to shock with his revelations of life in the East End:

The Condition in Which They Live

We do not say the condition of their homes, for how can those places be called homes, compared with which the lair of a wild beast would be a comfortable and healthy spot? Few who will read these pages have any conception of what these pestilential human rookeries are, where tens of thousands are crowded together amidst horrors which call to mind what we have heard of the middle passage of the slave ship. To get into them you have to penetrate courts reeking with poisonous and malodorous gases arising from accumulations of sewage and refuse scattered in all directions and often flowing beneath your feet; courts, many of them which the sun never penetrates, which are never visited by a breath of fresh air, and which rarely know the virtues of a drop of cleansing water. You have to ascend rotten staircases, which threaten to give way beneath every step, and which, in some places have already broken down... You have to grope your way along dark and filthy passages swarming with vermin. Then, if you are not driven back by the intolerable stench, you may gain admittance to the dens in which thousands of beings, who belong as much as you, to the race for whom Christ died, herd together. Have you pitied the poor creatures who sleep under railway arches, in carts or casks, or under any shelter which they can find in the open air? You will see that they are to be envied in comparison with those whose lot it is to seek refuge here. Eight feet square – that is about the average size of very many of these rooms. Walls and ceiling are black with the accretions of filth which have gathered upon them through long years of neglect. It is exuding through cracks in the boards overhead; it is running down the walls; it is everywhere. What goes by the name of a window is half of it stuffed with rags or covered by boards to keep out wind and rain; the rest is so begrimed and obscured that scarcely can light enter or anything be seen outside... As to furniture – you may perchance discover a broken chair, the tottering relics of an old bedstead, or the mere fragment of a table; but more commonly you will find rude substitutes for these things in the shape of rough boards resting upon bricks, an old hamper or box turned upside down, or more frequently still, nothing but rubbish and rags.

Every room in these rotten and reeking tenements houses a family, often two. In one cellar a sanitary inspector reports finding a father, mother, three children, and four pigs.[2]

Clara had returned to London to take her MA just as these revelations were being printed. With her father's radical interest in newsworthy stories and her own involvement in academic arenas she must, like many another middle-class woman, have become only too aware of these atrocities involving citizens living within walking distance of where she was studying; and like many another middle-class woman, she became involved in philanthropic work.

She joined the Society for Organising Charitable Relief and Repressing Mendacity, more commonly known as the Charity Organisation Society or the COS, and she was won over by their philosophy. Rather than the indiscriminate handing out of money which they felt would exacerbate poverty by allowing the poor to depend upon charity, the philosophy of the COS was to encourage the poor to help themselves. Anyone perceived as a malingerer was not given aid. It was thought that if given something for nothing, the recipient with no further necessity to work would become dependent on charity. The COS wanted to help the poor to solve their problems for themselves. The free distribution of charity would, they speculated, encourage more people to use it to buy alcohol rather than joining the day's queue for casual labour. The COS principle was based on the idea that, 'Poverty is principally the result of a moral failure, and indiscriminate charity contributes to or aggravates the failure.'[3] In her obituary of Sir Charles Loch, the Secretary of the COS (1875–1913), Clara wrote:

> [his] work was largely educative and aimed at persuading workers and societies of all denominations, engaged in relief work, to join together...to discover the right method of relieving each case of distress, making the independence and self-support of the man or woman relieved the main objects pursued and promoted.[4]

Beatrice Potter joined the COS before Clara, at the height of the frenzy caused by the publication of Mearns' book. Beatrice joined the Soho committee in 1883. As a consequence of her work with the COS and her association with Samuel Barnett, by August 1885 she had become involved in helping with rent collection from tenants of a tenement block named Katherine Buildings. This tenement was classed as a 'model building' and had been constructed by Samuel Barnett's East End Dwellings' Company as part of his attempt to improve housing for the very poor. These dwellings were managed on the Octavian system of 5 per cent dividend for investors, an idea instigated by Octavia Hill, the housing reformer, some years before. They provided rooms at a reasonable rent which poor working people could afford. If the tenants became ill or unemployed and were unable to pay their rent, the regime was tough and although small arrears of rent were allowed, if the amount was allowed to accrue for more than a couple of weeks or the character of the tenants was considered questionable they were evicted. This work was demanding for an upper-middle-class woman like Beatrice Potter used to servants, but she was determined to do something to help the poor. Unlike Clara she did not need to earn a living as her father was a rich railway magnate. Unpaid philanthropy was one of the few occupations suitable for a lady, and Beatrice followed her sister Kate into this work. She continued for the next four months, helping Miss Pycroft with collecting rents, handing out notices to quit and evicting tenants. Such were the needs of her tenants that on occasion she would have to work a 40-hour week. She did not have a strong constitution and often found the work physically exhausting, 'I am constantly weary; life is a continual struggle, a real battlefield, both physically and mentally.'[5]

Despite these being known as 'model' buildings they would be considered squalid by today's standards. Most tenants occupied one room which sometimes housed their whole family. Although there was sanitation and running water, this was only supplied to a central block which was seldom kept clean due to the numbers of people using it.

As a result of this first-hand experience Beatrice became disillusioned with philanthropy as a means to solving the social condition and began to believe that legislation was the only answer. She thought that the problem was too big to be dealt with by individuals and that the situation could not improve until laws were laid down centrally.

Beatrice found the work especially hard as she was trying, after the death of her mother three years previously, to keep the household for her father and to look after her younger sister, Rosy, who was a teenager suffering from what appears to have been anorexia nervosa. In November 1885 her father suffered a stroke, necessitating her to curtail her philanthropic work and return as eldest unmarried daughter to care for both her father and sister. She was not able to return to social work until late 1886, by which time she had managed to organise a rota for the care of their father with her elder sisters, allowing her a little time off to pursue her own life. Instead of returning to rent collecting she chose instead to help her cousin Mary's husband, Charles Booth, in his venture of investigating the level of poverty throughout London. Beatrice agreed with Booth that, if the facts of London's poverty were known, it would be a basis upon which to legislate to improve conditions. It was at this time that she severed her links with the COS. Many COS members were suspicious of Booth's methods and motives and especially his desire for an old age pension which they saw as an indiscriminate handout. Although Booth managed to maintain a working relationship with C.S. Loch (they were on several committees together), Beatrice became less tolerant of the ways of the COS as her ideas matured. She later wrote that although the COS was,

> an honest though short-circuited attempt to apply the scientific method of observation and experiment, reasoning and verification, to the task of delivering the poor from their miseries by the personal service and pecuniary assistance tendered by their leisured and wealthy fellow-citizens,

she criticised its ideas that the 'mass-misery of great cities arose mainly, if not entirely, from spasmodic, indiscriminate and unconditional doles, whether in the form of alms or in that of Poor Law Relief'.[6] Beatrice had become a socialist.

The idiosyncrasies of the COS continued to fulfil a part of Clara's life for considerably longer than Beatrice. She continued paying her membership fees from 1884 until at least 1906 (the date of her last contribution to the Charity Organisation Review). Like Beatrice, Clara did not believe that the handing out of 'doles' could be the main cause of poverty. For her, poor wages were to blame for the poverty of those willing to work and she began a campaign writing papers, putting forward her plans for the introduction of a minimum wage. She wanted this to be set not by the government but voluntarily by the owners of businesses. She advocated the boycotting of factories and employers who paid wages below subsistence level. She wanted the consumer to control wages.[7] She was one of the first to see that people had power to control the behaviour of the owners of businesses.

Despite, on the one hand blaming poor wages for poverty, paradoxically Clara also blamed poverty on character in the same way as did other members of the COS. The COS came to every case with character in mind and before they would issue any assistance assessed the motivation of the individuals to work, whether they drank or whether they led a frugal, moral life. People of 'good' character were divided from those of 'bad'. People who had been working, yet whose work might have been of a temporary or precarious nature or who were paid a wage too small on which to survive, would be given help. It was these on whom Clara based her theory that wages must be made high enough for people to live. She was convinced that if people were paid more they would be in better health and thus able to work harder, thereby becoming more profitable. This, she argued, would make the necessary increase in wages cost productive. During her work for the COS, Clara studied the details of 400 families who had applied for help from the Society over a period of eight months. She divided them into four groups; the first were in receipt of low wages even when in full-time work; the second were victims of inefficiency; the third suffered from irregularity as a result of fluctuations in trade and the fourth group suffered from irregularity due to the nature of the occupation. Thus the COS served as a training ground for Clara's later statistical work with Booth and the Civil Service. She tried to shame her readers into boycotting goods produced by employers paying low wages. She wrote:

> Anyone who buys the articles thus made, because they are cheap, unless she herself is only paid at that rate, is deliberately living on the flesh and blood of some of her fellow creatures, and is practising a refined cannibalism...No-one should buy garments, for example, if it is obvious on calculation that only starvation wages have been given.[8]

In order to give the shopper knowledge of the unscrupulous employer she was pro trade unions being given the authority to disseminate this information. For Clara it was the consumer who had control over irregularity of employment providing shopping habits could be changed. Slack periods in the clothing industry could be eliminated, she argued, if shoppers purchased their goods regularly throughout the year, by having their winter outfits made in the period between summer and autumn when staff were traditionally laid off through lack of demand. She suggested that rates of pay could be increased by reducing shopping hours as the same amount of work would be done in less time and with less waste of labour.

> As the work done is the same, wages need not be lessened, but the hours of work would be shortened, and therefore the rate of wages would be raised. Unnecessary trouble to a shopkeeper also increases his work, and therefore rational and conscientious buyers should form some idea what it is they want before going into a shop and should not, on the other hand, allow themselves to be tempted to buy what they do not want.[9]

This article shows her independent mind and determined nature. It illustrates the ideals by which she lived. She would behave in just such a way should she be running a business. Her Unitarian beliefs of altruism and caring were deeply ingrained. The problem was she was unable to see that other people did not live by her exacting rules. She had, however, recognised that consumers had power.

In the November 1890 issue of *Our Magazine*, there is an article commenting that Clara had given an account of the work and principles of the COS illustrating the dangers its workers had to face 'By anecdotes of clever impostures within her own experience.' This is the only mention made of Clara being engaged in fieldwork for the Society. Her contribution was more via articles contributing regularly to the Charity Organisation Review (nine items in the years 1889–1906). Her obituary of Sir Charles Loch was written in 1923, after which she seems to have broken links with the organisation. In this it is noteworthy that whilst no longer positively supporting the views of the COS Clara does not condemn them.

On Monday 11 March 1889 she was elected to the Committee of the Charity Organisation Society as an 'additional member' to the Central Council.[10] Other members elected at the same meeting included Octavia Hill and Samuel Barnett. The Secretary was Loch. Collet did not often attend meetings as they were held on Monday afternoons when she was at work, but she did attend local meetings at St Pancras.[11]

Alongside her newly begun philanthropic work Collet settled into academic life enjoying the fresh challenges. She moved into College Hall, Gordon Square and within a year had been awarded an MA in Political Economy. She must have had money saved from her time as a school mistress to tide her over during this period of uncertain income. In addition to her savings she was, in 1886, awarded the Joseph Hume Scholarship in Political Economy which provided the small grant of £20 per annum for three years. She wrote scientific papers, a couple of short stories, and did some supply teaching at the NLCS, 'Miss Buss has asked me to teach two mornings a week...only for this term though.'[12] At this time her sister Edith had a holiday from teaching for a term. She may have been unwell. During this period Clara filled her place at the NLCS and taught Latin in the autumn term of 1892. These odds and ends seemed to have been her only sources of income from 1885 until 1893, a period of eight years. She did also draw upon her teaching experience and organised a series of lectures. She advertised in *The*

Athenaeum which was the 'Journal of English and Foreign Literature, Science, the Fine Arts, Music and the Drama'. In February 1887 the first notice appeared:

> Miss C.E. Collet, MA (Lond), Joseph Hume Scholar in Political Economy at University College, reads with students in Mental and Moral Science and Lectures to classes on Political Economy.

She gave her parents' address to which to send replies. The second advertisement was in January 1889 and read:

> Courses of Lectures for Ladies on Economics and History will be given by Miss C.E. Collet, MA, and Miss L. Macdonald, MA at Westbourne Park Institute, Porchester Road, W.
> Six lectures on the WAGES QUESTION by Miss C.E. Collet, MA, on Tuesday, February 5th and Following Tuesdays, at 3.30pm.
> Six lectures on the ROMAN EMPIRE from AUGUSTUS TO JUSTINIAN, by L. Macdonald, MA, on Friday, February 8th, and following Fridays, at 3.30pm.
> Fee for each course, £1 1s. Single lectures 4s. Special arrangements for schools. Apply by letter to The Principal, College Hall, Byng Place WC.

Despite keeping herself busy during this time of uncertain income the lack of regular earnings must have worried her and she took every opportunity to earn extra by lecturing or any other means offered her. Alongside all this extraneous activity she continued her studying. Using the money from the Joseph Hume scholarship she spent the years 1886–89 studying pure mathematics at University College, London.

NOTES

1. Walter Besant, *All Sorts and Conditions of Men – An Impossible Story* (London: Chatto & Windus, 1882), pp. 48–9.
2. Mearns, *The Bitter Cry*, pp. 4–5.
3. Charles Loch Mowat, *The Charity Organisation Society: 1869–1913: Its Ideas and Work* (London: Methuen, 1961), p. 68.
4. Clara E. Collet, 'Obituary: Sir Charles Loch,' *Economic Journal*, Vol. 33 (March 1923), pp. 123–6.
5. Norman MacKenzie and Jeanne MacKenzie (eds), *The Diary of Beatrice Webb*, Vol. 1 – *Glitter Around and Darkness Within* (London: Virago and LSE, 1982–1986), 8 November 1885, p. 143.
6. Beatrice Webb, *My Apprenticeship* (London: Penguin, 1971), pp. 252ff.

7. Clara E. Collet, 'The Economics of Shopping', *Wyggeston Girls' Gazette* (July 1887), pp. 150–7.
8. Ibid., p. 154.
9. Ibid.
10. Charity Organisation Society archives, London Metropolitan Archives.
11. MSS diary, 1 May 1890.
12. Ibid., 8 May 1890.

2

Jack the Ripper and Charles Booth

Annie Chapman's body was found at about 6 a.m. on 31 August 1888, at the back of a cheap lodging house at 29, Hanbury Street, Whitechapel. It was one of the 17 lodgers, an elderly man by the name of John Davis, who made the gruesome discovery. He came downstairs as the church clock was striking six o'clock in the morning, opened the yard door and saw the body. The police report described her as

> lying on her back, dead, left arm resting on left breast, legs drawn up, abducted, small intestines and flap of the abdomen lying in a large quantity of blood above the left shoulder; throat cut deeply from left and back in jagged manner right around the throat.[1]

This was the second woman to be found murdered in such a way in the vicinity within two weeks. Over the next two months a further three women were found, each seemingly more mutilated than the one before.

Vigilante groups were organised to patrol the streets. 'Any passer-by who aroused the suspicion of a street crowd was forcibly seized and hauled into the local police station.'[2] The Home Secretary refused to offer a reward for the capture of the culprit for fear that the 'danger of false charge is intensified by the excited state of public feelings'.[3]

To the people living outside the East End and especially those with dealings in the adjacent City of London, there was an increased fear from this so-called 'outcast' London. The militant poor had spilled out of the slums to riot and demonstrate in Trafalgar Square in 1886 when the Fair Trade League met to demand for measures to be taken against unemployment. Around 20,000 dockers, building workers and other working-class people assembled for a peaceful demonstration. They were met by members of the Social Democratic Federation who encouraged rioting and looting causing around £50,000 worth of damage.

During the following days a heavy fog hung over London both metaphorically and actually. Many local shopkeepers barricaded their shops against possible further looting.

The following year homeless people began setting up camps in Trafalgar Square. Charitable organisations donated free food. It took some months before the Home Secretary and the head of the Metropolitan Police agreed on what would be the best action to take. The decision finally made was to ban all meetings and processions in Trafalgar Square. On what was to become known as 'Bloody Sunday', 13 November 1887, a march was planned by the Metropolitan Federation of Radical Clubs to protest about the government's policy in Ireland. The police dispersed the demonstrators before they reached their destination but not without bloodshed and rioting.

The middle classes increasingly began to call for reform. Even those who cared little for the well-being of the 1 million inhabitants of 'Outcast London' cried out for something to be done to preserve their own safety and livelihoods.

It was into this abyss that Clara Collet voluntarily launched herself. She now looked upon herself as a 'student of social conditions'.[4] Exactly how she first became involved with Charles Booth's plan to conduct research into the extent of poverty in London, concentrating on the East End, is not known. Booth first read his paper on his planned scheme at the Royal Statistical Society (RSS) in May 1886. It was entitled *Occupations of the People of the United Kingdom, 1801–81*. It is possible that she first met him as a result of their common membership of the RSS or the COS.

In late 1888, Booth was looking for someone to take responsibility for conducting research into women's work in the East End. This was to be just one section of the investigation which was to make up his *Life and Labour of the People in London*. Booth 'employed hardly any routine workers and there was no section of work in which he did not take an active part. He was resolved to make use of no fact to which he would not give a quantitative value.'[5] This was a radical new approach to statistics and a concept to which Clara attached importance throughout the rest of her working life. The workers Booth did employ were mostly graduates of Oxford or Cambridge. They were mainly men and almost all had contacts with Toynbee Hall. There were, however, a few exceptions.

Beatrice Potter, unlike Clara and the male members of Booth's team, had little formal education but like many upper-middle-class ladies her education had been obtained informally with the aid of her father and the family library. She had ambition and the advantage that Booth's wife Mary was her cousin. Beatrice had been fortunate to have been involved in the early planning of the work as a result of this family connection. She later thought of her input as part of her 'apprenticeship'. At the time she lacked some of the skills necessary to process the information she was collecting. Her work was not always of the highest standard. Her association with Booth's work continued sporadically from 1886–88, collaborating with him on work on 'The Docks', 'The Tailoring Trade' and 'The Jewish Community'.

Mrs Alice Green was another exception to the normal investigator working for Booth. She had set out initially to investigate 'Women's Work' in the East End. As the wife of John R. Green she spent nine years supporting his work as a minister to the poor in East London. Mrs Green had been widowed in 1883 when her husband had died from tuberculosis. According to Beatrice, with whom she later became friendly, Green's work was more a means to an end:

> Now that she has climbed the social ladder, social success based on her husband's achievements does not satisfy her. She aims at the position to be gained by personal merit. But she does not love her work for its own sake, but only for what it brings her, not for what it may bring others.[6]

Beatrice's cousin Margaret Harkness (later, using the pseudonym John Law she was to become a respected novelist of social conditions), wrote asking, 'Why did not Mr Booth employ me on his enquiry into the work of women in the East End? I know more than his lady Sec. who amused me vastly by her importance when she called.'[7] Green may have viewed the work with Booth as a means for her social advancement, but it was either not delivering that aim or she was finding it too demanding, for by 1887 the work was at a standstill and Booth was not happy. In a letter sent from Mary Booth to Beatrice Potter in 1887, Mary thanked her for asking about Charles' work and continued:

> He seems rather at a stand still just now over his 'Women's Work and Wages' which Mrs Green is undertaking. Otherwise the work goes on; as well as East End life which he is really enjoying. I think it rests him and makes a change from business thought and worry more in some ways than even Gracedieu [their country home] quiet and beauty...He likes the life and the people and the...food! Which he says agree with him in kind and time of taking better than that of our class.[8]

Green must have terminated her work for Booth shortly after, as by November 1888 he had asked Beatrice if she would take it on. She was not keen to do so as she had other commitments and, having put her name to the anti-suffrage manifesto drafted by Mrs Humphry Ward, felt it might appear hypocritical.[9]

Potter was in a quandary as to whether or not to take the work on:

> In dreadful perplexity about my work. Charlie wants me to do 'Women's Work at the East End' and have it ready by March, which means sacrificing part of February to writing ... It would indefinitely postpone 'Co-operation' [she planned to undertake an independent investigation into this subject and terminate her work with Booth]. On the other hand, 'Female Labour' is a subject of growing importance, one which for practical purposes is more important than 'Co-operation'. It touches very nearly on home industries, a subject fraught with interest considered by the light of the steady cry for labour regulation. Then the work is needed to complete Charlie's book and I owe him consideration. I have already a mass of material in my head which could be used for it and it would be doing the work which lieth to my hand instead of seeking far afield for it.[10]

A few days later she was filled with depression having heard of the forthcoming marriage of Joseph Chamberlain, with whom she had once harboured hopes of marriage, and which caused her to suffer from a period of nervous collapse; all thoughts of undertaking Booth's Women's Work had gone from her head.

Booth looked elsewhere for a suitable candidate to take on this important chapter in his book which was by now nearing completion. He needed someone reliable, educated and level-headed to finish the work by the spring deadline. He chose Clara Collet.

Thus Beatrice Potter's collaboration with Booth was virtually at an end by the time Clara's began. Beatrice and Clara did maintain contact over the years, although they were never close friends. In March 1942, Clara sent Beatrice her article, 'Some Recollections of Charles Booth', which had been published in the *Social Services Review* in 1927. Collet wrote in the covering letter, 'I am only two years younger than you. [Collet was 81] This will interest you.'[11]

She had more in common with Booth's male collaborators than his previous women workers, as she had a good university education, was planning a paid future career and saw this as an ideal opportunity to improve her career prospects which were so uncertain at this time.

Thus it came about that in November 1888, at the height of the terror caused by Jack the Ripper as he had become known, Clara moved into the East End. On 9 November, Mary Jane Kelly's mutilated body was found in Millers Court, off Dorset Street. This murder was more terrible than the others. The *Illustrated Police News*, reported that:

> The throat had been cut across with a knife, nearly severing the head from the body. The abdomen had been partially ripped open, and both of the breasts had been cut from the body, the left arm, like the head, hung to body by the skin only. The nose had been cut off, the forehead skinned, and the thighs, down to the feet, stripped of the flesh. The abdomen had been slashed with a knife across downwards, and the liver and entrails wrenched away. The entrails and other portions of the frame were missing, but the liver etc., it is said, were found placed between the feet of this poor victim. The flesh from the thighs and legs, together with the breasts and nose, had been placed by the murderer on the table, and one of the hands of the dead woman had been pushed into her stomach.[12]

As Clara did not keep her diary during this period, the picture of her contribution to Booth's work has to be pieced together using the final written chapter on women's work and comments by others. Booth gave evidence for the Royal Commission on Labour in which he discussed her assistance. What we do not know are her impressions of living in the East End. She must have felt fearful, as any single lady in the area would have been. The logically minded Clara would have rationalised that it had only thus far been prostitutes whom the Ripper had chosen as his victims, and the crimes had all been committed in the early hours of the morning when she was safely in bed – but then had not Mary Kelly been in her bed?

The aim of Booth's work, to be entitled *Life and Labour of the People in London*, was to show the extent of poverty by statistical means. Once the levels of poverty were discovered then the means of dealing with the problem could be decided upon.

For the Labour Commission, Booth was asked how the statistics on women's work had been collected. He answered that, 'The enquiry was conducted by Miss Collet on my behalf and it was in the winter of 1888–9 that this enquiry into women's work was done'.[13] He said that they took as the 'general basis the census figures', and that the:

> Registrar General was good enough to give me access to the detailed sheets, so that I had more information than had been published,

which gave me the number of women employed in 1881 in their various trades...I next obtained, by the kindness of the Factory Department of the Home Office and the assistance of the factory inspectors, a list of all the workshops and factories known to them employing women, and I arranged these in a sort of directory according to the trades and localities of the trades. This part of it referred solely to East London. From the factory inspectors (especially Mr Lakeman), Miss Collet and myself also obtained a large amount of information, very valuable information...We then sought assistance from some societies that interest themselves in the condition of the factory girls. I think the principal one is called the Factory Girls' Helpers' Union...the object being to obtain introductions to the girls, to find a road, so that we might become acquainted with them. And Miss Collet in connexion with that took up her residence in the East End, and lived there for three months (she gave altogether four months to the work), and during that three months she was continually engaged in trying to come in contact with the girls, and those who were working amongst them...She would become acquainted with the girls and invite them to her house and become acquainted with them. She found it very difficult to get information that was satisfactory; but in the end she did succeed with them. That covered only factory girls. And we had also to try and get information with regard to home work; and for this purpose she went mostly to the clergy. We knew from our previous inquiries whereabouts...these home workers were to be found and we asked from the clergy for introductions to those whom they knew were working at home work, and who might be expected, with that introduction, to give honest evidence. Miss Collet visited with those introductions home workers in their homes – a number of them – and again she found it difficult to get as much as she wanted, in the time so limited.[14]

After Clara had collected all the information she could from the workers she turned to eliciting information from the employers:

We sent...a circular letter to most of them, or most of the addresses that we could find; at any rate we sent a large number of letters informing them what we were doing and asking them if they would be willing to give us information from their side of the question, and such as consented to receive Miss Collet were called upon.[15]

Any factory where she was not made welcome she would not try to gain entry but most owners were happy to allow her to conduct her survey and she was soon wandering freely amongst factory workers and employers in the East End. She would return to her lodgings where she received working women to interview and befriend. The whereabouts of these lodgings is not known

other than that they were in the East End. One could conjecture
that they would be near to what she would have perceived as the
relative security of Toynbee Hall, in whose halls of residence many
of Booth's male investigators lived but which did not accept
women lodgers.

The local vicinity was inhabited mainly by Jews. Canon
Barnett's philosophy was to improve the area for everyone and,
although a Christian himself, did not try to influence people's
religious persuasions, unlike some of the later Settlements. Several
of his associates and students were Jewish. Toynbee Hall provided
social, philanthropic and leisure activities, with the aim of self-
improvement. Its most important function was to provide local
people with educational facilities. Initially Barnett did not approve
of Booth's plan to collect statistics in London, believing it to be too
large a task to accomplish and was unable to see any benefits. Once
Booth had begun, however, Barnett gave him his whole-hearted
support including allowing Toynbee Hall to be used as a base in
the area.

Clara's work for Booth was important enough for her to be
allocated her own secretary to help collect the information. George
Arkell, whose contribution to Booth's work was enormous over
the years, who had assisted Potter in her tailoring investigation
and who was later responsible for much of the revision of the
Booth map, seconded Clara.

Little is known about Arkell on a personal level. His
contribution to Clara's enquiries consisted of interviews with fur
trade employers and of an abstract he made on the women
employed making trousers, vests and juvenile suits, but it is likely
that he accompanied her on many of her visits to factories acting as
her chaperone. There is no question, though, that he was acting on
her orders and working for her. The finished chapter was written
by her alone. In Booth's summing up for the Royal Commission, he
concluded that:

> She made full notes as she went along. At first I was sharing in the
> work, as long as it was confined to interviews with the factory
> inspectors, and so on; and afterwards Miss Collet went on alone, and
> wrote down almost everything that happened in full, and those
> notes I read as they were written. She then wrote her own chapter –
> it is entirely her writing. I simply revised what she had written to see
> that it contained everything that seemed trustworthy. [He did that
> with all his assistants' contributions]. I might say that she did her
> work exceedingly well.[16]

The working girls were invited into her home incognito as one friend to another. Booth said that she did not inform the girls as to the nature of her work as it was decided this might make them suspicious and less likely to tell the truth. She managed to gain their confidence by leading them to believe that she was a working-class woman like themselves and invited them round for tea whence she casually asked questions about their lives as working girls and the wages they earned. She also gathered information on their working conditions and made observations about the girls' character and social class. There must also have been a great many discussions about the Whitechapel murderer. Many women who worked for the 'sweated trades' were part-time prostitutes during slack periods when little or no work was available. They may have discussed other ways of making a living whilst Jack the Ripper remained on the streets in their vicinity. The better-looking and younger prostitutes worked earlier in the evening – the Ripper had thus far committed his murders late at night – leaving the older less attractive women on the streets in the early hours of the morning trying desperately to earn enough to pay for that night's lodgings.

The chapter on women's work, when it was written up, consisted mainly of statistics and their interpretation. Clara made mention of her indebtedness to George Arkell. Intermingled amongst these 'dry bones' of statistics, there comes insight into her views and ideas for improving the area. Trade unions are mentioned frequently throughout the chapter showing her interest in them and belief in their worth. Her complaint was that not enough women were combined in unions and this was to their detriment. The recently formed match girls' union was one in which she was especially interested:

> The prolonged strike in July 1888 resulted in the formation of a union, the largest union composed entirely of women and girls in England. Nearly 800 women and girls belong to this union, of whom about 650 have kept up their weekly payments. Such trade unions are really productive of good both to the members and to the employers. So far from encouraging strikes, they diminish the number of ill-judged disputes arising from faults on the part of the women, as often as from injustice on the part of the employers. If employers are in the right, a practiced committee responsible for consequences will much more readily yield to the force of logic; and if the employers are in the wrong, sensible representations made to them by the committee of a strong union will be attended to and acted upon much more promptly than if put forward by girls on

strike. Not only is friction diminished, but friendliness between employers and work-people may be promoted.[17]

Another subject she tackled was the problem of low wages. Throughout her life Clara was scathing about employers paying less than a living wage. In 1888 she decided that the wage below which a person was unable to live should be set at 9 shillings a week. She argued that if a wage is fixed it gives an incentive to those:

> whose working power has hitherto been below par through indolence or lowness of standard, to raise themselves to the required level. Those who are left are the physically or mentally incapable, or the idle. Secondly, if these are left as the wholly unemployed, they can be dealt with much more easily than the half-paid or partly unemployed, who drag down population to their level. They are not left to starve. The parish rates and charitable contributions, which at present are spent in doing harm to the many, and in lowering wages, could be wholly devoted to the improvement of the condition of the few, either in pleasure houses or workhouses, according to the circumstances of the case.[18]

Clara argued that it was better to pay a viable wage to fewer employees than a non-viable wage to more. Higher productivity would result from competition and the better health of the employed and this would compensate for the increase in wages.

Another issue of concern about which she was to write regularly was that of the:

> middle-class parent [who] imagines that he is doing his daughter a kindness when he pays the cost of her board and lodging for her, and lets her work ten and a half hours a day for what she is proud to call 'only pocket money'. He is in fact making a present to his daughter's employer which may or may not be shared by the employer with the consumer.[19]

On the subject of prostitution she believed that it was more likely to be the poorer middle-class girl worried about 'appearances' than the working-class girl, who, in order to try to maintain her standards of dress:

> often sacrifices maidenhood itself. The substance is thrown away for the shadow. These girls do not sell themselves for bread; that they could easily earn. They sin for the externals which they have learnt to regard as essentials... [Clara had] no hesitation in asserting that if

these girls worked for their living instead of working only for pocket-money, their wages would rise considerably; early marriages would be much less common and the greatest temptation to immorality would be removed. It is among these skilled workers that union is most needed and that the economic question of wages is of the most importance.[20]

The survey concentrated on working women some of whom may have turned to prostitution to subsidise their wages. The women that Jack the Ripper murdered did not fall into this category. They were all alcoholics with a catalogue of broken relationships behind them and who at the time of their murder did little if any work. They were, thus, unlikely to have been included as one of Collet's interviewees.

Clara cited unreasonably low wages as a cause for many of the social problems in the East End, including prostitution. She also blamed the girls themselves for not working hard enough and, sometimes, not being interested in working in a reputable job. Unlike many Victorians, she did not blame the girls' inheritance, but their poor environment for their moral failings. They often came from poor families and had been brought up in:

stifling rooms, with scanty food, in the midst of births and deaths, year after year. They have been accustomed to ups and downs. One week they have been on the verge of starvation, another they have shared in a 'blow out'...They care nothing for appearances, and have no desire to mix with any but their equals.[21]

The concept that environment played a part in producing personality was a new one at the end of the nineteenth century and one which Clara, with her modern outlook on life, embraced with enthusiasm.

Another radical view she introduced in her chapter on women's work is the concept that the rate of infant mortality might be linked to irregularity of the father's employment. Many Victorians believed that the very poor were almost a different species and that heredity was responsible for the condition they were in. This meant that, with these views, no manner of intervention could change the way that they lived, as this was how they were born. Clara had begun to make links to external causes such as unemployment, irregularity of work, poor environment, deprived upbringing and poor wages for their condition.

Despite believing that it was environment which contributed to the problems in the East End, she was not convinced that state intervention was the answer. Whilst her contemporaries Beatrice Potter and Eleanor Marx had both been converted to the belief that it was the responsibility of the state to legislate to improve conditions for the poor, Clara continued, for the time being, to cling to her idea that it was individuals who should be responsible for change:

> The something which should be done is to some extent being done already by quiet workers among the East End working girls, who, coming in contact with them in their clubs, their evening classes and social gatherings and in their homes, know well that improvement in the condition of these girls is identical with improvement in their moral character. What is needed for working women in general is a more practical education in the Board Schools; greater facilities for the exercise of thrift, and definite instruction in the advantages and best methods of saving... And lastly, and not least, trade union is wanted; not union against employers, but union with them... The question of wages is trivial compared with the question of regularity of employment and kind and just treatment.[22]

Clara survived her three months living in the East End. Jack the Ripper had completed his reign of terror by the time she left the area.

NOTES

1. Whitechapel Police Report, 31 August 1888.
2. *The Times*, 17 September 1888.
3. Parliamentary Papers, House of Commons, 12 November 1888, 330:904.
4. Collet, 'Obituary: Charles Booth', p. 482.
5. Collet, 'Some Recollections of Charles Booth', *Social Services Review* (1927), p. 384.
6. Mackenzie and Mackenzie (eds), *Diary of Beatrice Webb*, 4 August 1889.
7. Passfield Collection 2/1/2/2.
8. Ibid.
9. Potter's views later changed and she justified her earlier stance by saying that: 'At the root of my anti-feminism lay the fact that I had never myself suffered the disabilities assumed to arise from my sex. Quite the contrary; if I had been a man, self-respect, family pressure and the public opinion of my class would have pushed me into a money-making profession; as a mere woman I could carve out a career of disinterested research.' Mackenzie and Mackenzie (eds), *Diary of Beatrice Webb*, p. 233.
10. Ibid., 3 November 1888, p. 264.
11. Correspondence of Charles Booth, University of London Library, Senate House. MS 797I/xxxx

12. Donald Rumbelow, *The Complete Jack the Ripper* (London: Guild Publishing, 1987), p. 93.
13. British Parliamentary Papers – Industrial Relations, Vol. 27 Labour Commission Session 1892 (Shannon, Ireland: Irish University Press, 1970), p. 489.
14. Ibid.
15. Ibid.
16. Ibid., p. 490.
17. Booth, *Life and Labour of the People of London*, p. 287.
18. Ibid., p. 315.
19. Ibid., p. 320.
20. Ibid., p. 322.
21. Ibid., p. 324.
22. Ibid., p. 326.

3

The Interim Years 1890–93

After a four-year gap Clara recommenced her diary in 1890. She wrote that 'The real failure of the last three years has hardened me in many ways. I have burnt my ships; I do not regret it; but I doubt whether I should have done it if I had known what it would be.'[1] To the outsider assessing her work during the years 1887–90 she appears to have been very productive. She continued studying pure mathematics at University College from 1886–87 and 1888–89; she organised and ran several series of lectures; undertook her own independent surveys and made her important contribution to Booth's volumes. What can she have meant by 'failure'? It is most likely that she referred to her failure to find a permanent well-paid position. She said herself, later in the same entry:

> This investigating work has many drawbacks and just now I feel thoroughly unnerved by the expectation of pin pricks. I would give it up and will give it up whenever I see a chance of earning a certain £60 even by lecturing on economics. Not that I do not like the work when it is done or that I do not feel a kind of enjoyment in the risk involved in facing unknown people but although I enjoy the personal contact with so many people I should never see otherwise, the work leaves no roots behind.

She was, understandably, concerned about her future and not altogether happy about the work she was undertaking as it had no continuum, nor did it provide a regular income. A bit of investigating here and there when she could find it, intermingled with whatever else she could manage to do, did not provide security. When she left Leicester to move to London she had ambition and expected to have settled into a permanent position by the time she had been back for five years. Instead she felt she was being

> pulled in so many directions by different interests. I no longer have any vague dreams of success in something or other or even desire for it ... I am a visitor everywhere and at home nowhere and the inability to find a resting place in any one line makes me useful in a way. But it is the old story; I am constantly feeling that I do nothing properly.[2]

Her despondency was understandable. Five years was a long time to have been without definite employment and there seemed to be no foreseeable end to the uncertainty. Things had not improved by the end of November when she wrote, 'What I am going to live on next year I don't in the least know.'[3]

Despite fears for her own poverty, her time in the East End served her well in the future. During the course of her work for Booth, she made contacts at Toynbee Hall. Despite the Settlement being an all male institution, she soon found that it was possible for a woman to participate in certain areas of the Settlement's work. As she was a practised teacher and lecturer, and as the principal aim of Toynbee Hall was of an educative nature, she soon began to work as a locum when other lecturers were away sick or on holiday. She made a lifelong friend of Henry Higgs who was a member of many committees to which she also belonged and in 1890 she gave five lectures on rent for him at Toynbee Hall as he was unable to meet his commitment. The two first became acquainted when Clara was entering the Civil Service bread shop opposite the British Museum. Higgs entered at the same time. The two had been aware of each other for some time, as he had won the Joseph Hume scholarship in the same year as she had, but they had not spoken before. On recognising her he approached to give her a message from Professor Edgeworth,[4] who had asked for her address so that he could thank her for writing the article 'Maria Edgeworth and Charity'. Maria Edgeworth was the professor's cousin, and someone whose work Clara admired. Higgs informed her that he had been lecturing for four years at Toynbee Hall to supplement his income whilst taking a law degree. Unlike most of the other men at Toynbee Hall, Higgs did not come from a moneyed background and like her had to earn a living. His interest by the time he met Clara had changed from law to economics. He was proud of the large numbers of people he had attending his lectures on economics at Toynbee Hall. He later became a leading 'Le Playist' economist contributing to a book authored together with Booth and Ernest Aves entitled *Family Budgets* (1896).

Higgs soon found a permanent position as a clerk in the War Office, where he remained for 40 years, working his way up by passing the Civil Service examinations. By 1905 he had risen to become Private Secretary to the Prime Minister, Campbell Bannerman. After retiring he stood for Parliament as an Independent Liberal. He and Clara never became anything other than good friends and in her diary she said he was like a cousin. The two met frequently over the years, she would listen to his lectures, dine with him, attend meetings with him at the Economic Club and later at Fellows' dinners at University College. When he married, Clara became friendly with his wife, the three of them going on river boat trips in a rowing boat, one of Clara's favourite occupations. On Higgs' death in 1940, when Clara was 80 years old, she wrote a lengthy obituary on him in the *Economic Journal*.[5]

Another lifelong friend whose acquaintance she first made during her Toynbee Hall and Booth days, was Hubert Llewellyn Smith. He was an Oxford graduate and a resident at Toynbee Hall in 1887. He also began working for Booth in 1888 and joined many of the same societies as Booth, Higgs and Clara. Although he was four years her junior and without an MA, he entered the Civil Service as Commissioner of Labour, several ranks above Clara when she finally joined, becoming the Permanent Secretary to the Board of Trade in 1907. Beatrice Potter was also on friendly terms with him and they planned to write a book together on trade unions. She said of Llewellyn Smith that:

> He is able, unselfconscious though ambitious, a good colleague, loyal and honourable, an eminently 'outside' man – as a worker a better executant than originator... formal-minded but has ability, and is generous in his helpfulness to others working on the same lines.[6]

Clara regularly visited Llewellyn Smith and his family, often staying for the weekend at their home in Ashford, Kent, and returning with him to work on Monday morning. It was a special treat for her staying in a household with children. Their little boy Arthur she found a 'delightful child', and thought their daughter, 'Margaret will be interesting but is not yet as attractive as Arthur.'[7]

Clara and Llewellyn Smith worked closely together throughout the years and remained good friends. In 1928–35, Llewellyn Smith produced an update to *Life and Labour*, entitled *New Survey of London Life and Labour*. Still in contact with him Clara contributed a chapter on domestic service.[8]

Clara was involved with these men both as friends and as members of the same clubs. In Henry Higgs' obituary written by John Maynard Keynes, he says that 'Higgs was a very "clubbable" man'.[9] This comment could have equally been made of Clara Collet. From the late 1880s onwards she joined every organisation that was relevant to her statistical work. This proved useful to her as she became acquainted with many eminent men working in the field of economics, statistics and social investigation.

Before she returned to London, she had already been involved with the Association of Assistant Schoolmistresses and the Charity Organisation Society, and in 1890 Collet was responsible for the establishment of three new societies.

Just a month after she became acquainted with Higgs, he wrote to her old teacher from University College, Professor Foxwell, informing him that Clara wanted to,

> form a little London group of students in Social Science. She thinks that University College in particular ought to furnish a band of progressive economists who have had the blessing of a training under you. I hinted to her that the junior ought not to be born before the senior.[10] But she [thought] the two bodies would have neither common aims nor common members; and with the usual impulsiveness of women she is convening a meeting of students for next Friday.[11]

On the following Friday, Clara convened the meeting at University College and the Junior Economic Club was formed. The initial membership consisted of over 20 people and the committee of 12 included Professor Edgeworth, Ernest Aves, Hubert Llewellyn Smith and Professor Foxwell. They decided against having a president. The first topic they chose for discussion was 'The Consumption of Wealth'. Charles Booth, Professor Marshall and J.M. Keynes also attended these early meetings. Henry Higgs was Secretary from the formation of the Club until 1905 when he resigned due to pressure of work as a result of his new position as the Prime Minister's Private Secretary. Clara took over in that year and remained in the post until 1922.

Later meetings included Dr James Bonar, William Beveridge (who became President in 1920, the rules by then having changed), C.S. Loch, Beatrice Potter, Sidney Webb (who joined in 1892, the year of his marriage to Beatrice) and Mrs Bryant (by then Headmistress at NLCS).[12]

The Economic Club, as it became known from the end of its first year, was still meeting in 1920 when Clara sent a belated letter of condolence on behalf of the Club to her friend Mary Booth after the death of her husband. There had evidently been a lapse in the meetings for some time – Booth had died in 1916. She wrote that 'The Economic Club desires to express its deep sense of the loss it has sustained by the death of...Charles Booth and Ernest Aves and to place upon record its appreciation of the high value of their joint and separate work on social and economic life.'[13] She was at this time hopeful that, 'The Economic Club has every prospect of continuing with renewed life and vigour with the promised support of Sydney Chapman and Sir William Beveridge.' She was correct in her prediction, as the club was still in existence by the time that A.L. Bowley wrote her obituary in the *Economic Journal* in 1950. It was by then meeting at the London School of Economics (LSE) which had taken over from University College as the centre for the study of economics at London University. Bowley described the purpose of the Club as being for the holding of monthly meetings to discuss economic papers, with the result of sometimes expanding the original, often resulting in further publication. It was, therefore, a ground-breaking organisation.

In its early years the Economic Club also debated problems such as the future teaching of economics, including a debate initiated by Clara, voicing concern over the future curricula and examinations, organising fund raising to increase staffing levels and voicing her dissent over the setting up of the LSE when she felt that UCL (University College, London) was the prime site at the time for economic excellence. Her relationship with Beatrice Webb, as Beatrice Potter had now become, must have been strained as the establishment of the London School of Economics had been inaugurated by her and her husband.

Clara also helped to launch the Club referred to initially as The British Economic Association. This was formed at a meeting in University College on 20 November 1890. Professor Edgeworth was voted Secretary and sole Editor of the *Economic Journal* in which Clara had so many articles published over the following years. Higgs took over as Secretary in 1892 and by 1896 joined Edgeworth as Assistant Editor. Both Higgs and Clara later became members of its Council, Clara from 1918 until 1940.

Membership of the two clubs overlapped. Apart from Higgs and Edgeworth, others present at the inaugural meeting included Professor Alfred Marshall, Dr Bonar, Henry Fawcett and George Bernard Shaw.

The British Economic Association later changed its name to the Royal Economic Society and members included A.J. Balfour (at the time when he was Conservative Foreign Secretary), Viscount Haldane (who was the Lord Chancellor with the Liberals 1912–15 and with Labour in 1924), A.L. Bowley, Professor Foxwell, Hubert Llewellyn Smith, Sidney Webb and John Maynard Keynes.

Not content with the initiation of two clubs in 1890 for the promotion of economics, Collet also became involved in the setting up of the Toynbee Economic Club in November 1890. The first

President of this club was Ernest Aves, Clara's collaborator in Booth's work. Henry Higgs and Clara Collet were voted as Vice Presidents. Exactly a year later, she gave a talk to the Toynbee Economic Club on 'The Occupations of our Mothers and Grandmothers'.

> The Toynbee Economic Club has been formed to help in the study of Economics among the students of Toynbee Hall by means of:
>
> 1. Reading and discussion of papers
> 2. The arrangement of conferences
> 3. Collection of statistics and investigation of economic questions.
>
> The Club is open to all who take a serious interest in Economics.

This was the description of the aims of the Club printed on the back of a card advertising a forthcoming lecture to be given by Clara. The annual subscription was 1 shilling and the meetings were to be held on the first Tuesday of the month at 8 p.m.

Apart from being involved in the setting up of the three economic clubs, Clara also joined the well-established and respected Royal Statistical Society (RSS). Hubert Llewellyn Smith and Charles Booth were both Fellows of the RSS and in 1892–94 Booth became its President. As part of his duties Booth led a campaign for the introduction of a permanent statistical body within the Board of Trade. Partly as a result of Booth's involvement and also with the influence of A.J. Mundella, a Fellow of the RSS and the President of the Board of Trade, the Labour Department was set up. Clara, also a Fellow, could hardly be better placed to benefit from the acquaintance of these men. Other members of the RSS included Professor Marshall, Arthur Acland and Graham Balfour.

The Denison Committee had the honour of having Clara amongst its members. This society was named, like Toynbee Hall itself, after an early 'slummer', Edward Denison. He came to the East End in 1867, when he was 27 years old, like Toynbee, that he might live amongst the poor, to understand life there more fully and to enable him to help in any way he was able. This was several years prior to Arnold Toynbee's own short 'slumming' experience and before any formal institutions had been set up. Like Toynbee, Denison was doomed to a short life, dying in 1870 aged just 30. In his honour:

> A number of Gentlemen who have long been engaged in dealing
> with the social questions of the Metropolis, and some of whom are
> themselves members of the Association [the British Association for
> the Advancement of Science] are engaged in founding a society to be
> called the 'Denison Club', which will meet weekly for the
> consideration of such matters. It has been proposed that Toynbee
> Hall shall become the head-quarters of the club, and the council are
> prepared to give a cordial welcome to the proposal.[14]

Little is known about Clara's connection with this Society but it
is to be assumed that the 'Gentlemen' must have allowed a 'lady'
to join with them in their Society as in May 1890 she reported in her
diary about a meeting of the Denison Committee.

Finally, also in 1890, Clara joined the British Association for the
Advancement of Science. Again many of the names, such as
Charles Booth, A.L. Bowley and Professor Edgeworth, were
common to other societies. Another member was Mrs James
Ramsay Macdonald. She and her husband went on to become very
close friends of Clara.

The friends and acquaintances she made through the
membership of these clubs turned out to be useful for her future
career, although she cannot have been sure at the time. For
someone with her level-headedness, ambition, intelligence and
confidence in her ability these contacts could only be to her
advantage both intellectually and in regard to her future, as yet
unknown and undecided, career. In the meantime she was
beginning to concentrate her energies on statistical investigation of
social issues with a bias towards women's work.

Not all of her time was taken up with committee work. She also
engaged in leisure pursuits with her new friends. Professor
Edgeworth invited her to join him on his walking parties; the first
of which took her through the area around St Albans.[15] She wrote
in her diary that this was the first of a series of such expeditions
mostly around the Thames. In November 1890, despite all her club
activities, Clara found time to go for a week's walking holiday in
Yorkshire with Edgeworth and his group. She joined them after
attending a meeting for the British Association in Leeds. A fellow
walker was Mrs Bryant, with whom she was, by this time, on very
friendly terms.

The despondency recorded in her diary in May 1890 may have
been responsible for Clara establishing and joining so many clubs
later in the year. Her way when despondent was always to work
harder. She became less candid and more formal in her entries

6. James Ramsay MacDonald in 1911 by Solomon Joseph Solomon. (By courtesy of the National Portrait Gallery, London.)

around this time. Sometimes a page was removed and on the page following, she would make a comment about becoming too frank. Other than the comments about her relationship with E.W. whose name she kept anonymous, she rarely remarked about her personal feelings for people. Later a portion of several years of her diary entries are missing, corresponding with a period of personal upheaval about which more will be said later. Did Clara still have ideas that her memoirs might eventually be read by posterity, despite her misgivings as to her future, and did she wish to keep her private life out of such a document? Beatrice Webb had no such concerns about the nature of her diary which was full of personal comments and sweeping character judgements, and was quite unlike that by Clara Collet. This reflects the very different personalities of the two women. Beatrice was a woman led by her emotions whereas Clara Collet was led by her head.

It was around this time that Clara began making contributions to the various journals of her new societies and continued writing for the *Charity Organisation Review.* These papers show us how her opinions and ideas were being shaped. Her views on the low salaries of middle-class working women and especially teachers were made known in two papers written in 1890 and 1892 respectively. The first was for the *Journal of Education* and was originally a paper she read at a meeting of the University Association of Women Teachers. In this she made it clear that the Association's trade union functions met with her approval. She dispelled two myths which she believed people held with regard to trade unions and made her own position clear. She did not believe that trade unionism had to involve antagonism. On the contrary she was convinced that trade unions diminished antagonism rather than caused it. The public only saw disputes for which no resolution had been made rather than the myriad for which solutions had quietly been found. A rare reminder of her Victorian values is found in this paper. She commented that,

> If the intelligent foreigner were to ask me if I would give in brief one proof of our superiority to every other nation, I would answer at once, 'Our long established national trade unions, which have taught our employers and our working men to treat each other with mutual respect.'[16]

The concept of superiority of one nation over another was discussed regularly during this period. Karl Pearson, the famous mathematician and eugenicist was working at University College in the 1890s. Clara had read and was conversant with his famous work, *The Grammar of Science* (1892) and commented upon it in her diary.

In the paper entitled 'Salaries and Cost of Living' and a second paper on the same subject, 'Prospects of Marriage for Women',[17] she returned to the subject of low pay for women and called for a minimum salary, especially for teachers whom she was convinced were being paid below a working wage on the supposition that as the job was vocational poor salaries were acceptable.

In 'The Economic Position of Educated Working Women',[18] after once more demanding living wages for women teachers, she continued by requesting an increase in the areas of work acceptable for educated middle-class women. She did not see why the only profession considered suitable for these women should be teaching. She was writing about her own dilemma. Here she had found teaching to be of limited scope and had struggled on the poor pay, but having left the profession five years before, finding an alternative was proving difficult. Her suggestion was that if fathers in business considered their daughters' future and involved them in their work as they did their sons, they would be surprised to find that:

> many a bright, clever, lazy girl would suddenly develop a most unexpected taste for study, if she had before her the prospect of doing practical, and to her most interesting work, as one of her father's managers, or as foreign correspondence clerk, or as chemist or artistic designer in a large manufactory.[19]

Despite wishing for increased career opportunities for women, she recognised that there were differences between the sexes. She saw their emotional nature as being different and urged her readers not to be afraid that women would take over jobs from men. 'I do not urge women to compete with men because they can do what men can, but because I believe they can do what men cannot.'[20] Clara was a pragmatist. She wanted to be taken seriously. If her ideas were seen as extreme she would have been disregarded by the average Victorian, male or female. In showing there would be no threat to the work and livelihood of men, her views were more likely to be treated as credible, resulting in an advance in her cause. Nonetheless, she was not expecting women to act impassively. Her expectation was that,

> Instead of bemoaning the ill-treatment of women in general, [they should] persuade those in authority of [their] fitness in particular.

And when [they had gained their co-operation] help every girl...
who shows similar capacities.[21]

The ethos of this paper was that:

> The economic independence of women is as necessary to men's happiness as to women's. Their true interests can never be opposed or antagonistic, however much those of an individual man or woman may be. There is no hardship to women in working for a living; the hardship lies in not getting a living when they work for it. And the great temptation from which all women should most earnestly strive to be freed is that which presents itself to so many at one time or another, the temptation to accept marriage as a means of livelihood and an escape from poverty.[22]

When she wrote this, Clara must have had her relationship with E.W. in mind. She wanted women's financial independence in order to enable them to be able to remain single if that was their desire; an extension to the work considered suitable for them to undertake and a call for them to be treated equally. She also paid tribute to those women, 'who, at the risk of great unpopularity and much social loss, fought the battles by which the doors were opened, through which others passed without one effort of their own'.[23] The battle was an ongoing one, however, and Clara Collet was already playing her part.

In 'Prospects of Marriage for Women', she highlighted, once again, the need for middle-class women to be able to find employment and independence. There was an imbalance in the ratio of men to women in the population as a whole and especially in London. As Mary Paley Marshall (Professor Marshall's wife) in her review of Clara's work in the *Economic Journal* remarked, 'In 1881 there were 112 females to 100 males...and in 1901, 116.'[24] These 'odd' women, that is those unable to marry through lack of available men, had to either be able to earn a living, be dependent on their family, or starve.

For middle-class women Clara saw increased work opportunities, coupled with a minimum wage as being the answer to the problem. Unlike many contemporary feminists who were concentrating on increasing opportunities for their middle-class peers, she did not forget her working-class sisters. She recognised that for many working-class women, wages were simply not high enough to allow them to survive. Unlike their middle-class counterparts they did not have the luxury of being able to turn to their fathers for help. Prostitution, for these women, was often their only alternative.

Clara believed that the solution would lie in the improvement in women's education. She differentiated between the education needed by working-class women and that of their middle-class counterparts. Working-class woman, Clara believed, should be offered a practical education including, 'cooking, cleaning, baby management, laws of health and English literature'.[25] With mothers educated in this way she envisaged a raising of standards in the working-class home with the resultant improved health of its occupants and, therefore, of the ability of the breadwinner to earn more money. 'Bad cooking, dirty habits, overcrowding, and empty-headedness are the sources of the drunkenness, inefficiency, immorality, and brutality which obstruct progress among so many of the poor.'[26] Despite her recognition that working-class women had, by necessity, to work both before marriage and during it, she did not agree with mothers working.

> The dock labourers' wives, having learnt to be useful at home, would appreciate how much is lost by going out to work. Their withdrawal from the labour market and the increased efficiency of their children, brought about by better home management and education, would both tend to raise wages, provided that a trade union existed to secure that the workers should keep the result of their increased efficiency.[27]

These two papers highlight her developing ideas. Her earlier papers on 'Socialism' and 'The Economics of Shopping' printed in the *Wyggeston Girls' Gazette*, outlined her politics, but these latter two give us best the idea of Clara Collet, the person, the promoter of women's rights, whose views on women's changing roles allowed her to make her important contribution in the investigation of women's work from the 1890s until the 1930s.

Despite her interest in women's rights from this time on, she did not lose her desire to eliminate poverty, nor did her early love of literature wane throughout the years. She found an outlet for these two interests in the work of George Gissing which she had discovered around this period. By 1891 his output consisted of nine novels and a few short stories. Such was her interest in Gissing's accomplishments that she was prompted to write an article entitled, 'George Gissing's Novels: A First Impression'. She recommended that people should read Gissing's books saying that those 'who wish to know more about the working-classes particularly will find few better instructors than Mr George Gissing'. Clara recognised that Gissing was speaking from personal experience and that his novels were based on social realism.

It is the combination of idealism with the most accurate and deep knowledge of working class life that gives George Gissing's novel *The Nether World* a place above all others in which the same task has been attempted.[28]

She believed that Gissing's aim could be summed up by the words spoken by one of his characters. Harold Biffen, in the newly published *New Grub Street* said, 'I want to take no side at all, simply to say, "Look, this is the kind of thing that happens."'[29] Gissing, she said, was not trying to suggest remedies, he was leaving that to someone else. He simply wished to highlight the plight of the people in the same way that Charles Booth was doing in *Life and Labour*. In Gissing's earlier novels it was the working classes he wrote about but later he turned to the middle classes and to that other disadvantaged group – women.

In his books on the working classes, Clara was able to recognise many characters similar to those she had met in the East End while she was working for Booth. Gissing was conversant with Booth's work. He made an entry in his diary on 6 December 1890 commenting that he was going to the British Museum Library in order to study *Life and Labour*. Gissing was also influenced by Dickens although Gissing's characters are more real and less caricatured than were his mentor's. He had an extensive knowledge of Dickens and in 1898 wrote a full length critical study of his work.

It was the class system which occupied the main theme of the majority of Gissing's books. Many of his characters lived in poverty despite being educated. They often felt trapped within the wrong class, and were made miserable by their plight. They had a longing to be able to earn enough money to enable them to escape and improve themselves but this was difficult for them to achieve. This idea runs through much of Gissing's work and is distinctly autobiographical – Gissing had a good education himself, yet was forced by circumstances to live in poverty amongst the poor.

It was at this time that Clara herself dabbled in writing fiction. She may have been exploring this as an alternative career as her investigative work was proving unpredictable and financially unrewarding or she may simply have been trying to add to her income. Two of her short stories are extant. One was published and the other not. For both her fiction pieces Clara chose the pseudonym, Clover King. 'Over the Way' was published in 1891 in *Home Chimes*, a women's magazine which folded three years later. She offered the other story to the same magazine but it was rejected. Gissing later commented in a letter that it was, 'amusing that [the editor] accepted the piece of mere romanticism, and would have nothing to do with the bit of real life'.[30] He expressed his pleasure that she had not been overly successful at this genre as he recognised that, 'We know that story-writing would never have satisfied you; and what a remarkable instance of rare fitness of things that you were so promptly put into just the right place!'[31] Had she been more successful with her stories, Gissing feared her future career might have been jeopardised, which would have been a great loss to society in general and to women in particular.

The 'piece of mere romanticism' was a melodramatic story about a man, dying of consumption, who fantasised about the woman who lived 'over the way'. Diana, the woman in question became his 'raison d'être'. She accompanied him spiritually as he faced up to death. His life had been one of misery. His mother had died when he was a small boy and his father as a serious follower of Calvin had constantly read depressing sermons to his son about fear and sin. Mark, the young man, had worked as a clerk in a repetitive routine job. When he looked back at his bleak life and bleaker future he found solace in Diana's unwitting presence, 'He stood by his father's grave dreading death and fearing life, and Diana stood there too, and he became aware that the skies were blue, and the birds were singing, and the trees were putting forth buds, and that there was joy on earth and peace in heaven.'[32] As he reached the end of his life he had a desire to meet Diana face to face. He sent a note over to her lodgings inviting her to meet him, explaining that he had been watching her and that as he was dying he wished to see her. As soon as she received his note Diana called on this unfortunate man. She was horrified at the sight of his wizened dying body yet she overcame her revulsion and:

> As she listened to Mark Hailstone's words, she told herself that God was revealed to her in him more truly than Mark had conceived Him. Mark should know before he died that there was something far better than selfish life and happiness; something Diana hardly hoped to realise herself, self [sic] had so much strength within her. With a quick movement she pushed the chair aside, put her arms round the dying man's neck, kissed him with sisterly love and tenderness, and then laid her head on his pillow with her cheek touching his. A passion of love flooded his soul, love that asked nothing but to love and to be known; love that filled him with infinite pain, but with divine ecstasy.[33]

Having experienced love for the first time in his life, Mark died. Clara's piece of melodramatic romanticism is typically Victorian in its subject matter of death and love. The piece was written to appeal to the reader's emotions and sympathy. It achieved its aim.

The second and unpublished story was based upon the 'women problem'. Its title 'Undercurrents' deserves comment. This is the same name as chapter 22 of George Gissing's novel *The Unclassed*, which was published in 1884 and was known by Clara and mentioned in her article on Gissing's novels. This choice may have been made unconsciously; however, on studying the two works it is possible to see that she may have deliberately chosen the same title. Her piece begins with a group of educated middle-class women, like herself, discussing the merits and demerits of marriage for women in their position. Alternatives can sometimes raise more problems than they solve. The dilemma for a woman as to whether or not to marry was a new one. In the late nineteenth century it was usual for a middle-class woman to be barred from working once she married even before she had children. The central character of Clara's story, Marian Bligh was ambivalent in her views. She believed in women being given the opportunities, but at the same time she still believed in the institution of marriage and the duties she saw that this imposed upon a woman. This character is autobiographical. Unlike several of the other characters in this tale, Clara was never a radical feminist who would have put her career above all else. She would have married had the right man appeared. Yet neither she, nor her character Marian, subscribed to the view that marriage meant, 'A whole career sacrificed in order to look after the meals and soothe the temper of one person whose only work in life is to make money'[34] – the view of one of Marian's more extreme friends. Working-class women usually continued in their work and drudgery, being given no financial choice in the matter. Clara was exploring this predicament to clarify her own thoughts on the issue. Her position later was that whilst she believed married women should be allowed to work before they had children, once they became mothers it was important, for the well-being of their offspring, to cease employment.

Marian met a 'young demonstrator at University College', named Frank Rust who had a guilty secret. He had married 'beneath himself' to an attractive working-class girl of 17 who loved him unconditionally. Unfortunately after the marriage he discovered that she had a serious drink problem. His wife arrived uninvited and inebriated to a University Extension lecture at which her husband was the lecturer. Marian was in the audience. The drunk girl stood up and shouted, 'That's my 'usband, that is. My! ain't he a toff? Three cheers for Frankie.' So embarrassed was

Frank by this outburst that he denied knowing her. Later Marian met him unexpectedly and he explained that the reason he married her was because of the love she gave which no woman had before offered him. His honesty with her led to Marian offering to introduce Frank's wife to a woman doctor friend of hers who might be able to help with her drink problem. He was forced to resign from his lectures and believed he must end his career at University College. Marian persuaded him that this should not be necessary and wrote a letter to them explaining the situation and as a result they allowed him to withdraw his resignation.

By this time, Marian had fallen in love with Frank despite his being married. His alcoholic wife became seriously ill and died, thus leaving the way clear for Marian. However, Frank's opinion of himself was so low that Marian knew he would never ask her to marry him despite believing that his feelings for her were reciprocated, so she planned an elaborate plot to 'trick' him into marriage. She told him that she was shortly to marry and that she would soon be seeing him for the last time as she was leaving the country with her future husband. Frank was made jealous and at their supposed last meeting, declared his love for Marian and thus she obtained what she desired.

Did Clara wish that she would meet a man like Frank and did she, like Marian, secretly wish to marry despite being a well-educated woman with ambitions? The question one has to ask when looking at 'Undercurrents' is when was it written? If, as some believe,[35] she penned this in 1891, we know that she was financially insecure; her career was not progressing as she would have liked and a husband would have solved many problems. Despite this, we know that she was, however, quite insistent that she would only marry for love.

The content of the story is so similar to that of Gissing's life (see Part IV, Chapter 2 for more detail on this) that it seems uncanny that Clara could have produced such a tale unwittingly. Had it been written before she met Gissing, it is possible, due to her detailed knowledge of his work, that she may have unconsciously picked up details of his life which he had included autobiographically in some of his stories. In *Workers in the Dawn* (1880), Gissing's first published novel, the principal character, Arthur Golding, is a philanthropist who wishes to improve conditions for the poor. Whilst 'slumming' he meets and falls in love with a poor, disreputable girl by the name of Carrie Mitchell whom he decides to marry. As in Gissing's life and in Clara's story, the hero is under the illusion that he will be able to reform and educate the girl. This proved an impossibility and she left. Consequently he met and fell in love with an educated middle-class woman. This relationship is doomed to failure when the woman discovers that Arthur is already married. In the later *Born in Exile* (1892), Godwin Peak, the main character, has a secret which, like Gissing's own, could threaten to destroy his reputation. Peak also fell in love with a woman for whom class prejudices and conventions made it impossible for him to marry. In Gissing's life his wife was an alcoholic prostitute and therefore, below his class, whereas in *Born in Exile* the woman of Peak's attentions was from a higher class than himself. Clara's story was more like Gissing's real life than his novels. In *The Unclassed*, the prostitute Ida Starr was striving to improve herself intellectually, unlike Gissing's own prostitute wife who, like Frank Rust's first wife, was beyond help.

It appears as though it must have been a coincidence that Clara composed a story mirroring Gissing's life, however hard it is to believe that she was not aware of his past when she wrote it. She did meet Gissing in 1893 but we know that he did not tell her about his first marriage until 1897 when he wrote about it in a letter. 'Undercurrents' must have been written at the latest by 1894 as the publisher who turned it down went out of business that year, so it seems impossible that she could have known about his life when she wrote her story, unless she had surreptitiously discovered details of Gissing's past.

If Marian was conceived by her as a result of her knowledge of Gissing's situation, then Marian's relationship with Frank Rust may throw light upon her feelings for Gissing. He was, by the time he met Clara, married to a second working-class woman and, therefore, she would have been unable to let him know of her feelings for him and, like Marian, 'She had entered into his life; she had never asked him to enter hers.'[36] Clara involved herself in the author's life from the onset of their relationship. She did not expect anything in return. Like Marian, she would have liked romance, but Gissing's wife was omnipresent.

Whatever the motivation or inspiration she had for writing 'Undercurrents' one can only imagine that when she sent these two stories to Gissing to read in December 1895, the contents of 'the bit of real life' must have shocked him although he made no comment in his correspondence to her about her short stories.[37]

In 1892, the year after the publication of 'George Gissing's Novels', Clara gave a lecture on Gissing at the South Place Ethical Society at which her father had been the musical director. This centre of nonconformist ideas had provided the venue for many radical speakers over the years. A review of the lecture in *The Queen* was read by Gissing's sister Ellen who subsequently informed her brother. At last he believed recognition was being given to his work. 'The Ethical Society is known to me; the lecturers are people of very good standing. Things go forward, you see!'[38]

Despite her digression into short story writing, Clara's focus remained upon her investigative work. In 1890 she became part of the team working on Graham Balfour's Battersea Enquiry. This research was undertaken as an extension of Charles Booth's enquiry in the East End but was less detailed. Balfour was another member of the group of intellectuals who had a close association with the Royal Statistical Society. The methodology used in this survey was similar to that used for Booth's investigation in the East End. Many of the notes taken for this survey are kept in the British Library of Political and Economic Science at the London School of Economics, and several of the notebooks contain information written in Clara's hand although there is no further information as to the part she played in this study. As with all her work, the notes kept are methodical and systematic. The information is laid out in a manner similar to that obtained in the census. Details were taken of every family under the following headings: street name; number of house; number of rooms; class; occupation; wife; number of children; others.

Towards the end of the year Clara began some further work for Booth. This was his investigation on 'Pauperism, A Picture; and the Endowment of Old Age, An Argument', written as part of the Royal Commission on Labour. Booth was a great believer in the provision of a state pension for the 'deserving poor'. The section on 'Pauperism at Ashby-de-la-Zouch' was taken on by Clara. Notes were taken at this country workhouse chosen to contrast with pauperism in London. Her findings were based upon personal observation. Despite conducting this survey Clara's own attitude towards a universal pension scheme was ambivalent as is illustrated in a letter sent in 1919 to Mary Booth thanking her for sending a copy of *Charles Booth, A Memoir* which had recently been published. She agreed with the idea of pensions in principle but was worried about their implementation. 'The financial basis and the appeal to sympathy with the aged were the aspects which seemed to me unsound.'[39] The Charity Organisation Society was opposed to the granting of universal old age pensions and Clara had always believed in the importance of individual responsibility for financial remuneration in old age and illness.

The following year, Clara engaged upon an investigation of her own choosing. The results were worked into an article entitled 'Women's Work in Leeds' which was published in the *Economic Journal*. She based her survey upon the secondary sources of Baines' *Woollen Manufacture in England*, and Jubb's *History of the Shoddy Trade*. She used census material about which she found much to criticise and finally she gathered statistics from her own investigative work in the area. This included visits to flaxmills, ragshops and cottages where she made personal observations. In total 800 questionnaires were sent out, which might not seem significant today, but it was Booth who had first introduced the questionnaire pro forma and Clara was thus applying very modern research methods.

Her investigative writing was basically factual, although she did add some personal observations. 'In the ragshops…in every room the girls were singing, and in one "I am the Ghost of John James Christopher Benjamin Binns" chanted in chorus, was quite impressive. Especially noticeable, too, was the air of vitality, of enjoyment of life.'[40] This is not the stereotypical impression of work in a sweated trade.

As a result of her growing reputation as an investigator she was asked to work as an Assistant Commissioner, compiling evidence for the Royal Commission of Labour on 'The Employment of Women'. This work was begun at 44, Parliament Street, London, on 7 March 1892 with a meeting at which the four Lady Assistant Commissioners were given their instructions by the Chairman of the Commission. Eliza Orme was appointed the Senior Assistant Commissioner. She remained in contact with Clara for many years. May Abraham[41] and Margaret Irwin were Clara's other two colleagues. The aim of the reports was to ascertain the differences in the rates of wages between men and women, to investigate women's grievances and to look at the effects of women's industrial employment on their health, morality and the home. They were also to inquire into the 'existence and causes of the exclusion of women from trades in which women's work is not unsuitable'.[42] The methods of investigation were to be those with which Clara Collet was by now more than familiar. They were to make use of other parliamentary papers, to visit centres of industry and take evidence directly from employers and employees. Their findings were to be written up in a report. Clara's researches began in London. She investigated women's work in tailoring, book sewing, mantle-making, feather curling, stay-making, silk hat trimming, shirt-making, jewel polishing, gold embroidering, wig-making, jewel-case-making, fur pulling, rope works, india rubber works, mineral water factories, sweet factories, printing and from women engaged in shop work, millinery, dress-making, laundry work, and match-making. Many of these trades she had already encountered during her investigations for Booth, but this new inquiry was to cover the whole of London. By June 1892 she had finished the section on London and moved on to look at 'Conditions of Work in Luton and Bristol', which took her three months to complete before she moved on to Birmingham, Walsall, Dudley, and the Staffordshire Potteries. Finally in January 1893 she began work on Liverpool and Manchester. The report was completed in September 1893 having taken 19 months to complete. It was the first Commission to look into the employment of women as a separate category. Clara's written report ran to almost 100 pages, and included many tables.

Work of this type today for Royal Commissions is paid work. In 1893 it may have carried with it some remuneration. This would have provided her with a further temporary means of earning her living. What she wanted was to be employed on a permanent basis.

Clara's work as Lady Assistant Commissioner proved very fortuitous. In August 1892, Anthony Mundella, who had headed the Commission, was appointed President of the Board of Trade. One of his first tasks was to create the 'Labour Department' as a separate branch of the Statistical Department. Hubert Llewellyn Smith was the first 'Commissioner for Labour' and 'three additional Labour Correspondents (one a lady) were appointed'.[43] The 'lady' was Clara Collet.

The North London Collegiate School Magazine summed up her new position thus:

> She has for some time been working as Sub-Commissioner in the Labour Commission, and for years has made a thorough study of economic aspects of women's work. No better nomination could have been made. The appointment is not only a distinguished one, and an opportunity for doing good work, but, as it is Governmental, it carries a high salary and a pension. Our School may well be proud of numbering among its alumni a woman, who is the first to receive such a State appointment.[44]

NOTES

1. MSS diary, 1 May 1890.
2. Ibid., 1 May 1990.

3. Ibid., 16 November 1890.

4. Edgeworth was Professor of Political Economy at Oxford, and a brilliant mathematical economist. He became the first editor of the *Economic Journal* to which Collet contributed many articles.

5. Clara E. Collet, 'Obituary: Henry Higgs', *Economic Journal* (December 1940), pp. 546–55 and 558–61.

6. MacKenzie and MacKenzie (eds), *Diary of Beatrice Webb*, pp. 268 and 352.

7. MSS diary, 2 July 1905.

8. Hubert Llewellyn Smith, *New Survey on London Life and Labour 1930–35*, Vol. 2, ch. 8, 'Domestic Service', (London: P.S. King, 1931), pp. 427–69.

9. John Maynard Keynes, 'Obituary: Henry Higgs', *Economic Journal* (December 1940), p. 557.

10. The 'senior' was to become established as the British Economic Association.

11. Letter from Henry Higgs to Professor Foxwell, reproduced in Collet, 'Obituary: Henry Higgs', p. 558.

12. See 'Herbert Somerton Foxwell: Obituary', *Economic Journal*, (December 1936), pp. 614–19, by Clara E. Collet and 'Henry Higgs: Obituary', *Economic Journal* (December 1940), by Clara E. Collet and John Maynard Keynes, pp. 547–61 for more information.

13. Booth's letters, University of London, Senate House, ULL MS 797 I 6183.

14. First Annual Report of the Universities Settlement in East London, Toynbee Hall Archives.

15. MSS diary, 8 May 1890.

16. Clara E. Collet, 'Salaries of Women Teachers', *Journal of Education* (London: 1 August 1890), pp. 412–15.

17. 'Prospects of Marriage for Women' (1890) was later published as part of a compilation which became *Educated Working Women* (London: P.S. King, 1902).

18. 'The Economic Position of Educated Working Women' was first delivered to the South Place Ethical Society in 1890 and was later published by P.S. King, in 1902.

19. Ibid., p. 18.

20. Ibid., p. 16.

21. Ibid., p. 21.

22. Ibid., p. 25.

23. Ibid., p. 5.

24. Mary Paley Marshall, 'Review of Clara E. Collet "Educated Working Women"', *Economic Journal*, Vol. 12 (June 1902), pp. 252–7.

25. Collet, 'Prospects of Marriage', p. 46.

26. Ibid., p. 47.

27. Ibid., p. 46.

28. Clara E. Collet, 'George Gissing's Novels: A First Impression', *Charity Organisation Review* (October 1891), p. 375.

29. Ibid.

30. Paul Mattheisen, Arthur C. Young and Pierre Coustilla (eds), *The Collected Letters of George Gissing*, Vol. 6 (Athens, OH: Ohio University Press, 1995), pp. 68–9.

31. Ibid.

32. Clover King, 'Over the Way', *Home Chimes* (May 1891), p. 300.

33. Ibid., p. 305–6.

34. MSS 29/3/13/4 Modern Records Centre, Warwick, manuscript of 'Undercurrents' by Clover King. NB: This is a photocopy of the original. The

story has been published in *The Gissing Journal*, Vol. 31, No. 4 (October 1995).

35. Dr Bouwe Postmus, University of Amsterdam, in *The Gissing Journal*, Vol. 31, No. 4 (October 1995), is of the opinion that this was written simultaneously with 'Over the Way' in 1891.

36. Mattheisen *et al.* (eds), *Letters of George Gissing*, Vol. 6, pp. 68–9.

37. Ibid., 18 December 1895.

38. Ibid., 14 March 1892.

39. Booth's correspondence, University of London, Senate House, I/4805 (i).

40. Clara E. Collet, 'Women's Work in Leeds', *Economic Journal*, Vol. 1, Part III (1891), pp. 460–73.

41. Later to become one of the first two women factory inspectors. Became Mrs H.J. Tennant on marriage in 1896. Her contact with Collet continued as a result of their joint membership of the British Association for the Advancement of Science.

42. British Parliamentary Papers: Industrial Relations; Labour Commission Session 1893–94, Vol. 34 (1893; Shannon: Irish University Press, 1970), p. iii.

43. Hubert Llewellyn Smith, *The Board of Trade* (London and NewYork: G.P. Putnam's & Sons, 1928), pp. 218–19.

44. *Our Magazine* (March 1893), p. 34. North London Collegiate School.

Part IV

A New Way of Life
1893–1910

1

The Civil Service – A Suitable Career for a Woman?

In 1890 two female typewriter copyists, were employed in the place of three men in a Civil Service department.

> Great care was taken to protect them. They worked in a locked room in the upper part of the building and their work and meals were served to them through a hatch in the wall. They left a quarter of an hour before the men, and no man was allowed to take work up to them without a special permit from a responsible official – only granted with great difficulty. The only time they were let loose in the office was when they went to draw pay, and even then, in the early days, and as their number increased, they are said to have been marshalled in a crocodile by the Superintendent.[1]

Not only did women have to cope with conditions such as these, but also to contend with the men who objected to their presence and did not believe them to be intellectually capable of undertaking more than the most mundane of tasks. Patrick Comyns, a first-class clerk gave evidence before the Playfair Commission which in 1873, was examining the possibility of employing women in the Civil Service. Comyns said:

> So far as the female returners [these were women engaged in the post office returning undelivered mail], are concerned, as long as the work is simple and straightforward, the mere returning of a letter for instance, which involves merely copying the address from the inside to the official cover, they get through it; but at any time when tact, discrimination, or judgement is required, I find that they are perfectly at a loss in the matter...I think generally where women perform official duties, their minds are wanting in those respects; that they are timid to a certain extent, and will not act without applying to another person if there is anything out of the ordinary way...I am, however, not in favour of having a number of young women returning letters, because I think it is demoralizing, and that it is not a proper atmosphere for young women to be in.[2]

The few women employed within the Civil Service in the 1890s still had to contend with such attitudes at the time Clara began her employment in the Labour Department. As a Labour Correspondent, she had a far more demanding and senior position than that of returning letters, which Comyns had felt women were unfit to do.

Women first entered the Service in 1870 when the telegraph system was nationalised and taken under the control of the Post Office. Several of the companies to be nationalised had employed women, which meant that the Post Office became, by default, the first department in the Civil Service to include women in its staff. An official by the name of Scudamore worked in the Post Office. Unlike Comyns, he realised the benefits of employing women. He was pleased with their work:

> They have in an eminent degree the quickness of eye and ear, and the delicacy of touch, which are essential qualifications of a good operator. In the second place, they take more kindly than men or boys do to sedentary employment, and are more patient during long confinement to one place. In the third place, the wages, which will draw male operators from but an inferior class of the community, will draw female operators from a superior class. Female operators thus drawn from a superior class will, as a rule, write better than the male clerks, and spell more correctly... They are also less disposed to combine for the purpose of extorting higher wages, and this is by no means an unimportant matter.[3]

It was becoming recognised that women could be employed for less money, do better work and generally cause less trouble than their male counterparts. In addition women usually left to marry after they had only been employed for a few years which had the added advantage that higher scales of pay for long service did not have to be paid and pensions for women were almost unheard of – another saving.

Initially they were employed only by being nominated by an influential person. In 1881, after reforms introduced by Henry Fawcett, the appointment of women clerks was opened to public competition in the same way as it was for men.

As a result of these financial advantages, women's employment in the Civil Service began to spread to other departments. They mainly carried out routine clerical tasks. As early as 1873, James Stansfield, President of the Local Government Board decided that he needed a woman's view on the education of girls in pauper schools. He employed Mrs Nassau Senior as the first woman inspector. The prejudices of her male colleagues caused her great distress yet she continued her employment for more than a year until she had to resign from ill health. In 1883 the Board of Education employed the first woman inspector but her job was restricted to the investigation of needlework in schools.

Prior to Clara's employment at the Board of Trade, women were generally employed to do simple tasks. In 1886 the House of Commons passed a resolution to arrange for the collection of labour statistics. This was at the suggestion of Charles Booth who, as President of the Royal Statistical Society, had led a delegation campaigning for the collection of these statistics. Once the resolution was passed, the Labour Statistical Bureau was set up. In 1893, with the appointment of Mundella as President of the Board of Trade, the Labour Department was created. Mundella was committed to the collection of statistics, being a member of the RSS at the time of Booth's campaigning. Due to the employment of Booth's investigators including Clara, Llewellyn Smith and David Schloss, it was inevitable that the methods used in the new department owed much to those Booth had used in *Life and Labour*. Clara Collet herself was more than aware of Booth's influence within the department and in a note penned later to his wife Mary, wrote:

> I feel and have always felt that Mr Booth's influence at the Board of Trade has been abiding and unceasing, although few people are aware of the fact. Both his scientific methods, and his personal character, working through Llewellyn Smith, raised the standard and purified the aims of the Labour Department. Outside also, all the economic thinkers started from a new standpoint, with a much wider outlook, as a result of Mr Booth's pioneer work.[4]

Clara was appointed early in 1893, with a special responsibility for collecting statistics concerning women's industrial relations. Her salary at £300 a year was double that of her closing salary as a teacher.[5] Clara 'who was a recognized expert on statistics, was the first woman to be appointed to an important inside post of an administrative character'.[6]

As the employment of women increased, her job expanded beyond the capabilities of one person. She was given her own assistant investigator:

> She chose a woman who had had a brilliant university career; she married, however, within two years and left the service. Miss Collet chose a second, a third, and finally indeed a fourth outstanding

university woman with similar shattering results, and it was not until 1903, when she was appointed Senior Investigator for Women's Industries in the Commercial, Labour, and Statistical Departments of the Board of Trade, that she had the assistance of a woman who 'stayed the course'.[7]

Scudamore had realised it was financially advantageous to the Civil Service if unskilled women left upon marriage. It was not so advantageous if skilled workers, like Clara Collet or her assistant left as it took several years for them to acquire their knowledge. In the early years of employment of women it was not a regulation that when they married they should leave their job. By 1894 when a number of women had become established within the Civil Service, many departments began to make it a condition of employment that once they were on the permanent staff with its attendant privileges, such as pensions, the rule of resignation on marriage should be upheld. For those staff who had been employed for over six years, a 'marriage gratuity' was handed out as the women left the Service. By 1895 the Treasury decided that the extension of this rule should be made to all departments to include all female staff. Although this rule was in place it was not adhered to 100 per cent and by the time of the MacDonnell Commission in 1912 the majority report stated that, 'There are many cases, especially in the higher grade of work or where women are appointed for highly specialised knowledge, in which the enforcement of this rule would act to the public disadvantage.'[8]

Therefore, for most of the years that Clara was working for the Civil Service the majority of married women left the Service on marriage. A person in Clara's position could have been taken as a special case and might have been allowed to stay on as to lose her would have proved too costly.

Comments about her personality both within and outside her working environment have portrayed her as ruthlessly pursuing her own ends and making enemies. She has been described as serious and formidable, and cold and emotionless. She may have appeared so by her later years. In her younger days using material from other sources and studying comments made by contemporaries, a rather different picture emerges. She certainly had, 'vigour and alertness of mind and body, sincerity and directness, practical commonsense, independence of judgement, and the courage of her opinions'.[9] She was a very capable woman. Although her early diary entries contained references to upsets and uncertainties in her life, from the time she joined the Civil Service onward, no such doubts are mentioned. Once her new career was established with its inherent security she had no regrets. Her single-mindedness, independence and ability to stick to her beliefs even when they went against the majority were 'traits...probably not entirely ingratiating to her immediate official superiors'.[10] She was in a role outside that normally acceptable for a woman. That she was able and willing to challenge men's views was bound to be a problem for some. In contrast, it was also said of her that:

> Her colleagues and subordinates found her 'very pleasant to work with' and her friends noted her readiness to listen and to give weight to the opinions of others. She was indeed kindly; but she refused to be fettered by convention, custom, or anything that stood in the way of what she thought should be done...a characteristic gesture was her arrival at the Ministry, during the General Strike, in a hearse, which had offered the simplest way of getting there. She was in fact, thoroughly practical and applied economic principles in her daily life.[11]

Her large circle of loyal friends and acquaintances, with whom she remained in regular contact throughout most of her life, show her as able to maintain relationships over a great many years. She also 'had a keen sense of humour, and made many witty remarks...She had a brilliant mind, and a charming personality; and always looked on the brighter side of things.'[12] She may have been single-minded and tough enough to speak up for what she saw as right, despite being a lone woman among often hostile men, but she was also very human, lively, uncomplaining and enjoyed fun.

The year 1893 thus became pivotal for Clara. For not only had she begun working in what was to be her lifelong career, but this was also the year in which she began her relationship with George Gissing who was to become the most important person in her life.

NOTES

1. Hilda Martindale, *Women Servants of the State, 1870–1938. A History of Women in the Civil Service* (London: George Allen & Unwin, 1938), p. 67.
2. Ibid., p. 22.
3. Ibid., p. 17
4. Booth's correspondence. Letter from Clara Collet to Mary Booth, 25 November 1916. I/4804 MS 797, University of London.
5. Mattheisen *et al.* (eds), *Letters of George Gissing*, to Nelly Gissing on 19 November 1893.

6. Martindale, *Women Servants of the State*, p. 48.
7. Ibid., pp. 47–8.
8. Ibid., p. 150.
9. C.T. (Charles Trevelyan), 'Obituary: Clara Elizabeth Collet', *Journal of the Royal Statistical Society*, Series A, Vol. III, Part III (1948), pp. 252–3.
10. Ibid.
11. Ibid.
12. Professor P.C. Mahalanobis, 'Obituary: Clara Elizabeth Collet', *Journal of the Royal Statistical Society* Series A, Vol. III, Part III (1948), p. 254.

2

George Gissing – 'Born in Exile'

On my way home at night an anguish of suffering in the thought that I can never hope to have an intellectual companion at home. Condemned for ever to associate with inferiors – and so crassly unintelligent. Never a word exchanged on anything but the paltry everyday life of the household. Never a word to me, from anyone, of understanding, sympathy or of encouragement.[1]

So wrote George Gissing seven months before he first made the acquaintance of Clara Collet. If anyone was in the need of a friend able to give him hope and fulfil his need for intellectual conversation it was Gissing. What was it that led Gissing to be in such a despairing frame of mind in the early months of 1893? All his problems stemmed from an event which had occurred way back in his youth, and which destroyed his ambitions and paved the way for his future discontent both in his career and in his social life. It was also responsible for producing the wonderful novels he wrote based on his angst-ridden life.

Gissing was born in November 1857, three years before Clara. His early life was spent in Wakefield, the northern town of his birth. His father was a pharmaceutical chemist. The shop in which he practiced his business was still being used for the same purpose 100 years later. He was the oldest child and had two brothers, William and Algernon and two sisters, Ellen and Margaret. The first tragedy in Gissing's life occurred when his father died when Gissing was only 13 years old. Thomas Gissing had nourished his son's early thinking by providing a stimulating environment. Despite a lack of intellectual sophistication, he had a strong interest in botany and wrote two books of local botanical interest. His house was full of books. Gissing was encouraged to read literature and poetry from an early age. His father was a religious sceptic whose unorthodox rationalist ideas rubbed off on his son, although his two daughters, as if to make up for what they saw as a failing in their father and brother, became fervently involved in the Church.

Gissing was determined to improve himself. Realising his

intellectual ability from an early age, he aimed to attain the high scholastic achievement necessary to fulfil his ambitions. Hard work and diligence led him to early academic brilliance. His excellent results in the Oxford Local Examinations led to a scholarship to the nonconformist Owens College, Manchester, after which he hoped to continue his studies at the University of London. He expected to become a don.

His academic career was not to come to fruition. In order to attend Owens College, Gissing, at the age of 16, had to live alone in lodgings in Manchester. Although his intellectual development was precocious, he had been unable to mix easily with his contemporaries. In this vulnerable condition, lonely and friendless he fell in love with a prostitute. His feelings for Marianne Helen Harrison (known as Nell), soon spiralled out of control. Gissing expected to reform her and save her from working on the streets – at this time, he believed that prostitutes were victims of society and if given a chance would be able to change their way of life and become respectable once more. He purchased a sewing machine to provide Nell with the means of pursuing a reputable job. The naive Gissing had not recognised that his young lover was suffering from severe alcoholism. In his innocence he believed that once Nell had been provided with an opportunity to escape from the life she was leading, she would be able to resist both prostitution and alcohol. She was unable to comply with his wishes and made more and more demands upon him to fund her addiction.

Gissing's financial resources did not amount to much. His mother had been left with little on the death of her husband and George had to rely on the scholarship he had been granted to attend his college. He became desperate to save Nell from returning to prostitution to fund her drinking and in his desperation resorted to crime. Nell's demands for money proved more than Gissing could manage himself and he began stealing from his schoolmates. Not just once, but on several occasions, he raided the common room for cash or items to sell. The college authorities were concerned enough to engage a detective to discover the culprit. To everyone's dismay it was not a college porter or a lowly employee but the boy who had shown the most academic promise. George Gissing was the thief. His life's ambitions were ruined. The college dismissed him and he was sentenced to one month's imprisonment.

At the end of his sentence one or more of his former classmates appealed to their fathers to raise some cash to enable him to go to the United States where he would have the opportunity to start afresh and escape Nell's influence with whom he continued his relationship on release from prison.

Thus it was that in 1876 Gissing landed, alone, aged 19, in Boston. He had a letter of introduction to William Lloyd Garrison through whom he came into contact with Dr Marie Zakrzewska who was to prove very helpful. Many years later, in correspondence with Clara Collet, she wrote about Gissing's semi-enforced exile. She met him in the year of his arrival in the United States where his stay was planned as a three-year trip on account of

> a passionate attachment to a young woman perfectly unsuitable to become his wife. An attempt would be made during his absence to train and educate her to see...[if they would] both be of the same mind after these three years. As my house was a kind of liberty hall for young people as well as old, whose education was of a higher order, Mr G. found himself not only entertained every Saturday evening during the whole winter of 76/77 but quite at home.[2]

Dr Zakrzewska helped to find a temporary assistant teaching post for Gissing. He began the job immediately, seemed to enjoy the work and continued visiting the 'kind of liberty hall' every Saturday. However, two months later, for a reason unknown to Dr Zakrzewska, or anyone else, Gissing went missing:

> leaving all his belongings...As we had no sign of his life we all guessed that he must have sailed to England or committed suicide in one of his moody conditions. So Mr Smith examined the things left behind, packed them except the great number of love letters from his young woman in England, the contents were chiefly 'Come back, George, I can't study or learn anything they want me to learn. I love you so much,' and much more. The contents ill written and spelled like that of a child. After several months in the autumn of '77, Mr Garrison told me that Mr Gissing had presented himself at his office in a wretched and dilapidated condition asking for money to return to England.[3]

Gissing had, during this period travelling around the United States, been trying unsuccessfully to make a living from writing for the local press.

On his return to England, the still lonely and now socially alienated Gissing moved in with Nell. They left Manchester for the comparative anonymity of London and Gissing made a poor living from tutoring whilst writing the first of his novels. The mismatched couple moved from one squalid lodging to another, setting the pattern for the rest of his nomadic life, never settling anywhere, never belonging, never putting down any roots. Nell's drinking continued and, thus, to Gissing's intense dismay and embarrassment, did her prostitution to pay for her habit.

Gissing was desperate to belong to the social class for which he had been educated, yet with Nell as his wife this was impossible. His writing reflected this dilemma with several of his novels using as their theme the subject of men being forced to live in a social class for which they were not intended. His work is highly autobiographical and often appears to prefigure the future. His characters undergo experiences which he later encounters himself. In one of his last works, the semi-autobiographical *Private Papers of Henry Ryecroft*, the narrator comments that, 'Persistent prophesy is a familiar way of assuring the event',[4] and this certainly seemed to be the case.

Gissing and Nell lived together for about five years during which time, if he were entertaining, he would confine her to her room in order to hide her from his intellectual friends. Morley Roberts, one of his old Owens College colleagues had contacted him through his publisher after seeing his name in a review of his first published book *Workers in the Dawn*. The two remained in close contact until Gissing's death, and nine years after Gissing's death Roberts wrote a fictionalised biography. Roberts used false names, to safeguard identities, but it was clear to whom he was alluding. In this book Roberts establishes that despite the number of times he visited the household, he never once saw Nell. On one occasion he commented that:

> Twice in the course of an hour our conversation was interrupted by the servant knocking at the door and beckoning to Gissing to come out. In the next room I then heard voices, sometimes raised, sometimes pleading. When Gissing returned the first time he said to me, 'I am very sorry to have to leave you for a few minutes. My wife is really unwell.' But I knew by now the disease from which she suffered. Twice or thrice I was within an ace of getting up and saying, 'Don't you think I'd better go, old chap?' And then he was called out again. He came back at last in a state of obvious misery and perturbation, and said, 'My dear man, my wife is so ill that I think I must ask you to go.' I shook hands with him in silence and went, for I understood. A little afterwards he told me that that very afternoon his wife had gone out, and obtaining drink in some way had brought it home with her, and that she was then almost insane with alcohol. This was the kind of life that George Gissing, perhaps a great man of letters, lived for years.[5]

7. George Gissing, author and close friend of Clara Collet.

Nell's health began to deteriorate and she started to suffer from epileptic fits brought on by excessive alcohol consumption. She was unable to abstain from drinking and found it difficult to fulfil her husband's idealistic aims of rehabilitation and education. His attempts to control Nell led to her leaving home periodically and returning to prostitution as a means to fund her drinking, returning after a time full of remorse and begging forgiveness. Gissing would be forced to go without food to pay for her drink.

In the autumn of 1881 Nell had an alcoholic fit in public. Gissing took her to hospital but they refused to help her. He had by now realised that she was beyond his help and that the disturbance she was causing him was making it impossible for him to write. As he had few financial resources upon which to depend, he had no alternative but to have Nell taken into an invalid's boarding house run by two old ladies in Battersea at the cost of 15 shillings per week that he could ill afford, but which he felt was the only course open to him. By the following summer Nell escaped her incarceration and began writing abusive letters to Gissing, accusing him of neglect. In reply, he increased her allowance but stood firm in his resolve not to have her back.

Crisis point was reached in September 1883 when Nell was arrested for her part in a public disturbance in which she was involved with three men. Gissing was so ashamed at this that he tried to sue his wife for divorce. He employed a private detective to catch Nell working as a prostitute to provide him with grounds for his action. This made him feel guilty as he still had feelings for his wife, so he withdrew the detective and to make amends increased her maintenance to £1 a week. He never saw her alive again.

Once Nell was no longer disrupting his life, Gissing was able to extend his social engagements. Despite the episode at Owens College as well as his reluctance to mix easily, Gissing maintained a small circle of like-minded intellectuals with whom he could engage in conversation. Eduard Bertz and Morley Roberts were his most regular visitors. With Bertz he had become acquainted in 1879 after the German had placed a newspaper advertisement in the personal columns asking for company. The impecunious Bertz was finding his stay in London lonely and was in need of friendship. Uncharacteristically, Gissing answered the advertisement. During most of his working life, Gissing shunned association with strangers as it disturbed his work, but after his return from the United States and subsequent unsuitable marriage, someone with whom he could enjoy intellectual conversation appealed to him. A foreigner would be less likely to find out about his past or question his present circumstances than would an Englishman. Bertz was making his living from writing books but after his return to Germany found journalism more profitable. He continued corresponding with Gissing until the latter's death.

Gissing's other friend, Morley Roberts, met Gissing every Sunday when they would cook a stew over the fire and treat themselves to what was often the only decent meal Gissing ate all week. They would discuss intellectual matters and classical civilisations, of which Gissing was so fond, until late in the evening. Roberts would have stayed later but Gissing's hours and consumption of alcohol were moderate. He did not wish to lose writing time the following day.

Gissing's life continued in this way from 1883 until 1888, during which time he had four moderately successful books published but had to supplement his writing with tutoring, which he disliked.

In February 1888 as he was feeling pressurised, he took a winter holiday to Eastbourne to alleviate the depression from which he was suffering. Roberts spent a week with him there. The weather was terrible. It snowed and a bitterly cold easterly wind blew through the draughty lodgings. On 29 February, Gissing went to Lewes for the afternoon returning at 5.30 p.m. to find a telegram awaiting him. It announced starkly, 'Mrs Gissing is dead. Come at once.' He returned to London that evening. Roberts and Gissing spent the night together in Gissing's flat deciding what to do. He was unsure as to the truth of the telegram. He thought it may have been a trick Nell was playing to discover his whereabouts in order to extract more money from him. It was decided that Roberts should travel alone to Lucretia Street, Lower Marsh, to determine the truth. Nell had indeed passed away the previous morning at about 9.30 a.m. Roberts returned to fetch his friend. Gissing was devastated when he saw the conditions in which his wife had been living. In his diary he left a description of the scene:

> It was the first floor back; so small that the bed left little room to move. She took it unfurnished, for 2/9 a week; the furniture she brought was: the bed, one chair, a chest of drawers, and a broken deal table. On some shelves were a few plates, cups etc. Over the mantelpiece hung several pictures, which she had preserved from old days. There were three engravings: a landscape, a piece by Landseer, and a Madonna of Raphael. There was a portrait of Byron, and one of Tennyson. There was a photograph of myself, taken 12 years ago, to which, the landlady tells me, she attached special value, strangely enough ... On the door hung a poor miserable dress

and worn out ulster; under the bed was a pair of boots. Linen she had none; the poor covering of the bed had gone save one sheet and one blanket. I found a number of pawn tickets, showing that she had pledged these things during last summer, – when it was warm, poor creature! All the money she received went in drink; she used to spend my weekly 15/- the first day or two she had it. Her associates were so low that even Mrs Sherlock [the landlady] did not consider them respectable enough to visit her house.

I drew out the drawers. In one I found a little bit of butter and a crust of bread, – most pitiful sight my eyes ever looked upon. There was no other food anywhere...In a cupboard were several heaps of dirty rags; at the bottom there had been coals, but none were left...She lay on the bed covered with a sheet. I looked long, long at her face, but could not recognize it...she had changed horribly.[6]

He made a pledge never to 'cease to bear testimony against the accursed social order that brings about things of this kind. I feel that she will help me more in her death than she balked me during her life. Poor, poor thing!'[7]

With Nell's death to avenge, Gissing set to work two weeks later writing his darkest and most depressing comment on London's poor. This became *The Nether World*. It was completed in July 1888.

With a little more money to spare as a result of no longer having to pay maintenance for Nell, Gissing decided to take a trip abroad. He left for the south of France by train on Wednesday 26 September 1888 and travelled from Marseilles by ship to Italy. He did not return to England until the following March when he was forced for financial reasons to commence writing another book.

Gissing spent from March until November in England. During these few months he wrote *The Emancipated*, before setting off to Europe once more. He travelled to Greece to visit the ancient civilisations with which he had always felt a great affinity. For the rest of his life, Gissing looked back on his time in Italy and Greece with affection bordering on obsession. He returned to England at the end of February. He disliked the English winter with its dark evenings and cold weather which he believed were exerting a detrimental effect on his health and saw his trips abroad as a way of avoiding the ordeal.

Gissing's travels were mostly solitary affairs and by the time of his return from this second trip he was becoming lonely and desirous for the company of a woman. He would have liked to have found a suitable, educated, middle-class woman, but he was still suffering the results of his youthful folly. His income was low and his past prevented social intercourse with ladies. Like so many of his fictional characters Gissing felt trapped in a class beneath that of his intellect and education. He could see, like his character, Godwin Peak in *Born in Exile* that his secret would eventually surface if he tried to lie about his past. Yet he knew that he could not remain single for the rest of his life. He had sexual urges which plagued him. He wished for a companion with whom to share his time. He needed someone to organise the domestic tasks in order that he might concentrate on his writing. In his correspondence on this issue there is no mention of a need for love. As he believed that a middle-class woman would not be suitable, a working-class woman would have to do. As with Nell, he believed he would be able to teach the woman and elevate her mind so that she could, in time, provide him with intellectual company.

In a short story which Gissing said was based on his own experience and which he composed a couple of years later, he wrote:

> I am a fool about women. I don't know what it is – certainly not a sensual or passionate nature...there's that need in me – the incessant hunger for a woman's sympathy and affection...Day after day we grew more familiar...I didn't persuade myself that I cared for Emma [a servant girl], even then. Her vulgarisms of speech and feeling jarred upon me. But she was feminine; she spoke and looked gently, with sympathy. I enjoyed that evening – and you must bear in mind what I have told you before, that I stand in awe of refined women...Perhaps I have come to regard myself as doomed to live on a lower level. I find it impossible to imagine myself offering marriage – making love – to a girl such as those I meet in the big houses.[8]

Gissing believed that a marriage of convenience would be more commendable. His first marriage for love had been a disaster. With the idea that his new wife must be chosen from the working classes and with an impetuosity not seen in other aspects of his life, Gissing went into the streets of London to commit the second folly of his life.

In September 1890, on what can only be described as an impulse, he went to the Oxford Music Hall and either there or en route to or from, became acquainted with Edith Underwood. She was the daughter of an artisan and Roberts

> disliked the young woman at first sight, and never got over my first impression...She was of medium height and somewhat dark. She had not, however, the least pretence to such beauty as one might

hope to find even in a slave of the kitchen. She possessed neither face, nor figure, nor a sweet voice, nor any charm – she was just a female.[9]

At the beginning she was pleasant company and Gissing believed he would be able to educate her enough that they might be able to converse at least a little. He began the patronising task by reading to her from poems by Tennyson and Browning and taking her to serious theatrical shows.

Early the following year, only three months after meeting her, Gissing made up his mind to marry Edith. He went, on 9 January 1891 to see her father, to ask for her hand in marriage and to say that he was planning to move to Exeter. The following day, after having been given an assurance from Mr Underwood that he agreed to the marriage, Gissing set off for Devon. After a few weeks' uncertainty fearing that Edith had changed her mind about the union, Gissing returned to London and on a foggy 25 February 1891, the two were married at St Pancras Register Office in the morning, returning immediately to Exeter after the wedding.

Gissing's second marriage began auspiciously enough. The couple spent many a happy spring hour walking around the nearby Devon countryside. By May his wife began to suffer from a mysterious illness, 'Edith ill with dyspepsia, or whatever it may be. – Constant sickness and misery',[10] which in their naivety the young couple did not immediately realise heralded her pregnancy. The 'illness' did not put a stop to outings to the coast, nor to Edith's education, which was continuing with Hardy's *Far from the Madding Crowd*. Winter came and with it the baby. On 9 December Gissing's diary entry stated, 'Rain and wind. E beginning her troubles…At 8 in evening came Dr Henderson.' The following morning, he complained about having been up all night:

> A furious gale blowing. E in long miserable pain; the Doctor has just given her chloroform, and says that the blackguard business draws to an end. 5.15 a.m. Went to the study door, and heard the cry of the child. Nurse speedily coming down, tells me it is a boy. Wind howling savagely. So, the poor girl's misery is over, and she has what she earnestly desired.

The baby had an 'ugly dark patch over right eye', and whether it was his unattractive appearance, the painful birth or his difficult early weeks, but Edith failed to bond with Walter, or 'Gubsey', as his father affectionately called him. The baby proved to be of a difficult constitution and by 30 December, as a result of the stress of dealing with him, Edith went down with influenza and Gissing recorded the first signs of the problem which was to become a feature of their future life together,

> Wed Dec. 30. Windy, mild. Horrible day with E., who seems to have got the influenza. Henderson came. She in brutal temper, reviling everyone and everything. A day of misery, once more, and bitter repentance. Did nothing.

The baby's behaviour did not improve and by 12 January Gissing felt that the only course open to him was to find someone to take him in for a few weeks' respite for the sake of Edith's health as she was finding Walter increasingly difficult. He was worried as to how he would find the opportunity to return to his work, for another book was, as usual, necessary for the continued livelihood of the new family. Walter was sent away for three months to be nursed in the nearby village of Brampford Speke and Edith's life continued as before the baby's birth except for an occasional visit to see her child.

It was during this period that Gissing first became aware of Clara Collet. This was when his sister Nelly had written to tell him of the report in *The Queen* on 5 March about 'A lecture deliv'd by a lady to the London Ethical Society on "The Novels of George Gissing". I must inquire about this.'[11]

Both Clara and Gissing had attended lectures at the Ethical Society. It is possible that they attended one together in which case Clara may have noticed the author. They were not introduced at this venue. Gissing was good-looking and his looks may have attracted the young woman's notice. According to Morley Roberts:

> His grey eyes were very bright and intelligent, his features finely cut, and at times he was almost beautiful; although his skin was not always in such good condition as it should have been, and he was always badly freckled...It will be observed that he brushed his hair straight backward from his forehead without any parting...It was a very fine hair of a brown colour, perhaps of a rather mousy tint, and it was never cut except at the ends at the nape of his neck.[12]

Gissing was impressed that his work had been the subject of a lecture. He wrote to Bertz to inform him of the event:

> Certainly my position improves. I am told that, recently, a lecture was delivered before the London Ethical Society on 'The Novels of George Gissing'. Of this I heard nothing at the time, but it is very

important. I don't even yet know who the lecturer was. The Society is not contemptible; I used to attend its lectures occasionally.[13]

Gissing discovered the identity of the speaker and reported back to Nelly:

The lecture at the Ethical Society was by a Miss Clara Collet, MA, whom I do not know, but who has a sociological article in the current *Nineteenth Century*.[14] Obviously a woman of brains. The report in *The Queen* was very bad, & only allowed me to gather that she maintained that G G's mind was healthy & not, as many people say, morbid. The fact of the lecture astonishes me. It is surely significant.[15]

Significant it was, but not only for the reason Gissing meant.

Whether or not Clara planned to meet with Gissing purely as a result of reading his work or whether she had seen him at some time, she was quite unconventional in her approach and single-minded in her determination to make his acquaintance. The lecture may have been the first plan to get herself noticed by Gissing. She followed this by writing to him. *The Odd Women*, Gissing's latest novel, had just been published and she may have used this as the excuse she needed to make contact with him. In this work he explored the 'woman question', highlighting the problem middle-class women had if they remained unmarried yet needed, like Clara, to earn an income. In Gissing's own words this book, 'deals with the lot of women, who, for statistical or other reasons, have small chance of marriage. – Among the characters, militant or conventional, are some who succeed, and some who fail, in the effort to make their lives independent.'[16] On 10 May 1893, Clara wrote suggesting that the two of them should meet; an unconventional and bold move for a woman at that time. Gissing rejected her offer, and wrote to say that he lived too far away – he was still in Exeter – to be able to visit her. He did not usually respond positively to requests to meet with readers whoever they may be. He was fundamentally shy and embarrassed by his domestic circumstances.

Clara was not to be put off by this rebuttal and three days after her first letter, sent a parcel of her publications. She was determined to make an impact on the author.

Gissing had tired of Exeter. He could not get inspiration for his work from Devon's pleasant surroundings and was finding the rural atmosphere stifling to his creativity – he needed the poverty of London. The local libraries were not of the same standard as those in the metropolis and he was suffering from the lack of mental stimulation he could count on from his small circle of friends. He had, therefore, been planning to return to London shortly and informed Clara of his plans. She seized her opportunity and suggested that Edith and he should spend the first weekend of their return to the City with her at her house in Richmond. Gissing replied that this was impossible. He was determined that no-one should become aware of his worsening marital situation.

The Gissings returned to a flat in Brixton and his correspondence with Clara continued. By 28 June he felt comfortable enough in his letters to comment that, 'The great kindness of your letters encourages me to write to you in this off-hand way: I feel as though I had a friend in you – tolerant and human...I will write again very soon. This is only to show you that I am not ungrateful.'

Her single-mindedness finally paid off. Gissing agreed to meet her. It was unusual for him to agree to meet with an admirer of his work. On the whole he had a rather derogatory attitude towards them, although he would sometimes agree to send an autograph or a quick note. However, a date was set, and the venue was to be Clara's home at Richmond. Edith was not included in the arrangements.

NOTES

1. Pierre Coustillas (ed.), *London and the Life of Literature in Late Victorian England: The Diary of George Gissing, Novelist* (Brighton: Harvester Press, 1978), 24 January 1893. (Hereafter *Gissing's Diary*).
2. Letter from Dr Zakrewska to Collet, 10 August 1901. MSS 29/3/9/i, Warwick University, Modern Records Centre.
3. Letter from Dr Zakrewska to Collet, 10 August 1901.
4. George Gissing, *The Private Papers of Henry Ryecroft* (first published 1903, London: Constable, 1923), p. 87.
5. Morley Roberts, *The Private Life of Henry Maitland* (London: Eveleigh Nash, 1912). The real names have been inserted in place of the fictional ones in this version.
6. Coustillas (ed.), *Gissing's Diary*, 1 March 1888.
7. Ibid.
8. George Gissing, 'A Lodger in Maze Pond', *The House of Cobwebs* (London: Constable, 1926), pp. 257–60.
9. Roberts, *Henry Maitland*, p. 125.
10. Coustillas (ed.), *Gissing's Diary*, 17 May 1891.
11. Ibid., 14 March 1892.

12. Roberts, *Henry Maitland*, p. 126.
13. Mattheisen *et al.* (eds), *Letters of George Gissing*, Gissing to Bertz, 17 March 1892.
14. This was 'Prospects of Marriage', April 1892.
15. Mattheisen *et al.* (eds), *Letters of George Gissing*, 11 April 1892 to Ellen Gissing.
16. Coustillas (ed.), *Gissing's Diary*, 15 March 1893.

3

George and Clara – An Intimate Friendship?

Tuesday. July 18 [1893]. Worked [in British Library] from 9.30 to 12.30, then ate some sandwiches brought from home, and went out for a glass of beer, walking for half an hour. Back at a little after 1, and worked till 3.30, then home and had dinner at 4. To Waterloo to catch the 5.45 express to Richmond, where, by arrangement, I called on Miss Collet at 34 Hill Street. We at once went out on to the river, and rowed to Kingston and back. Home by the 8.45 train. Miss Collet younger than I had expected. She wishes to come and call on E[dith]., but I fear.[1]

Thus Gissing recorded in his diary the first occasion he met Clara. The two of them met at her house, a newly constructed building in Richmond. They walked down to the river, a distance of only a few hundred yards. Clara owned a rowing boat which was looked after by a boatman named Frank Thornson with whom she remained in contact for many years. In 1906 she recalled a trip on the river at Richmond when she took Mr Thornson with her as company and in the course of the journey he informed her that a book entitled *The Pilot of Mississippi* which she had given him 12 years previously had by then been read by every boatman on the Thames. Did Thornson act as chaperone on the inaugural voyage of Clara and Gissing? It is possible, although Gissing mentions no one, and we know from several diary entries that Clara was able to row.

Clara's diary appears to have been destroyed for the years 1892–1904 save for some scanty entries in 1898. This was the exact duration of her friendship with Gissing. She did not wish for anyone to read what she had written about him.

The rendevous was successful. Gissing agreed to her suggestion that she should meet Edith despite his having serious misgivings as to what her impressions would be of his lower-class wife. Of his friends only Morley Roberts, Clara and later Eliza Orme were given an insight into his domestic situation. H.G. Wells, despite being one of Gissing's friends in his later life, was never to be introduced to Edith.

On Wednesday 2 August 1893, Clara arrived at the Gissings' Brixton household at 6 p.m. after she had completed her day's work at the Board of Trade. She stayed for tea, departing at 9 p.m., but not before inviting Edith to spend the day with her at Richmond the following Thursday. She took her on a river trip to Kingston whilst her husband looked after young Walter at home. What can have been her motivation in taking the uneducated, unfriendly Edith out for the day? In later years she had nothing good to say about her. Her first impressions may not have been unfavourable; but most likely she saw befriending Edith as a means of gaining welcome access to the household.

Gissing saw Clara as the unattainable middle-class woman with whom he could never envisage having a relationship. On 14 August, less than a month after their first meeting, he wrote his short story, 'A Lodger in Maze Pond', in which one of his autobiographical characters surmised, 'I find it impossible to imagine myself offering marriage – making love, to girls such as those I meet in the big houses.' Despite many years since his crime, Gissing still felt unable to relate to middle-class women other than as a friend. He may not have found Clara attractive. Even had he done so, she would never have outwardly indicated that she wished for anything other than friendship with Gissing as he was married. Although her attitude towards others was one of tolerance, especially as she grew older, her own behaviour was exemplary. Gissing may have been attracted to her but, like her, never gave any outward appearance of so doing. Despite remaining outwardly indifferent she became emotionally involved with the author. It must have soon become apparent to her that the Gissings' marriage was not happy. Edith was becoming increasingly difficult. Her constant arguing with her husband, with Walter, the landlords and the servants, was by this time causing Gissing great stress. Edith was not able to live contentedly with anyone. The first signs of her mental illness were beginning to manifest themselves.

Clara took the opportunity at this early stage in their relationship of making herself indispensable to Gissing. Even though they could not become partners, her feelings ran deep and she was determined to play a continuing part in his life. If other women had proved to be the bane of Gissing's life, she would become its blessing.

On 16 September 1893, only two months after their first meeting, she arranged another outing with Edith. She took her to a matinée performance at the Globe Theatre, leaving Walter with his father again. Much to Gissing's surprise, Clara sent a letter that she timed to arrive whilst Edith was absent from home, in which she made the extraordinary offer of accepting financial responsibility for Walter's upbringing should Gissing's health fail him. Gissing commented in his diary that it was, 'A wonderful piece of kindness.'[2] In his reply to her he wrote,

> It is difficult to answer such a letter as this with which you have surprised me; – difficult to express…the strong feeling of gratitude for a proposal dictated by such thoughtful kindness…You have made my mind very easy in the thought that, if my own life were to be as short as that of my father, (who died at 42, & when I, his eldest son, was not fourteen,) my dear little boy would have not only a sincere, but a very capable, friend to stand by him. I know only too well the miseries & perils of a child left without strong, wise guidance [he had in mind his own folly at Owens College]…Let us, then, say no more about this; sufficient to remember that you have given me the highest proof of friendship possible, & that I have acknowledged it with sincerest gratitude…And is it not something that you make me think more kindly of the world than is my habit?[3]

Her proposal had its desired effect. Gissing would always think of Clara differently from his other friends. She had elevated herself in his mind above anyone he had previously encountered. He could never forget her.

Gissing and Edith were sent an invitation by Clara to attend a Gilbert and Sullivan opera at the Savoy, with her sister Edith. They went on 14 October and afterwards had tea in the Strand. Thus the relationship began.

For the next few years the pattern was set. The two corresponded regularly, writing on various subjects including literature, providing Gissing with the intellectual stimulation which had been lacking in his previous life. They would discuss his work. Clara made it clear that she did not like the title he had given to one of his books, *In the Year of Jubilee* which she thought was 'prettyish'. He decided not to change it to placate her, but did try to justify it saying she had not understood the reason for his choice. They discussed *The Odd Women*. Gissing asked her whether she knew of any establishments which offered training in secretarial work like the one in *The Odd Women* established by the feminist Mary Barfoot. She replied that she did not know of any such places at that time. Gissing believed he had come up with an original concept: the opening to women of clerical work – the type of work Clara Collet had been arguing should be accessible to them.

When Gissing wrote telling Nelly of his growing friendship with Clara, he said that she was, 'A remarkable person; full of energy. We see nobody else',[4] and to Clara he said:

> I myself, indeed, am not inhospitable, but the circumstances of my life – surely, in a measure, you begin to understand them? – compel me to seem so. It is on this very account that I shun all society; again & again I have had to tell people - in ambiguous language which, I fear, often offends – that I cannot ask them to come to see me, & cannot go to see them... You are all but the only person in London with whom I can talk of intellectual things – for Roberts has gone I know not whither.[5]

Gissing developed a high opinion of his new friend, commenting that she had, 'a great deal of brain to the square inch, in everything [she] wrote'.[6] He also thought her emotionally strong so that he could discuss his problems with her without causing her alarm:

> A strange thing that, but for our having come to know each other, these struggles and gaspings of mine, would have been unspoken of to anyone. I suppose my reason for telling you of such miseries is the assurance I have that you cannot be depressed by them; you are the sole & single person of my acquaintance who is living a healthy, active life, of large intercourse with men & women. To other people with whom I correspond I am ashamed to complain much, as they have more than enough morbidity of their own to endure.[7]

Clara would make an extra effort to visit Gissing on any special occasion such as birthdays or close to Christmas. Little Walter was not forgotten, she would often bring him gifts such as a large bucket of bricks on Gissing's birthday and a book on her return from a holiday in Switzerland. She remembered Edith's birthday and brought gifts for her when she called or sent presents by post. She had to prevent any jealousy which might jeopardise her relationship with Gissing. Edith was prone to paranoia and in the relationship between her husband and Clara maybe this was with a degree of reason. Edith must have recognised that Clara could provide her husband with the intellectual stimulation that she was unable to offer. If Edith's paranoia was to become worse she could make the relationship between her husband and his friend difficult.

When the couple required advice it was to Clara they would turn, on subjects as diverse as medical matters, to where the family should go for their holidays. She suggested that Gissing should try terebene for his chest condition. It was a liquid obtained by the action of sulphuric acid on turpentine which could be inhaled. He tried it although it did little good. Gissing took her advice on where to stay at St Leonards-on-Sea (near Hastings) and congratulated her on her choice, 'We have cause for endless gratitude to you. These lodgings are remarkably comfortable, & the people extremely decent.'[8] It was rare for Gissing to be satisfied with a holiday. On most occasions he found much about which to complain regarding the lodgings and especially the landladies. At St Leonards, Clara not only advised them where to stay but also joined them for a week. If Edith had ambiguous feelings about Gissing's friend her goodwill was being pushed to its limits.

After her initial futile attempt to befriend Edith, Clara abandoned the idea and simply accepted her presence. In a letter she sent many years later, she summed up her feelings for Edith, commenting on her 'absence of affection for anyone and her mental laziness'. She continued:

> In the four years I had known them [1893–97] I had hardly ever talked to G[eorge] alone after the first evening when I made his acquaintance. She had spent a day with me afterwards on the river & in the early spring of 1894 they had gone with Walter to lodgings recommended by my sister, & I went down to another part of St. Leonards & had a longish walk with her. Listening to her alone always made me vaguely uncomfortable & not at all anxious to know her better. I wanted to make the best of her & never criticized her at all.[9]

This last pledge must have been hard to maintain, for in his correspondence to Clara, Gissing had begun discussing the problems he was encountering in his marriage.

In January 1896 another baby, Alfred, had been born. The birth was easier although Edith had wished for a girl and was disappointed at having another son. She again found it difficult to cope with her new baby and dealt with her anxiety and depression by episodes of what Gissing called 'sullen rage'. Edith's temper was becoming worse. She frequently had arguments with the servants, resulting in their resignation and the necessity of Gissing having to find replacements. She began to abuse her husband, sometimes to the point of physical violence, by threatening to throw things at him. Worse than all that, as far as George was concerned, was that she started to behave violently towards the children, especially Walter. Gissing wrote in his diary that he found work had become an impossibility.

It can hardly have helped matters at home, when just a month after Alfred's birth, Gissing decided to have gas installed in the house. This decision had been made after 'The flaring up (all but explosion) of hall [oil] lamp last night.'[10] This meant the upheaval of gasfitters in the house at a time when Edith was in a state of near exhaustion and anxiety trying to cope with a new baby.

On 2 March a disaster occurred. As Gissing recorded in his diary,

> A black day in memory, though weather fine. Went to town, to get measured for clothes etc. Bought some seeds for garden. Had dinner with Tinckam [his old Brixton landlord who had become a friend]. Got home by 11 o'clock, and to my horror found all the front windows standing open. During my absence, man was to test the gas pipes; this he had done with a candle, and there resulted a bad explosion. Ceiling of drawing room completely blown down, and a patch in the dining room. In front bedroom a chair burnt up, bed clothes damaged by fire, carpet drenched with water. All this happened at 3 in afternoon and on my return, E. with Walter and baby and two servants were sitting all together in the kitchen. Drawing room a hideous wilderness of plaster. With difficulty made ourselves beds for the night.[11]

Walter had been in the room watching the workman when the explosion had occurred and his hair had been singed at the back. The workman was seriously injured.

It was lucky that none of the family had been hurt but the accident caused further problems for them. Gissing found rooms in Dorking for Edith and the children and bemoaned the fact that he had no insurance to cover the repairs, which he had to pay for himself, despite the accident being a result of the incompetence of the workman. As Gissing wrote to Clara the following day:

> What had happened was simply this; the man (who came early in the afternoon) [to test the system] in his wisdom searched for the gas-leakage with a candle...the tee junction left to supply gas to lower front room was quite open. He also noticed that the floor above had not been removed, so that the pipes could not have been properly tested. The hall lamp was supported only by a piece of broken slate batten, which rendered it very unsafe, & likely to fall at any moment. An elbow in scullery was stopped up with a cork. This should have been an iron plug.[12]

She replied instantly offering assistance, suggesting she take Walter to be looked after by herself and her new sister-in-law Mary.

Clara had, the previous December, moved house into one she had purchased herself at 36, Berkeley Road, Crouch End, around the corner from her parents' house. She lived there alone for 15 months, after which time her sister Edith joined her. Mary Ewins had married their brother, Wilfred, who was in the Colonial Service and was abroad at the time, so that Mary had little to do. Gissing did not accept her offer of help as he had found rooms for the whole family. His wife, already at breaking point, found this added difficulty especially problematic.

Gissing looked for a solution to his domestic situation. He knew that Walter was suffering. Edith's behaviour, strange almost from the beginning of their married life, deteriorated quickly after the birth of her first son. She began to suffer from a form of neurosis or even psychosis exacerbated by post-natal depression. Edith had never enjoyed a good relationship with Walter right from his birth and with his disfiguring mole, and the prolonged separation after his birth, it is easy to imagine that there was little opportunity for the unstable Edith to bond with her elder son.

The exact nature of her illness is difficult to ascertain. The symptoms were frequent outbursts of temper often culminating in violence. She suffered from paranoia and by 21 April 1895 Gissing informed Clara that his wife was becoming increasingly unwilling to leave home, suggesting agoraphobia. When Clara invited Edith to stay with her at Richmond, Gissing wrote:

> Now is it not better that – as we now know each other pretty well – I should write to you with considerable frankness? In brief, then, all hope must be abandoned that she will ever find any pleasure or satisfaction away from home...I have made several efforts to bring about friendliness between her & my own people: with the sole result of making her regard them with a fierce antipathy, – so that I cannot, now, even mention one of their names, as I value my peace. The difficulty is very grievous; for I see no hope of ever being able to take her or the boy to Yorkshire...My people do not understand this...but Edith has determined not to go anywhere, & upon me, of course, falls the task of devising excuses. Plainly, I am at the end of my circumlocutions; to you at all events I must tell the truth.[13]

Gissing's determination to keep his few friends from meeting his wife can only have exacerbated her paranoia, but he believed that her behaviour was too bad to risk such rendezvous. Mental health problems were not something that Victorian men liked to discuss. As with Nell before her, Gissing kept Edith out of sight to hide her lack of education and her strange, often violent behaviour, from his friends. On 26 October 1893 Gissing wrote to Clara, 'Do not think that Edith disregards your letters. But she has long since given up the hope of learning to write. So I will answer for her.'[14] Edith may never have had any intention of learning to write or of educating herself but again, Gissing had the expectation that once married she would wish to become educated like himself, although he did understand that, like Nell, Edith was not interested or able to become an academic. Gissing had held out hope that the working classes would eventually be able to elevate themselves. First, Nell had been unable to educate herself as Gissing had wished, and now his second wife also appeared to lack the motivation and ability to improve herself. His idealism began to wane and his later books were more accepting that the working classes were as they were and attempts at self-improvement were likely to fail. For this reason he was not a believer in democracy as he was fearful of the country being run by what he saw as ill-educated people. This attitude was born from his own experiences and was in contrast to the beliefs of Clara Collet. They had more in common in their attitudes to women. Both had a fundamental belief that education was the answer. However, neither Edith nor Nell had the intelligence, the inclination, nor the health to benefit from the education which Gissing had tried to force upon them.

Edith has suffered from a lack of sympathy amongst Gissing's biographers. Compassion has been meted out to Nell. As an alcoholic her behaviour could be blamed on this affliction. Edith has just been seen as an old nag; a woman with a temper. She has been abused for her selfishness, lack of intelligence, ill-treatment of her children and of her husband. Whilst this is undoubtedly true, what must not be lost sight of is that, as with Nell, the reasons for her behaviour were probably beyond her control. Edith's bearing was not that of a normal, rational person. She suffered from a form of depressive illness. She had not a friend in the world. No-one wrote her a letter or visited her – even her own sister tired of her after the first two days of a week's visit. Edith would not leave her home unless absolutely necessary without her husband, signifying agoraphobia caused by her insecurity and paranoia. Knowing that her husband and his friends were literate and could discuss matters about which she knew nothing would not have helped to improve her self-esteem. Gissing often gave the impression of exasperation regarding Edith's intellectual failings, and she developed a hatred for his family as a result of her paranoia. They were middle class and in her mind (and that of her husband) better than her. She was unable to become a part of the intellectual world of her husband, and consequently, in her lonely existence the role she was forced into was the only one she was capable of – housekeeper to Gissing and even of that he was hypercritical, making her feel that she had failed. Her berating of the servants was the only area in her life in which she had power – her only way of being noticed in this household in which intellect was the only benchmark. She felt wretched and ill, unable to cope, irritable, depressed and with no-one to turn to. In marrying Edith, Gissing had made a mistake from which his wife suffered as much as he did. Edith might have become mentally unstable whomever she had married, but the lonely, socially isolated life she spent with a man who found her presence an embarrassment cannot have helped.

Gissing did not select emotionally or intellectually strong women for his relationships, which may have been a subconscious decision to ensure that he was able to dominate. He was not a confident man, and marrying someone weaker would give him some control, for in this one area of his life, he could be certain that he was 'better' than his partner, both intellectually, emotionally and socially. To have married someone like Clara Collet would have given him intellectual stimulation, but he would always have felt himself to be her inferior; a situation with which a Victorian man would have found it difficult to cope. He was hypersensitive about his social standing in the world. In a letter to Clara he said that:

> I have made up my mind never again to mix in the society of educated people. It is a necessity of my circumstances. I find it a wretched discomfort to pretend social equality where there can be none. My acquaintance must only be with a few individuals; in a gathering I am at once set in a false position, – I cannot talk, cannot listen, & become a mere silent misanthrope.[15]

Conversely, Clara treated her social 'superiors' with the same confidence that she treated anyone else. She did not feel the same need as Gissing to place people, of any class or position, on a pedestal. She may have been attracted by Gissing, but whatever he felt for her emotionally he would have found it difficult to conduct a relationship with someone of her social position as he would never have felt he was her equal. Throughout the whole of his life Gissing continued addressing Clara as 'Miss Collet' despite the intimacy, depth and length of their relationship. She was like a mother figure to him: someone with whom to discuss all his problems and who could be relied on to give advice when needed, a person to look up to, but not someone whom he could easily have loved on an equal basis. She was his superior.

Despite her outward appearance of being composed and confident, was she really so in control? Her early diary entries show a lack of confidence at times both in herself and in her relations with others. She may have appeared to Gissing to have been the rock on which he could depend but she also needed him to depend on her. Why did she destroy her diary entries for this period? Was it that she wrote down her feelings for the author and in the light of future events decided they had better remain unrevealed? Unlike Beatrice Potter or Eleanor Marx, Clara managed to appear cheerful most of the time: 'Now let me hear something from the sane world. It always does me good to think of you, for you are unassociated & unassociable with gloom', Gissing told her.[16] Was she unable to express her feelings for Gissing or did she have no feelings for him other than of friendship?

In a letter of 25 April 1896, he told her of the deteriorating situation at home:

> Most fortunately, the baby gives very little trouble. Edith cares infinitely more for him than she ever did for Walter. When she said to Walter, in her rage, 'I always hated you', there was a measure of truth in it; from the boy's birth onwards, scarcely a day on which she has not loudly regretted his existence...I shall hold very firm. Indeed, if I do not, I shall very soon be in penury.

Walter was a difficult child. Being brought up in an environment such as his, it was unlikely that he would be otherwise. Gissing decided that the only way to safeguard Walter's health and well-being was to remove him once more from the household. On 8 April 1896 he and Walter left Epsom for Wakefield where he was, unbeknown to Edith, planning to leave their four-and-a-half-year-old son with his two aunts. Not surprisingly, Walter did not like the idea and made a terrible scene a couple of days after his arrival when his aunt Margaret tried to give him a bath. He refused to get out and fought viciously with her until Gissing intervened. Walter was understandably becoming disturbed. However, Gissing's mind was made up and on 22 April, whilst still up north, he wrote to inform his wife that he was intending to leave their son in Wakefield. The following day he returned to London by himself.

He returned to Epsom to a 'terrible scene with E.; won't bear speaking of'.[17] The same evening he wrote a long letter to Clara, his only confidant, to justify his actions:

At last a crisis – the inevitable. I have left Walter at Wakefield, to be taught & cared for by my mother & sisters. On returning, I am met with terrible scenes, but nothing shall move me. The child's whole life is at stake. For the last two months there has been a daily quarrel here, in which, at any moment, the boy could hear venomous abuse of his father & all his father's relatives & friends. When, on the Sunday before we left, Edith told the child that she never wished to see him again, – that she wished he had died in one of his illnesses, – that he was a little wretch, – & so on, & so on, I quietly took the resolve... There he will be with other children, & surrounded with the warmest friends. If any attempt is made to disturb this arrangement, I shall take Walter with me to some great distance. I am responsible for his future, & I <u>know</u> I am doing the right – the only right – thing.

Impossible to make you believe the treatment – the ceaseless insult – to which I have been subjected for a year or two. Well, you must judge me as you feel able to. It has come to Edith's opening my letters (from relatives), that she may find new forms of vulgar abuse. In the presence (or hearing) of servants (even, I should think, of neighbours) she brings revolting charges against me, & prays fervently (her one prayer) for misery to befall me & mine. No one could bear it... Of course I write with a shaking hand, & feel miserable enough. It is bad to lose sight of my boy; but he, happily, stays on without the least reluctance.[18]

Gissing had not told his sisters and mother the true reasons for his leaving him there. They were told that there was servant trouble giving the family cause for concern. Edith in her paranoiac and troubled mind was sure that the 'Wakefield people' were 'in a plot to rob her of her child'.[19]

After Walter's removal from Epsom, life went on much as before. Edith continued abusing her husband and the servants, and Clara continued to visit the dysfunctional household, providing Gissing with an escape into the intellectual world which must in some small way have assisted his survival during this difficult time.

In July, Clara took a trip to Scotland. As on all her journeys away from London, she wrote regularly to Gissing. On this holiday she exhibited a side of her personality rarely revealed. She admitted to Gissing that she was depressed. He scoffed at such an idea. Surely dependable Clara Collet could not have human weaknesses such as misery? 'What, <u>you</u> depressed! Hoot awa! – as they possibly say at Perth. This must be the most transitory of moods; that grand northward journey will already have blown it away, when you get this.'[20] Hopefully it was just a passing mood for it would have been unfair for Clara not to be offered the sympathy of her friends on the rare occasion when she too suffered from a period of upset. She may have had the inability to show her vulnerability and a wish to always appear in control. To Gissing she often reprimanded him; pointing out a grammatical error in his work about which he was unaware or brusquely berating him for his attitude towards Edith. Like many men, Clara found it difficult to be soft and gentle – she had a reluctance or inability to show her feminine side – a fault into which she had insight as early as 1883 when in her diary she stated that, 'I undoubtedly possess to a remarkable degree the faculty of offending nearly everyone.'[21] With her sometimes over-confident, brusque manner, Gissing would have been unaware that she had feelings for him and, had he been interested in her, a lack of any signals would have made it difficult for him to respond to those feelings. That she often took the initiative in their friendship is highlighted by a letter from him in which he apologises for not having contacted her for so long, 'It is really very good of you to endure this arrangement, whereby you take my silence to mean that I am always glad to see you. Other people would long ago have taken offence; – but that is not your way.'[22]

In October of the same year, whilst she was touring the country once again, collecting statistics for an investigation for the Board of Trade, she wrote to tell Gissing that she would like to visit Wakefield to see Walter. Gissing made arrangements with his sister and sent a message to Walter with whom he corresponded regularly. She spent the night with Ellen, Margaret and Mrs Gissing, meeting them for the first time. She had already met Algernon, Gissing's brother, when he visited Brixton in 1893. Gissing's other brother William had died in 1880.

On her return she contacted Gissing to arrange to meet with him and Edith to report on the boy's well-being. Edith took exception, being sure in her paranoid state that her husband and Clara were in league regarding the removal of Walter to Yorkshire. Gissing had to send a telegram to prevent Clara from travelling to Epsom as he was certain Edith would be abusive towards her. Instead they met in London where they lunched together at a restaurant. Gissing broke Victorian social convention by taking Clara out to lunch with him on his own. It would have been a most irregular occurrence for an unmarried woman to eat with a married man in the absence of a chaperone, but Clara did not care much for convention, and Edith did not forgive her for some time – as late as December, she was still not welcome at the house. Gissing wrote:

Certainly you must come after Christmas. I feel uncomfortable enough in mind as it is. & I should be altogether too much ashamed of myself if it came to forbidding you the house. Happily you can see the humorous side of things, & you must often laugh in thinking of my grotesque position. Indeed, I often laugh myself – though with a sort of mortuary laugh.[23]

Later in the same letter Gissing made the comment that he would try to remain with Edith for another two years to allow him to sort out Walter's education, but he did not wish to do so. Would his future separation give Clara the opportunity she may have hoped for to make a bid for Gissing's emotions? Gissing was taking her increasingly into his confidence and their friendship could hardly have been any closer.

The following month Gissing met H.G. Wells for the first time and wrote to Clara with the news.

At the Omar dinner,[24] just as I was going away, a wild-looking man rushed up to me, & introduced himself as H.G. Wells. He mentioned, as a strange coincidence, that when he read <u>New Grub Street</u> he was living near Regent's Park, in great misery, & his wife's name was Amy.[25] A day or two after, I had a most amusing letter from him, inviting me to his new house in Worcester Park. You must see that letter some day. 'Mr Wells rarely washes. He is generally found in an unshaven condition, with dirty cuffs' &c. I think I shall like the man.[26]

The two became friends, visiting each other regularly. For the present, though, Gissing would bring no visitors, other than Clara, back to his home at Epsom as he had managed to re-establish her place as their one visitor, despite Edith's health and, as a result, her behaviour deteriorating still further.

On 10 February 1897 came a further crisis in the relationship between George and Edith over accusations that he was stealing her mail. He could take no more and went to stay with Henry Hick, an old school friend, who had recently re-established contact with him and who was, by this time, a doctor. Clara was not wholly sympathetic with Gissing's behaviour and he attempted to justify himself by explaining in detail about the relationship with his wife and what had prompted his recent action. Clara implied, or Gissing took her to mean, that he was being weak leaving his wife and that a stronger man would have managed to deal with her. He retaliated, explaining that Edith was even abusing him for his illnesses saying to him 'You knew [you were ill] all along, but what did you care. I wonder what my father was thinking of to let me marry such a man – the old idiot.'[27]

Gissing was concerned about his health as he had been suffering from a long-standing chest condition. Hick insisted that he see a specialist in London so the two travelled up from Hick's house in Kent. They met with Wells, and the three had dinner together. Hick and Wells formed a friendship and Hick became Wells' doctor as well. The prognosis from the specialist was cautious. He recommended that Gissing should not spend the rest of the winter in London as he could detect emphysema in one of his lungs. So with that in mind, and giving him the excuse he needed to escape Edith, Gissing left to spend the next few months in Budleigh Salterton, South Devon.

Gissing alerted his wife's relations that she would be on her own whilst he was away and asked Eliza Orme to keep an eye on her. Miss Orme was the woman who had been working with Clara on 'The Employment of Women' in 1892. She had, apparently coincidentally, made Gissing's acquaintance through his publishers Lawrence and Bullen in 1894. Clara wrote to Eliza Orme explaining the situation with regard to Edith, informing her that Gissing would be contacting her to ask for her assistance. Clara would have found it difficult to assist as Edith distrusted her. Gissing said, 'You, alas, could do nothing whatever, – as I fear you know.'[28] Nonetheless, she did visit Edith on two occasions and commented later that, 'The second day that I spent with her stands out as the most terrible in my life. Not because of any outburst but because of the revelation of her mind, its littleness, its selfishness, the entire absence of any affection for anyone and her mental laziness.'[29]

Eliza Orme provided a great deal of support to Gissing and his family over the next few years. She was nine years older than Clara and like her had a good education. She had attended Bedford College, studied law and political economy at the University of London, graduating in 1888 as the first woman with a law degree. She worked in conveyancing, developed an interest in women's suffrage and, in common with Clara Collet, was keener on working within the system, pouring scorn on women who were eccentric and outspoken as she felt they harmed the cause. Miss Orme, as an impartial observer of the Gissings' marriage, found Edith's behaviour impossible to tolerate and told Clara that she believed that Edith had a 'filthy mind & was always detecting evil in servants & accusing people'.[30]

In a letter written to Clara from London after his meal with Wells and before his appointment with the specialist in 1897,

Gissing finally informed her of his past, 'Not once but twice, have I made an ass of myself. My first wife was a hopeless drunkard, & died miserably in 1881 or 2, I forget the year [he was wrong about the date which was 1888, Clara corrected this in the margin of the letter]. This will seem to you incredible. Is there another such imbecile walking the earth?'[31] She was the only person other than Morley Roberts whom he had told about his first marriage and he did not mention that Nell had been a prostitute as well as an alcoholic. He did not divulge the details of his criminal past at this time, although he did allude to it in a letter written to her just after he arrived in Budleigh, when, commenting upon his present solitude he likened it to when, 'at 16 or so, I was most foolishly sent to live alone in Manchester in miserable lodgings. Hence all subsequent ills & follies',[32] implying that something may have been said verbally to Clara about this event.

Gissing was not sure that he intended to leave Edith for good. He felt guilty about the failure of his relationship and wished that his wife could be reunited with Walter in the future. Gissing had no plans for removing Alfred from the household as Edith treated him better than she had Walter. Clara intervened, trying to encourage a reconciliation, which Gissing did not view at all well.

> Your severe letter did make me rather miserable; but we must not discuss it. Whilst there is much truth in your accusations, I repeat what I have said before, that you cannot possibly understand the difficulties that have been put in my way.[33]

Whether under the influence of this 'severe letter', or as a result of good reports from Miss Orme of Edith's recent behaviour, Gissing decided to give her a last chance and returned to Epsom at the end of May, just over three months after he had gone to Devon.

During his absence Clara received regular letters, and Edith attempted a reconciliation by sending her little letters of her own.

It was at this time that Clara's sister moved in with her at Berkeley Road. Their father was very old and their mother becoming increasingly difficult. Carrie periodically suffered from ill-health necessitating periods of convalescence in Hastings and later at Sidmouth. Their brother Wilfred had been working in the Colonial Service, and had recently been transferred to Cyprus as District Commissioner so he was away for much of the time. Her move closer to the family home in Coleridge Road enabled her to be more of a help in supporting the family.

Gissing did not enjoy his time in Devon other than as an escape from Edith. There was, however, a brief respite from the solitude he felt, during a two-week visit by Wells and his wife. The friendship was growing and Gissing commented to Clara:

> We get on quite astonishingly well; this is the only case in which I have been able to make friends with a new writer. Wells's sole defect is his lack of a classical education; he makes up for this by singular sweetness of disposition, a wonderfully active mind, & a ceaseless flow of merriment. I believe he will do fine work, for he has a literary conscience & no touch of vulgarity in his views of life.[34]

On his return to Epsom, the old pattern of life re-established itself with Clara visiting on a regular basis and letter-writing in between. As a result of the growing rift between Gissing and his wife, she felt able to be more outspoken in her feelings towards her friend. On 11 May in a letter written just prior to his return, Gissing commented that 'I have delayed writing until I could let you know that your wish concerning the letters has been obeyed.' Clara was worried that Edith might find the letters and wished them destroyed. There appears, at this time, to be the formation of a less formal relationship between the two. Gissing commented 'Ten years hence, if I live, I shall think about you precisely as I do to-day, & be just as ready to resume happy talk.'

Gissing's reconciliation with his wife was to be short-lived. On 12 September 1897 he wrote once more that:

> Things have gone very badly. Our holiday in Yorkshire was a terrible failure. Useless to report the details. Enough that it all but drove me mad. In one of my sleepless nights, my good genius said to me: 'Make an end of it once and for all! Go to Italy for the winter, & there work in peace.' I clutched at the thought, & held to it in spite of everything. To Italy I am going, & I write this letter to say good-bye.

What must Clara Collet have felt on receiving this farewell letter? First she must have felt hope for her own future with Gissing, for even though a divorce was unlikely, she must have imagined the possibility of a close companionship unimpeded by Edith, whereby they would be free to see one another as and when they wished. Gissing, however, was going first to Italy. Why had he not involved her in the immediate aftermath of the separation? She could have been able to view this as his need to put distance between himself and his estranged wife since he would be afraid of her reaction. Miss Orme was again enlisted to help and she offered accommodation to Edith and Alfred at her own home.

Soon after his arrival in Siena, Gissing wrote asking Clara to be the joint executor of his will with his brother Algernon. He wished for them to be 'Guardians of my infant children to act as such Guardians jointly with my said wife during her life.' Gissing wished to avoid Edith becoming sole guardian as he did not feel that she was fit for such responsibility and with that in mind added that if,

> either of the Guardians hereby appointed decline to act I appoint my said sisters to act as Guardians. I direct and empower the majority of Guardians to decide all questions arising as to the Guardianship custody and education of such children ... And it is my desire if from any reason whatever my wife becomes sole Guardian of my infant child or children an application be made to the High Court for the appointment of a suitable Guardian or Guardians to act with her.[35]

Gissing knew he could trust Clara and regarded her as a 'very practical person'.[36] With a responsibility towards both of Gissing's children, she may now have expected more from their relationship.

Gissing's correspondence implied that he may have been planning to spend more time with her in the future. Nothing he wrote dispelled that impression. In a letter written in Italy on 22 November 1897 he ended, 'We shall have great talks, I trust, some day, about all I am seeing & learning. With very kind remembrances. Always sincerely yours, George Gissing.'

Clara was able to write freely to Gissing now that she knew Edith could no longer read her letters and the couple had separated. He noticed that she was indeed, 'gentler than of old', but that she remained, 'far, far above [him] – so far, indeed, that your sympathy for my troubles must for ever be imperfect'.[37] He commented that,

> We are now pretty old friends, & yet I find that I am only just beginning really to know you. I have always inclined to think of you as very self-reliant, rather scornful of weaker people, & especially impatient of anything like sentimental troubles. There is no harm in saying that your last two or three letters have pleased me just because they differed in some respects from those of a year or two ago.[38]

It was this moment that Clara chose to write insisting that, should Gissing find himself 'desperately ill' whilst abroad he should send for her as she wished to nurse him back to health or to support him at his death bed. This is very revealing of her true feelings for Gissing, for who other than a person in love would make such an extraordinary offer. He was a little taken aback and although he did not rebuff her for her suggestion he explained that should he find himself in such a predicament he would rather be with strangers as he had been during a recent serious fever suffered in Cotrone, Italy. He was, he said, pleased to be nursed only by people whom he had paid for this service. Despite turning down her latest gesture, he used this moment to remind Clara of her original offer of help to his sons in which he hoped she would:

> use [her] strong brain & pure woman's heart to guard my boys against the accursed temptations of early life! If necessary, tell them everything about me – everything. Don't let them wreck their hopes on that wretched mud-bank. Promise me this, in so many words, & to my last moment I will think of you with profoundest gratitude & trust.[39]

This prompted him to write to Walter to remind him to write to Clara Collet as she is, 'one of the best & kindest friends you will ever have, & as long she lives she will do whatever she can for you. You ought to write to her once every term, if possible.'[40]

Gissing continued to give Clara hope for a future together,

> Have no fear but that I shall come to see you in London. The old fetters – which had begun at length to poison the wounds they made – no longer hold me. To live in utter solitude, just because that poor silly creature wished me to do so, would be mere foolishness. I shall move about, in future, with perfect liberty.[41]

News from Miss Orme did not help to calm his fears. Edith's moods, tempers and paranoia had not been the sole result of the relationship with her husband. Eliza wrote early in 1898 to say that she was unable to continue to allow Edith to live with her. She described Edith's 'brutal insult and fury' and found her lodgings in north-west London in the house of a friend of hers who agreed to look after her. This prompted Gissing to sign an 'Agreement of Separation' in which he pledged to send her a pound a week on which to live.

No letter from Gissing to Clara has survived of those written between 10 February 1898 and 22 July 1899. She destroyed these letters yet we know the two continued to correspond during this period from references in Gissing's diary. She had been, 'writing to him endeavouring in every way to raise his self respect. He was passionately grateful.'[42] She continued to open up to Gissing, maybe even referring to his return to England and their future together. On 26 February she sent part of her diary to Gissing for his perusal. It was an 'old Diary of her girlhood'.[43] This was almost certainly the early part of her diary which she later made into a typescript possibly with a view to publication[44] and which dealt with her period as a school mistress. That Gissing describes this as of her 'girlhood' seems to preclude the possibility that she sent him the section dealing with her early relationship with him, although this is also missing, probably destroyed at the same time as the letters. The gesture of sending Gissing a section of her diary illustrates her more open relationship with him. Exposing herself in this way was not characteristic behaviour for someone who was generally a very private woman.

Gissing enjoyed his journey in Italy. He had, by February 1898, moved to Rome and had met up with Mr Price, a friend of Clara's, with whom he had dinner twice and struck up a good relationship. Wells and his wife arrived for a month's holiday in March. He took them sightseeing, trying unsuccessfully to develop Wells' interest in classical Rome.

On 24 March a new English guest arrived at his hotel. This was Mrs Williams, the youngest sister of Beatrice Webb, by now a widow with a little boy. Gissing was not immediately struck by Rosy Williams as someone with whom he would wish to form a relationship. 'Unfavourable impression; loud; bullies waiters; forces herself into our conversations', he wrote in his diary. However, he was not averse to befriending difficult women and the two of them soon began viewing the sights, lunching and partying together.

Beatrice Webb had found Rosy 'problematical'. She described her as, 'The least gifted, mentally and physically, of the whole sisterhood', and her deceased husband as, 'not up to the mark of the other brothers-in-law'.[45] Beatrice had taken over the task of acting as Rosy's guardian after the death of her mother and the illness of her father. Rosy suffered, like her sister, from a nervous complaint manifesting itself as what would now be termed anorexia nervosa. After the death of her husband her behaviour had become difficult again and Beatrice feared she may have been leading what she termed an 'immoral life'. In 1899 Rosy was unwell and Beatrice, and her elder sister Mary, even feared she might be pregnant. Beatrice visited her and was reassured that this was not the problem, although she 'should not be in the least surprised' if it was. She felt that, '[Rosy] is not likely to "keep straight" if she does not get married. I am not sure that <u>sanity and celibacy</u> are both within her capacity.'[46] In view of Gissing's apparent need for sexual contact with women and Rosy's desire to fulfil this function, it is possible that the two had a sexual liaison whilst in Rome together. Her diary alludes to such a relationship. As she was only there for a week, it is likely that they had a holiday romance with little expectation that it would continue into the future.

On his return to England in April, Gissing visited Rosy a couple of days after he arrived, staying for a meal, and from time to time over the following six months he walked or cycled over to Holmwood where she was residing. In a letter to Wells, written on 30 July, he described his feelings:

> I am not sorry that Mrs Williams has come to Holmwood. She is not at all likely to interfere with my working hours, & at other times I am very glad to be saved from melancholy madness. She is a good and sensible & honest woman; I like her better the more I know her, & respect her not a little. Her weaknesses are amiable – a great thing. And, as I begin to see, she has a quite unusual loyalty & right feeling in her friendships.[47]

Rosy had fond feelings for Gissing. 'I have seen Mr Gissing once or twice. He came to lunch and spent the day with us Sunday... I am so glad he likes to come here as I feel that if one could in any way make his life a little happier it would be a great thing.'[48] There is some suggestion in her diary that Gissing made the suggestion that the two of them should live together and that Wells was in favour of this plan. One can only guess at the scandal this would have caused within the respectable Potter family. If Beatrice's assessment of her sister's character at this time was accurate, and if an attachment had been formed between these two fragile personalities, Gissing would most likely have made his third disastrous liaison, although at least in this instance it would have been a financially more satisfactory one. The relationship with Rosy Williams came to nothing and Mrs Williams became Mrs Dobbs the following February.

Whether Clara was aware of this relationship, or was kept in ignorance, is not certain. However, of his next dalliance she certainly became aware and must have been devastated. On Wednesday 6 July 1898, Gissing met Gabrielle Marie Edith Fleury at Wells' house to plan a French translation of his book *New Grub Street*. The meeting went better than expected and, on 26 July, she made an unchaperoned visit to Gissing's house and by the following day he wrote a letter to this intelligent French woman,

I, sitting here in my quiet room, try to work; but it is not easy after such a day as yesterday. I see you too plainly; I hear your voice every moment. Perhaps it is well that I cannot see you again just now [she was already on her way back to France]. Your character is too sympathetic, & I should wish to have you near me always.[49]

Gissing was in love. He had fallen for Gabrielle immediately and his feelings were reciprocated.

During the period since his return to England, he continued his regular communications and meetings with Clara. He rushed around shortly after his return to visit her at her home at Berkeley Road, where he had previously been unable to visit prior to his split with Edith. It is possible to assume that as he visited Rosy Williams before Clara on his return to England this was evidence that Rosy had usurped her in his affections. It is equally likely that it was convenient to visit Rosy Williams first as it was a weekday when he visited her and Clara would have been at work. He may have wanted to clarify the status of his relationship with Clara in order to prevent any possible misinterpretation of feelings on his part. She had, after all, been more outwardly demonstrative in her letters and he may have wished to let her know that his feelings for her were unchanged and make it clear that he was not looking for romance in their relationship. As far as he was concerned it is quite likely that as he had not had romantic feelings for Clara, this visit was for him just a normal one and he may have been oblivious of any emotional attachment she may have had for him.

There is no evidence in Gissing's diary that his attitude towards her changed in any way during this period. However, on her side there is a clear indication that something untoward had occurred. The destruction of all her letters from him and her diary entries imply that she wished to eradicate all evidence of their correspondence and what she had written privately about him in her diary. It is not clear as to the exact time when Gissing informed his old friend of his feelings for Gabrielle. His relationship with Rosy Williams had been purely of a sexual nature but with Fleury the friendship soon grew deeper. Gissing wrote to tell Clara of his first meeting with Fleury, who was a French translator. Clara was away a great deal that year and later remembered to ask Gissing how the meeting had gone. He replied that Gabrielle was 'infinitely graceful & a Frenchwoman of the finest type'.[50] From that time on Clara noticed that there, 'was an indefinable change in his letters to me & in one he said he "was going through some strange things"'.[51] He must have sensed that she would be upset by the news of his new love affair and tried to shield her from the knowledge for as long as he was able. Even when he invited Gabrielle to his house in Dorking to stay with him in August when his mother was down from Yorkshire on a visit, he mentioned nothing, although Clara could tell that there was a, 'certain constraint which puzzled me'.[52] Gabrielle came over from France and stayed with Gissing in October 1898 and they made plans to live together in France as man and wife. Due to the difficulty of divorce and the scandal it would cause in Gabrielle's circle, it was decided that they would have a mock ceremony and simply pose as man and wife. The only French person to be let into the secret was to be Gabrielle's mother. Only days after definite plans had been laid, Gissing wrote to tell Clara the extent of his relationship – he wanted her to be party to his decision.

She wrote many years later to Gabrielle saying that, 'When he wrote to me about you I destroyed all those letters and told him to destroy mine.'[53] Because she and Gissing had become more open and she had been flattering him to boost his self-esteem, she was concerned that if Gabrielle came across the correspondence she might be upset. She told her that these letters were, 'not such as he would have written if he had ever dreamed of being loved by someone willing to give more than friendship'. As a married man, friendship would have been all that Clara could, at that time, have been able and willing to offer Gissing. She may have been hoping for this friendship to become close companionship and that in the event of Edith's death they would be able to marry.

Gissing had told Wells about his relationship with Gabrielle on 22 August 1898 and on 1 November 1898 he told Bertz. Clara, Wells, Bertz and Roberts were the only people informed about his secret plans. He told Gabrielle in a letter that,

> I called upon Miss Collet. She was admirable in her kindness, & spoke of you with great respect. Indeed, knowing all the fact of my life & my position, she looks upon you as my guardian angel. Her discretion is perfect; she will be at all times our best friend in England. Speaking of our difficulties, she asked 'Why not declare the truth, like George Eliot?' ... I replied that it seemed impossible, because of your numerous connections with the 'respectable' world.[54]

Whatever her feelings were about Gabrielle, she kept them to herself and only allowed Gissing to see how pleased she was that he would be happy once more. She admits in her letter to Gabrielle

8. Herbert George Wells by A.L. Coburn, 1905, at the time when Clara was engaged in a battle with him over the preface to Gissing's posthumously published novel. (By courtesy of the National Portrait Gallery, London.)

written in 1935 that initially she was shocked, but then she decided that Gissing's happiness was paramount and it would be better than 'leaving him to casual sexual relationships or a degrading permanent connexion, there is no doubt that you should be honoured not blamed by anyone who knows the facts'. She also realised that, 'if a man cannot lead a single life, to leave him alone if one loves him until someone might die is not only cruel but exactly the kind of attitude that leads to crime'. She recognised that Gissing was a man with sexual needs that she was unable to fulfil, as a sexual relationship outside of marriage was not one she would have considered and Gissing would have known this.

Not betraying any emotion to Gissing must have proved difficult, but she may have already lost any hope of a relationship with Gissing herself, and her love and respect for him by this time meant that she was glad that he had found someone with whom he could be happy; even if that precluded herself. One aspect of the affair Clara was not happy about was its secrecy. She would have been happier had they lived openly together. This opposition was probably the result of her upset that Gissing would apparently be lost to her forever, even as a friend, due to the distance which would now separate them.

There is one letter indicating her reaction to the news of Gissing's forthcoming liaison. On 6 February 1899, in a letter to Gabrielle Fleury, Gissing commented, 'Miss Collet will some day love you, I know she will.' Was her immediate reaction at the news of the forthcoming event negative? Gissing knew Clara well. He knew that if he loved Gabrielle then so would she. In this supposition time would prove him correct.

Even had Gissing wished for a relationship with Clara she had too much to lose to entertain such an idea. Gabrielle did not, she did not have a career which she would have to put an end to, and living in France would make it easier to cover the fact that Gissing was still married to Edith.

By July 1899, six months after she had been told of Gissing's plans for the future and a year after he had first begun his relationship with Fleury, Clara had come to terms with the situation – even to be pleased for Gissing and his happiness. No more letters were destroyed. Her diary, however, despite a couple of short entries written in October and December 1898 relating mainly to her attendance at various committees and work, does not recommence until 1904, after Gissing's death.

In the meantime, we can look at her life through Gissing's diary and after July 1899, through his letters to her which she began once more to retain. On 31 December 1898, Gissing made an entry commenting that he had read in the papers of the death of Clara's father, to which he immediately responded by sending a letter of condolence. In his next letter dated 2 January 1899, he consoled Clara by saying that at least the death had been painless.

Collet Dobson Collet had been 85 years old when he died. His work, the *History of the Taxes on Knowledge* was, at the time of his death, being serialised in the *Weekly Times*. His wife continued to be difficult, making impossible demands on her children without offering a word of gratitude.

During early 1899 Gissing's correspondence consisted mainly of letters to Gabrielle in which he discussed, amongst other things, their forthcoming 'marriage' and their continuing relationship with Clara. On 14 February he wrote to Gabrielle saying that Clara had written to him and quoted her as saying, 'I solemnly promise you that, whilst I live, Gabrielle shall never be without a friend & a home in England – Never!' On 5 March he told Gabrielle that:

> I have told of our coming marriage, truthfully, to the only two of my friends (besides Miss Collet) to whom it will be known: Eduard Bertz, at Potsdam, & Morley Roberts in London. I need not say that they both regard it as my salvation, for they both know that my life was drawing to an end under the old circumstances. Bertz is rather anxious lest you should feel a prejudice against him because of his nationality, but I have reassured him on that point...I doubt whether he & I will ever meet again for his health is very bad. As for Roberts he & his wife are occasionally on the Continent. If we met them, there would be not the slightest embarrassment... By the bye, I forgot to tell you that Miss Collet understands French perfectly. But do not write to her until after our marriage. Then, I am sure, it will give her great pleasure to hear from you.[55]

From these two letters, it is apparent that Gissing had entrusted the knowledge of his forthcoming 'wedding' to only three of his special and closest friends of whom Collet was one and she had completely come to terms with the situation by this time, to the point of offering her friendship to Gissing's future partner. Even H.G. Wells was being kept in the dark about the details of his plans at this time.

After he had told her of his plans, Gissing and Clara met only once more before he left England. This was during his convalescence from an illness which had worried her so much that she felt compelled to visit him. After his eventual recovery by 6 May 1899, he left the country and travelled to Rouen where the following day the 'marriage' ceremony was performed in the presence of Gabrielle's mother. After an extended honeymoon travelling around France and Switzerland, the couple returned in September to begin life together, with Gabrielle's mother in her Parisian apartment.

On 22 July 1899 Gissing wrote requesting Clara's forgiveness for not having written for some time. She began, once more, to keep his letters. Gissing sent Gabrielle's regards and commented that, 'If it should ever be possible for us to meet you in France or Switzerland, we should both be glad – more than glad. Indeed it is one of my hopes.' They did not have long to wait, for on 25 October she sent a note to say she was in Paris and would like to call on them. Gabrielle replied, in French, to the note expressing her delight at such an early opportunity to meet Gissing's good friend. She was invited to tea and Clara returned the compliment inviting them to the home of the friend she was staying with the following Monday. A friendship began immediately between the two women and whatever Clara may have felt for Gissing in the past, she did not allow her feelings to intrude upon her relationship with Gabrielle Fleury. From this time onwards she corresponded with both Gissing and Gabrielle.

Edith continued to cause trouble which inevitably found its way to Gissing in France. Within a period of only six months the friends of Miss Orme who had accepted Edith in their home were complaining that her behaviour had become unacceptable. Gissing was forced to pay for damage she had caused: 'She broke furniture, tore up the plants in the garden, & finally, after attacking the man & his wife with a stick, had to be removed by a policeman!'[56] To Morley Roberts after explaining the situation he added, 'In mild intervals she spread the rumour that she refused to live with me because I was a disciple of Oscar Wilde! A fact! She told that to many people, & some, doubtless believe it.'[57] Little more was heard of Edith until, in January 1902, Gissing received a further communication from Miss Orme informing him that Edith's violent behaviour now included regularly beating little Alfred. Edith was taken to the Brixton Workhouse infirmary, where after examination she was pronounced insane and removed to an asylum in Salisbury for which Gissing paid, using money saved from the allowance he sent her. The last we hear of Edith is from a letter she sent to Ellen Gissing in 1910. Ellen sent it on to Clara the same day asking for her advice as to what she should do. Clara could always be relied upon for sensible, helpful advice. Edith had asked if Ellen could do anything to enable her to be released from the asylum. Ellen told Clara that 'Of course, I do not send any reply to this letter', although she did ask her view as to whether it was, 'at all possible that she might recover her reason – & whether [she knew] at all what the Doctors think'.[58] Whether she was able to help Edith seems unlikely although she did keep the letter. Edith died from so-called 'organic brain disease', 15 years after being committed to the asylum.

On Edith's removal to Salisbury, Miss Orme helped to find suitable accommodation for the children. She ensured that Alfred was given hospital treatment, which he needed, for a urinary disease, after which she arranged for him to be sent to a farming family at Mabe near Falmouth in Cornwall. Gissing wished his children to be happier than he had been and he had an idealised romantic view of farming life. It proved to be a successful decision, however, and Alfred stayed happily with his foster parents for the next six years with regular reports being sent back to his family via Miss Orme. Gissing never saw either of his children again.

With Edith confined to the asylum, Gissing had the opportunity to return to England if he so wished – his enforced exile in France could end. An inability to settle in one place was something which was a feature of his life. Many of the moves made later on were as a result of the futile search for a climate suited to his lung condition, although his transit to France had been solely in order to live with Gabrielle, but wherever he lived he was discontented and wished to be elsewhere.

Even within France, Gissing was unable to settle in one place. In 1901, after 18 months in Paris (with an extended summer break in Nièvre), Gissing risked taking Gabrielle with him on a short trip to England as he was homesick. She was only able to stay for one week as she had to return to nurse her sick mother. Gissing planned to return about a week later. However, his health was in a poor state and his English doctor advised him to rest in a sanatorium to recover. One of the problems was that Gabrielle's mother, despite years of suffering from a weak heart, still ruled the household and half starved Gissing, who had a love of rich wholesome food. Mrs Fleury fed him on the same sized portions of cheap, plain food, as those on which she and her daughter lived. Consequently, by the time he returned to England in May 1901 he was seriously underweight. As his chest was still congested the rest in a sanatorium would allow him to regain his weight and strength. He admitted himself to Nayland Sanatorium in East Anglia. Gabrielle had been worried about her husband's cough and futilely tried to persuade him to reduce the number of hours he worked each day. She wrote of her concerns to her new friend, who encouraged Gissing to see a doctor. In practical matters, Clara was better able to influence him than his own partner could. The doctor advised a 'force' feeding regime, bed rest, injections of arsenic and told him off for neglecting himself for so long!

During her week in England, Gabrielle resided at the Wells' house in Sandgate on the coast. From the first, Gabrielle and Wells disliked each other. Gabrielle returned to France and it was after she had left that Gissing, suffering with an infection, visited the doctor and made plans for his stay at the sanatorium. Gabrielle was convinced that Wells was trying to force a separation between herself and her husband. She could not understand why he did not wait until his return to France to see a doctor and was upset by his extended stay in England.

Gissing realised that she was not happy with his decision although she was pleased that he was finally taking his health seriously. In order to placate her, he asked Clara to write to try and explain the situation. After receiving this letter Gabrielle, still not convinced that the decision Gissing had made to stay in Norfolk was a good one, wrote a long letter to Wells. In this she sounds neurotic and paranoid, voicing her concern that she believed Gissing might never return to her. She realised the strong ties Wakefield and his children had for him and that her own position was not legally secure. She knew also that Gissing had been unable to settle anywhere, or with anyone, for long. Her fear was that he had tired of France and life with her.

Gissing's main complaint had been lack of food, although why he was unable to simply ask for more seems strange. In her letter, Gabrielle dwelt at length on the fact that he had not informed his family of her existence and position. She believed that if he was unable to tell them the truth, this may have been because his intentions were not honourable. In the final paragraph she asks Wells to 'destroy this confidential letter'. Evidently he did not do so. Gabrielle never forgave Wells for what she saw as his attempt to persuade Gissing to return to live in England without her.

In a letter explaining the situation to Clara, her new friend and ally, Gabrielle shows her insecurity,

> I feel so unhappy, so miserable! I can't help feeling I sld [*sic*] not have been treated like that if I were a legal wife, all these grave decisions which disturb all our life, taken behind my back, imposed, forced upon me – not proposed – without a word of warning, my not being allowed to express an opinion, a wish about what concerns him.[59]

The problems Gabrielle was having with Wells caused Clara to also turn against him and their future relationship was to prove difficult.

In the event, two positive things came of Gissing's stay in the sanatorium. First, his health did improve with the intensive feeding and rest, and his weight increased. Gabrielle agreed to ensure that she would speak to 'Maman' about the future dining arrangements in order that he could have more say as to his menu and the quantity he was given. Secondly, realising Gabrielle's insecurities, Gissing decided to inform his mother and sisters about his relationship with her. Although they were not overly happy, they were reasonable. Ironically it was Wells who had persuaded Gissing that this would be the most honourable course of action and the one which would please his new partner best. His motive may have been to cause family disharmony rather than to help Gabrielle feel more secure. He may have expected that with the family informed Gissing could return to England. Both these actions would have exerted a further strain on his relationship with Gabrielle.

Wells proved unsuccessful in his attempt to cause a rift between Gissing and Gabrielle if this was what he intended. Nor did he persuade them to return to England, although Gissing may have ultimately planned to do so. The couple spent the remainder of the summer and early autumn 1901 in Autun in Burgundy. Gissing continued to gain weight on his immediate return to France, but in order to maintain the improvement he decided to spend the winter in Arcachon while Gabrielle returned to Paris to stay with her mother as they could not afford to pay for the three of them to go away. He wrote to tell Clara that the climate there was worse than that in Devon and since Edith's confinement at the asylum, he hoped that some time in the future he would be able to return to England and live there once more. His memory was poor – while in Exeter he could not wait to return to London and nor had he enjoyed his stay in Budleigh Salterton. Possibly he believed that now he was with a partner whose company he enjoyed he would find the experience of the country different.

On hearing from Miss Orme the latest news concerning Edith, it was to Clara Collet that Gissing wrote at length giving her all the details about Edith's constraint. He did not write to inform Gabrielle for a further four days and then gave only the scantiest of information,

> When we go to England, we shall no longer be subject to uneasiness. The poor creature (who I have no doubt has long been unsound of

mind) must pass altogether out of our thoughts, as one dead. I cannot distress myself about her fate, for it is infinitely better that she should be cared for in an asylum than live as hitherto, brutally & cruelly. So we speak no more of the matter.[60]

During the year 1902, when Clara published her book, *Educated Working Women*, she sent a copy to Gissing who wrote by return saying that he found the series of essays of interest and listed a number of points about sections which particularly impressed him. He agreed with her views on most of what she wrote in the book which aimed at putting a case for better education for women, higher wages in order that they could be independent if they wished and an extension of areas in which it was acceptable for them to work. She also voiced the opinion that women develop intellectually later than men. Gissing agreed with her upon this point. This was Clara at her most pragmatic. Had she written stridently and antagonistically the book would have been less well received by men, even Gissing.

There was one issue over which he did not agree with her and that was the Boer War. Gissing was an ardent pacifist. When she wrote a letter stating how pleased she was when the town of Mafeking, which had been defended for 31 weeks by the British, had finally defeated the Boers, with the assistance of a relief column, he did not share her pleasure. He had a strong hatred of patriotism. 'As for his feelings about the Empire and all that it implies, they are best put into a few words he wrote to me about my novel "In the Sun"', wrote Morley Roberts in his fictional biography of Gissing,[61] 'Yes this is good, but you know that I loathe the Empire, and that India and Africa are an abomination to me.' Roberts went on to note that Gissing had been considering sending Walter abroad to avoid his ever having to face military service, 'I would greatly rather never see him again than foresee his marching in ranks; butchering or being butchered.'[62] The irony of this prediction was that in 1916 Walter was to be butchered in the Battle of the Somme.

He had a dislike for the recent 'jingoism' and all that it stood for. Kipling was a staunch supporter of this nationalistic fervour and Gissing wrote,

> I have always dreaded Kipling & Co., but I hardly thought their sowing would so soon have come to harvest. I am sick at heart when I read of these things, & when I picture to myself what we English should think & say of any other nation which so disgraced itself. I entreat you, dear Miss Collet, to reflect on this sign of the times, & not to allow yourself to be carried away by a natural patriotism.[63]

He implored her not to write to him about the Boer War again. His continued horror of all things military surfaced later in the book that he wrote whilst living in France and which was published in 1903. He said with incredible premonition, 'The revival...of monarchic power based on militarism, makes the prospect dubious enough. There has but to arise some Lord of Slaughter, and the nations will be tearing at each other's throats.'[64] When the Great War was in progress Clara was hard at work planning the aftermath on the 'Reconstruction' committee, but we have little indication as to her view on the war itself. She must have been pleased in 1918 when women over the age of 30 were finally granted suffrage. The war effort had also led to an increase in areas of work open to women resulting in a move away from the poorly paid, demeaning, domestic work in which so many of them had been employed. By the time of the Second World War Clara was elderly and living by the coast. She did not make her views on this war known in any of her work. Gissing's disagreement with her over Mafeking is, therefore, the only evidence we have for her attitude towards war and patriotism. Probably, like most of the population at the turn of the century, she did support nationalism. With Gissing as fervently anti-war and Empire as he was, it is difficult to ascertain the degree of her nationalistic feelings.

In the last years of his life, despite his living abroad, Clara still managed to provide the practical advice and assistance she had always done. It was to her that Gissing wrote asking for any research he required to be done:

> I am writing now for a special purpose; I think you can answer two inquiries which I have promised to make for my friends here. First: does there exist in England an Anti-Tobacco League? If so, I should like to know the address at London or elsewhere. Secondly: what do you think would be the best English weekly paper for a French girl of 17 to take, who wants to use it for practice in English? I had thought of the Girl's Own Paper, but I don't know whether it still exists. If it does, would you kindly let me know the address. But perhaps you can suggest something better.[65]

He also continued to involve her in his family problems. When his sisters complained of Walter's continuing difficult behaviour, they suggested that he be sent to a boarding school, and it was to Clara that he turned for advice. They had suggested a school at Bakewell but the fees were 20 guineas a term, an expense which he would have found difficult to meet. In his letter to her he said:

I write simply to ask what you think about the situation? I suppose there can be no doubt that a boarding school will be less expensive than an arrangement for him to live somewhere & attend a day-school, & of course the discipline in his case will be better. I am writing to ask whether any arrangement can be made about the holidays; but I fear it is asking too much to ask my sisters to burden themselves with the care of Walter during their times of rest...Now, if I could find some school which was at once cheap & good. Have you anything of the sort in mind?...If you are of the opinion that 20gs [guineas] a term is the least I can expect to pay, well, I must manage to pay it – that is clear. Of course for a twelvemonth, I could easily find the money, & then I could review the situation again. But pray give me your advice.[66]

Within five days she had replied having investigated the alternatives and come up with the suggestion of a school that she knew, named Rawlings School in Quorn, Leicestershire. She may have known it from her time as a school mistress or have known the headmaster, Edward Walker Hensman, who had gained his MA at University College, London. Gissing was pleased with the suggestion and intended to send Walter there at the end of the school year. In the event his sisters did not wait for his decision and sent Walter to a school in Ilkley, Yorkshire which was cheaper than their original suggestion. He stayed there for just over a year when he was once more moved, to Holt Grammar School in Norfolk, where he was to remain until he left school in 1908.

During what were to be the last 18 months of his life, Gissing lived in the south-west of France, firstly in Ciboure near St Jean-de-Luz and then at Ispoure, near St Jean-Pied-de-Port. He was having increasing bouts of ill-health. The last diary entry he made was in November 1902. This did not stop his correspondence with Clara, although he wrote less regularly than before. He and Gabrielle were concerned by some serious problem troubling Clara during much of 1902 and the earlier part of 1903,

How very sorry I am to hear from George that you are having great worries of some kind! I do hope you will soon overcome them & that they will not affect you very seriously. I myself know so well what worries of nearly every kind mean, that I sympathise with you deeply & heartily...

wrote Gabrielle on 4 March 1902. It was most likely something relating to her family; possibly her mother who had always been difficult. What is known is that she once more moved house at this time from

Berkeley Road with her sister Edith, to 90, Woodside, Wimbledon. Could this move have had any connection with her troubles? It is just possible that there was a family rift but there is no evidence of any severing of relations between her and her sisters or brothers and once her diary recommenced in 1904 we can see that she continued visiting the household at 7, Coleridge Road as often as before.

Despite ill-health, Gissing managed to work most days and completed his highly acclaimed semi-autobiographical work, *The Private Papers of Henry Ryecroft* in 1902. He sent the usual inscribed copy to Clara. Wells, Gissing's relations and Miss Orme all had to make do with a copy sent from the publishers. In his last known letter to Clara (12 June 1903), he commented on the success of *Henry Ryecroft*; was disparaging about Walter who, was not doing very well at Holt Grammar School, and pleased with Alfred who, he said, had settled well into his new home in Cornwall and had made many friends. Gissing rather hoped Alfred would become a 'plain, healthy rustic', which he felt would be better for him than the life he himself had led. Finally he informed Clara that he had just heard that their mutual friend Dr Zakrzewska had passed away, although he said that he found it hard to believe that he had ever lived in Boston as it seemed such a distant memory.

Gissing's last few months were spent in virtual isolation in the tiny village of Ispoure, 30 miles inland, where he had been advised to move for health reasons. Many British residents lived in St Jean-de-Luz on the coast which, although he protested that social events disturbed his work, at least provided him with a link with home. He was, as usual, discontented with his place of abode and blamed it for all his ills. He was kept indoors for several months early in the year as a result of an attack of sciatica but by the summer was feeling better than he had for some time. His latest novel *Will Warburton* had just been finished and he was tackling his first historical novel over which he had spent a great deal of time in research. Living away from a town or friends, with Gabrielle's ailing bed-bound mother, proved very depressing for Gissing.

Despite the respite in mid-summer which lasted through to autumn, enabling him to take a trip to Pamplona in Spain, when winter came Gissing's spirits were as usual at their lowest ebb and he approached the bad weather pessimistically. 'I wish the summer & not the winter, were before me', he wrote ominously in a note to his agent in November 1903, enclosed with the first 22 chapters of his historical novel, *Veranilda*.

On 27 December 1903, Clara received a letter from Gabrielle informing her that Gissing was seriously ill:

G. is dying des suites [as a result] of a broncho-pneumonia from which he suffers since nearly 3 weeks. I am desperate beyond words & wish so deeply you were here, with me! Mr Wells came over, but only for 2 days; he has gone and the condition of my dear patient has become much graver nearly immediately after his departure. The end is awaited every moment. And what dreadful sufferings! It is terrible, to [sic] terrible![67]

This communication was followed the next day by another saying merely, 'Died yesterday 1 [in the] afternoon.'[68]

Clara responded in the only way she knew; by offering practical help, although she must have been as badly affected by his death as was Gabrielle. If Gabrielle wished Clara to be with her, then that is precisely where she would be. She telegraphed Gabrielle to ask if she wished to come to England or if she would prefer her friend to go to France, and then wrote to Wells enquiring as to the best method of travelling to Ispoure as he had only just returned. Despite his untimely death, Clara Collet was to spend many years yet involved with George Gissing, his family and his affairs.

NOTES

1. Coustillas (ed.), *Gissing's Diary*, 18 July 1893.
2. Ibid., 16 September 1893.
3. Mattheisen *et al.* (eds), *Letters of George Gissing*, 17 September 1893 to Collet.
4. Ibid., 13 September 1893 to Ellen Gissing.
5. Ibid., 2 May 1894 to Collet.
6. Ibid., 16 March 1894 to Collet.
7. Ibid., 17 June 1894 to Collet.
8. Ibid., 11 February 1894 to Collet.
9. Letter from Clara Collet to Gabrielle Fleury, 6 January 1935 (copy in the possession of Professor Coustillas).
10. Coustillas (ed.), *Gissing's Diary*, 15 February 1896.
11. Ibid., 2 March 1896.
12. Mattheisen *et al.* (eds), *Letters of George Gissing*, 22 March 1896.
13. Ibid., 21 April 1895.
14. Ibid., 26 October 1893.
15. Ibid., 11 November 1893.
16. Ibid., 17 June 1894 to Collet.
17. Coustillas (ed.), *Gissing's Diary*, 23 April 1896.
18. Mattheisen *et al.* (eds), *Letters of George Gissing*, 23 April 1896 to Collet.
19. Ibid.
20. Ibid., 3 July 1896 to Collet.
21. MSS diary, 11 November 1883.

22. Mattheisen *et al.* (eds), *Letters of George Gissing*, 27 September 1896 to Collet.
23. Ibid., 6 December 1896 to Collet.
24. This was the Omar Khayyam Club at which many eminent authors met and discussed literary matters and of which Gissing had been a member for some time.
25. The book was set in that area and the heroine's name was Amy.
26. Mattheisen *et al.* (eds), *Letters of George Gissing*, 29 November 1896 to Collet.
27. Ibid., 13 February 1897 to Collet.
28. Ibid., 17 February 1897 to Collet.
29. Letter from Collet to Gabrielle Fleury, 6 January 1935.
30. Ibid.
31. Mattheisen *et al.* (eds), *Letters of George Gissing*, 17 February 1897 to Collet.
32. Ibid.
33. Ibid., 27 February 1897 to Collet.
34. Ibid., 11 May 1897 to Collet.
35. Ibid., 31 October 1897 to Collet.
36. Ibid., October 1897 to Algernon Gissing.
37. Ibid., 3 January 1898 to Collet.
38. Ibid.
39. Ibid.
40. Ibid., 8 May 1898 to Walter Gissing.
41. Ibid., 3 January 1898 to Collet.
42. Letter from Clara Collet to Gabrielle Fleury, 6 January 1935.
43. Typed diary, 26 February 1898.
44. It is interesting to note that Charles Trevelyan had access to this typed diary when compiling Collet's obituary. It is possible that Collet may have given access to this portion of her diary to people before her death. Trevelyan does not mention the much longer hand-written diary.
45. MacKenzie and MacKenzie (eds), *Diary of Beatrice Webb*, p. 241.
46. Carole Seymour-Jones, *Beatrice Webb: Woman of Conflict* (London: Allison & Busby, 1992), p. 255.
47. Mattheisen *et al.* (eds), *Letters of George Gissing*, 30 July 1898, to H.G. Wells, Vol. 7, p. 126, note 3.
48. Ibid.
49. Ibid., 27 July 1898 to Gabrielle Fleury.
50. Letter from Clara Collet to Gabrielle Fleury, 6 January 1935.
51. Ibid.
52. Ibid.
53. Ibid.
54. Mattheisen *et al.* (eds), *Letters of George Gissing*, 29 January 1899 to Gabrielle Fleury.
55. Ibid., 5 March 1899 to Gabrielle Fleury.
56. Ibid., 6 February 1899 to Gabrielle Fleury.
57. Ibid., 6 February 1899 to Morley Roberts.
58. Warwick University Modern Records Centre, MSS 29/3/8/1, letter from Ellen Gissing to Clara Collet, 8 August 1910.
59. Mattheisen *et al.* (eds), *Letters of George Gissing*, Gabrielle Fleury to Clara Collet, 26 June 1901.
60. Ibid., 4 February 1902 to Gabrielle Fleury.
61. Roberts, *Henry Maitland*, p. 139.
62. Ibid.

63. Mattheisen *et al.* (eds), *Letters of George Gissing*, 23 May 1900 to Collet.
64. Gissing, *Henry Ryecroft*, p. 56.
65. Mattheisen *et al.* (eds), *Letters of George Gissing*, 2 November 1900 to Collet.
66. Ibid., 7 April 1901 to Collet.
67. Ibid., 27 December 1903, Gabrielle Fleury to Collet, p. 173.
68. Ibid., Gabrielle Fleury to Clara Collet, 29 December 1903.

4

Aftermath

One of the most unfortunate aspects of the circumstances in which Gissing died was the involvement of H.G. Wells. On realising that her husband was dying, Gabrielle had telegraphed Wells to come to his friend's deathbed. He sent a telegram to Morley Roberts saying that he was unable to go as he was unwell and asked if Roberts might go instead. Without waiting for Roberts' response, Wells changed his mind and later the same day sent a telegram informing Gabrielle that he was on his way. He arrived two days later and took control, nursing his friend and sending Gabrielle off to bed. In her own words written later she said:

> H.G. Wells urges me to take a couple of hours' rest while he keeps by George's side. I give him endless injunctions and explanations concerning what must be done while I am out of the room, and very reluctantly, yet listening to reason, as I have not had one moment's rest for 17 nights and as many days, – I retire to lie down. But uneasiness prevents me from closing my eyes, and an hour later, unable to bear it any longer, I return to my patient's room. – Alas! the moment I open the door I stand horror-stricken at the sight of the empty bottles, basins, glasses, etc., containing the fluids prescribed to feed the patient in doses of a spoonful every 30 minutes. Mr. Wells triumphantly announces that he has made him swallow <u>all that</u> during the fateful hour: tea, coffee, highly concentrated beef tea, champagne, milk, somatose etc!! I reply, 'You have killed him, Mr. Wells.' He rubs his hands gleefully protesting that the patient has refused nothing and that 'substantial nourishment in plenty' is all that is needed to cure him. Thereupon he returns to his hotel. In the night temperature rises suddenly to over 104 degrees and a fearful agitation begins, accompanied by violent delirium. G. throws himself out of bed...Next morning (Sunday 27th) the doctor is amazed at the change in the patient's condition, and on hearing what has happened, he exclaims, 'He has poisoned him!'[1]

Wells, with an arrogance of his own, was convinced that the doctor's prescription was incorrect and that he knew better. He had always believed that Gissing's problems came from underfeeding. Wells did not realise that the acute condition from which Gissing was now suffering was not comparable to his previous illness. Nevertheless, Wells decided to administer his own cure. The results were disastrous, although he probably only hastened the inevitable.

Wells left to return to England. Gissing died the following day, Monday 28 December 1903. Morley Roberts arrived on Wednesday and Clara a few days later. Gabrielle was devastated and convinced that Wells, whom she had never liked, had been responsible. Clara also became suspicious of Wells' behaviour and the two women's relationship with Gissing's erstwhile friend became worse than ever. Most of 1904 was to be spent feuding with him.

With Gissing dead, Clara launched herself into her duty as one of the two executors of his will. Relations with the other executor, Algernon Gissing, were also to prove difficult. He would make decisions without consulting Clara and she often made decisions without consulting him.

The problems were caused by the publication of Gissing's unfinished historical novel, *Veranilda*, which was set in ancient Rome. It was agreed that the book would be published despite its not being completed, as posthumous books often proved successful. Algernon decided that the book should be produced with a preface written by someone who knew and admired the author's work and chose Wells. Wells' fame would undoubtedly enhance the chance of success, and he agreed to the task. Wells was sent the manuscript and just four days later he had not only read the work but written the preface. It was to prove highly controversial.

Wells began the preface with a brief biography of Gissing in which he mentioned his schooldays in Manchester, saying, 'He truncated his career at Owens, with his degree incomplete...and from that time his is a broken and abnormal career',[2] – thus implying something improper had occurred, which of course it had. He went on to say that after his trip to the United States:

> He returned to London. By this time he had discovered what was not so much an artistic impulse as an ill-advised ambition to write a series of novels...More or less deliberately he set himself to the scheme of an English *Comédie Humaine*, and in the very titles of such novels as *The Unclassed*, *The Emancipated*, and *The Whirlpool*, lurks the faint aroma of his exemplar...His knowledge of the world was strangely limited, was scarcely existent.

He continued in this same derogatory vein, implying that Gissing's novels on the working classes were a mistake:

He wrote for the most part about people he disliked or despised, and about people he did not understand; about social conditions that seemed to him perverse and stupid, and about ways of life into which he had never entered.

Ironically, considering the arguments Wells had with Gissing about what Wells saw as dead civilisations with little to offer the modern reader, after he had destroyed the worth of the vast majority of Gissing's work, Wells came out in support of *Veranilda*, his work on ancient Rome.

It needs some practice in the art of imaginative writing to gauge quite how skilfully this magnificent conception has been wrought, to detect the subtle insistence, touch by touch, that keeps its mellow and melancholy atmosphere true. The whole learning that was possible of this period lies behind this book...Gissing carries his learning as a trained athlete carries his limbs, as it were unwittingly.

Algernon was the first person to read the preface. As a failed impecunious writer he was in awe of Wells' status. His initial reaction was muted, although he did voice concerns as to Wells' description of Gissing's schooling implying, as it did, some kind of impropriety. Why should a first-class scholar such as Gissing have left school to travel to the United States if it were not on account of a scandal? His sister Ellen was more scathing in her condemnation saying that the effect of the preface, 'with the exception of the last four pages, would be to stir in the mind anything but a pleasing, and anything but a true picture of my brother'.[3]

Morley Roberts did not become involved in the condemnation of the preface. In his book *The Private Life of Henry Maitland*, Roberts wrote that, 'The executors did not approve [of the preface], again for reasons which I do not appreciate, for on the whole it was an admirable piece of work.'[4] Roberts believed that the objection was entirely due to the reference to Owens College and the scandal this might cause for the family if the reasons for his having to leave were made public. Roberts, however, had reservations about some of Gissing's work. Gissing, he said, 'could, and did write great fiction, I know his best work in other circumstances would not have been fiction'.[5] And again, 'It was no doubt very strange that he should have spoken to me about my having little faculty for writing fiction when I had so often come to the same silent conclusion about himself.'[6]

Wells was unable to see that there was anything wrong with his preface. Apart from the danger in mentioning Gissing's schooling, the remainder of the article can be seen as an attempt by Wells to ensure that this book would be taken seriously. Wells' remit was to write a preface to sell *Veranilda*, a book wholly different from any Gissing had written previously. In condemning Gissing's previous work, Wells may have been intending to highlight the brilliance of this, his last book, in order to push the sales. He could not see that by showing how good *Veranilda* was, to the detriment of all his previous work, Wells was implying that Gissing's past novels were of less importance. Wells became defensive, pointing out that the accusations against him were incorrect and that his preface in no way showed Gissing's work in a derogatory manner. However, as Roberts wrote to Clara, 'Wells is a very good chap but he has arrived at a frame of mind when he finds it rather hard to admit that he can be wrong.'[7]

Instead of demanding alterations to the preface, Algernon allowed the work to be sent to the printers. No copy had at this point been sent to Clara for her opinion, and with the relationship prevailing between Wells and Gabrielle, she had also not been sent a copy, although, as Gissing's common-law wife she would have had the most to lose from any scandal involving either Gissing's life or his work. She did not wish for her relationship with the author to be made public.

Clara demanded to see a copy. She was not happy with what she saw and was the only one of Gissing's friends or relations to demand alterations to the preface which she saw as a slur on his work and character. Frederic Harrison, a friend of Gissing's from the time when he was commencing his writing career, suggested that he would write a replacement preface. Constable, the publishers, were upset that the preface would not be written by Wells, who as a well-known writer would have helped sell more copies than would Harrison despite his reputation as a Positivist. The publisher was concerned that the book would no longer be viable and threatened not to publish at all if the original preface were not used. Clara placed the matter in the hands of her solicitor, whom she authorised to halve the advance on *Veranilda* from £300 to £150 and offered to pay the price of resetting the new preface in order that the publisher would not be out of pocket. She wrote to Algernon to inform him of her decision. He initially agreed to the proposal, but she had an objection to one of the paragraphs which she wanted deleted. He became angry and

> told me to return the preface to him at once; questions of this kind
> were for the family to settle and if they did not mind it was not for

me to raise any objection. As I happened to have a fairly free day and thinking his objection was solely to offending the Harrisons, I went to Hawkhurst saw Mrs Harrison & got her to ask Mr Harrison to strike out the paragraph.[8]

She wrote to Algernon to inform him and as she was concerned that the Gissing family might not know the full facts of George's early life, she 'definitely stated what these facts were as I felt it necessary he should know them'. She received back 'a furious note – written I believe before he had received my letter – that he had heard of my extraordinary behaviour & had written to Mr Townsend [the solicitor] to try to bring me to reason. Mr Townsend regretted that he could not fall in with AG's views.' At this time, Clara realised that it might be better if she humbled herself to Algernon:

I felt that whatever AG's faults might be, it was my business to make the best of him & not the worst. So although I did not really think I had done anything but what I ought to have done in the interests of the children, I felt sincerely enough to confess myself at fault.

She went on to say that her attitude to Algernon had, 'been more of an antagonist than of a friendly co-worker'. She wrote him a 'general enumeration of my natural tendencies to tactlessness & overbearingness & said I would agree to anything he wanted'.[9] A resolution was then reached although Algernon did not make any mention of either of her letters and conducted his business via the solicitor. Eventually Algernon also backed down and agreed terms directly with Clara.

She had prevented Wells' preface from being published in *Veranilda*, but there was, of course, nothing Gissing's family or friends could do to stop him from publishing it privately. This is exactly what he did, and 'George Gissing: An Impression' was published in the *Monthly Review* in August 1904. It resulted in a flood of correspondence in the literary journals, only a few of which agreed with the sentiments of the article.

Concurrent with the wranglings over the preface, Clara was involved in other matters concerning Gissing's estate. She spent time in Paris in June with Gabrielle where the two of them sorted out his belongings which were still stored in a small apartment at rue de Billancourt, Boulogne, near Paris. Clara arranged for Gissing's book collection to be sent back to England where Ellen Gissing organised a valuation of the contents. They were shocked at how little the total collection was worth. If the books had been sold individually they would have been worth more but the whole collection was valued at only £5. Clara offered to buy them with the proviso that Walter and Alfred could, if they wished, buy them back later at the same price. This act of kindness did not prove necessary as Gissing's mother agreed to purchase them herself. The rest of his possessions, including his writing table, chairs and bookcases were sold to Gabrielle.

Gabrielle returned to England with Clara, staying with her for a week and then went on for a week to Wakefield where she cemented the relationship with Gissing's sisters and met Walter for the first time. On her return to London she stayed for another two weeks with Clara in her new apartment at 4, Vernon Chambers. Clara wrote in her diary, when she recommenced writing it (or stopped destroying sections she had written) after the death of Gissing, that she had moved to Vernon Chambers, 'after many vicissitudes since I last wrote any kind of diary',[10] she did not elaborate further so this period remains a mystery.

Aside from seeing Gabrielle regularly during this first year after Gissing's death, and spending a great deal of time arguing over the preface to *Veranilda*, Clara also became involved in organising the reprinting of much of his work, and dealing with his publishers and agents. Unsurprisingly, she argued once again with Algernon. She did not always notify him of her decisions until after she had made them because she was in London and more easily able to make physical contact with the relevant people. Algernon felt that she was not consulting him enough, while he irritated her with his indecision. He was an ineffectual man whom even his sisters felt could not be trusted to do things the right way.

Over the next 30-odd years Clara Collet and Gabrielle Fleury continued in regular correspondence and visited each other on many occasions. At some time before 1910, Clara wrote that their:

> friendship is the one bright spot in all this. In bringing me near to you George has filled a blank in my life, which I have felt most keenly during these last few years...It has been too a great happiness to me to know that in those last years George found his ideal realised in you – that for a brief period at least he was allowed to be himself living with the woman he would have chosen out of the whole world above all others.[11]

If she still harboured feelings of love for Gissing, it was of the purest kind. To have been able to see him in a relationship with a woman whom he loved and who loved him had become more important to her than her own happiness. Any feelings of jealousy towards Gabrielle had long since disappeared.

Wells, paradoxically, appeared to hold an irrational grudge against Gabrielle which may not be wholly explained by her Frenchness, which made him suspicious, or her neurotic personality, which he did not understand. Wells' behaviour may have been due to the jealousy that one would more have expected from Clara. Gabrielle Fleury had usurped his affections and taken Gissing away to France. Clara wrote a letter to Wells to try to explain her reasons for vetoing the preface. She never received a reply.

Nothing more is heard of Wells in Clara's diary until 14 November 1908 when, while she was sitting in the reception room at the Writers' Club, Violet Hunt, a woman she vaguely knew, came in with an entourage of people with whom she was lunching. Clara heard their voices in the dining room and went in. She recognised several of the party including Wells. She felt sure that Wells would rather not acknowledge her as he might be embarrassed considering their past animosity, so she acted as though she had not recognised him. However, one of the women leant forward and said to her, 'Excuse me, it is Mrs Hawkins is it not?' Clara, feeling that it might not be politic to explain who she was, simply denied that she was Mrs Hawkins. The woman replied, 'Oh, I beg your pardon, Mr Wells felt so sure.'[12]

On 17 December 1904, Clara left for France to visit Gabrielle in order to be with her for the first anniversary of Gissing's death. She arrived at St Jean-de-Luz and found her friend much improved since the summer. She stayed with Gabrielle and her mother at the Pension Larréa in Ciboure. The two younger women discussed Gissing a good deal during her visit. Clara felt it might be prudent to inform Gabrielle about the scandal to which Gissing's thefts at Owens College had given rise, in case it should at any time be made public. Gissing had confided more to his friend about his past than he had to Gabrielle. The shame remained until his dying day.

In May 1905 Gabrielle visited Clara in London and was taken sightseeing by her to Lincoln's Inn, Temple, Regent's Park and the following week to Stratford-upon-Avon in the Midlands where they met up with Arthur Bullen, one of Gissing's publishers. They discussed Gissing's work and whether Bullen would sell his rights to various books. He contacted Clara on her return to offer her Gissing's rights and stock for £200 and £4 with the royalties due. She accepted the offer and the transfer was completed a couple of days later. Only after the transaction was complete did she write to let Algernon know what she had done. Again she had acted before conferring with her co-executor; and he was not pleased. According to her diary he used words such as, 'simply furious', 'illegal', 'gross impertinence', and he told her to stop all the proceedings immediately. He contacted Bullen who assured him that all was legal and that she could act without his permission in this case. Algernon accepted the situation but not without complaining that Clara had excluded him from the decision which he found to be 'offensive'. She realised that she had been less than tactful, instantly backed down and apologised, explaining that her motivation had been merely to release Gissing's books, enabling them to be reprinted for others to read. Unwin's were keen to take over the business of reprinting the books, and this time she ensured that Algernon was involved in the transaction, although she felt that,

> It is AG's dislike of me that makes him move in this matter; his wounded vanity is too great for him to be able to see that he is not limiting my authority or increasing his own, but is limiting Gabrielle's ownership.[13]

In September, Algernon wrote, seemingly having forgotten their recent difficulties, to ask Clara to lend him £50. 'Too bad to worry me with his Grub Street difficulties.' She sent him £20. 'He said it would be repaid by Christmas but, of course, he knows perfectly well that he will never repay a farthing.'[14] She knew of Algernon's poor reputation for repaying his debts through Gissing whom he often asked for 'loans'.

Whilst in England, Gabrielle again visited Wakefield, where, according to Clara, the Gissing family, 'With their usual peculiar sense of humour... ran me down to her as they always do.'[15]

On Gabrielle's return, they both spent the day in Richmond, where they lunched, walked through the park to Kingston from where they took the bus and train to Hampton Court and returned home by the electric train to Shepherds Bush and finally by tube.

By September 1905 Clara had arranged for a new publication of *The Odd Women*. This was not without its irony as she had initially disliked the book so intensely that she had almost changed her mind about wishing to meet its author. It is strange that she should have had an aversion to this of all Gissing's books as it deals with the 'woman question' upon which much of her own work was based.

It is likely that Clara's problem with *The Odd Women* stemmed from her dislike of the main character Rhoda Nunn, whose views were too extreme for her pragmatic beliefs. Rhoda falls in love but abstains from marrying as that would be against her principles. She exhibits the militant behaviour of which Clara so vehemently disapproved. Her ideas were for women to join with men rather than work against them. She liked men. Rhoda did not. Whilst Clara recognised the need for change, as in all things, she advocated change by evolution, not revolution. In her view changing things too quickly would be counterproductive. Her later acceptance of *The Odd Women* may have been due to her closer study of the other characters in the story with whom she would have had more sympathy, such as Mary Barfoot whose brand of feminism was toned down and more like her own. She may also have gained a closer understanding of Gissing's aims in the book. He aimed to make the reader think about the dilemma which middle-class women without means faced as they were unable to make a living. In his view there were several alternatives, all of which he thought were unsatisfactory, other than marriage, the most socially acceptable and conventional solution. This was not always possible due to the excess of women in the population. One of his characters, Monica, does marry, despite not loving the man, in order to find the financial security that she lacked. The marriage is a disaster as her husband, a stereotypical Victorian man, tries to control her absolutely. Monica's older spinster sisters, Alice and Virginia, struggle to maintain an aura of respectability despite having only a very small inheritance which only allows them to live on the breadline. They supplement this by periodic teaching work. Virginia develops a drink dependency as a way of coping but they are both unhappy. The only other choice, as Gissing saw it, was for women to have improved educational opportunities such as Rhoda Nunn and Mary Barfoot were providing for their students, enabling them to compete in arenas not previously open to women. This would give them economic independence which both Gissing and Clara agreed was the answer to improving the situation for 'odd women'. But even this option was not without its problems. Women might, like Rhoda, lose their femininity and in their struggle to become independent become too much like men. The book comes to no conclusions but suggests that all contemporary options open to single women were unsatisfactory and that alternatives needed to be found. Had Gissing seen Clara as another Rhoda Nunn? She could be arrogant, and in Gissing's eyes she too may have lost some of her femininity.

Gabrielle was back in England the following spring, 1906. There was some discussion about Clara taking a flat at St Jean-de-Luz.

Whether this was for a holiday or whether she was thinking of moving there permanently is not clear. She later wrote, announcing her decision not to go. This pleased Madame Fleury who was against the idea, possibly not wanting another intruder distracting Gabrielle from her nursing duties as Gissing had done previously.

Gabrielle must have found Clara's company therapeutic for during this visit two years after Gissing's death, she began to play the piano for the first time since that tragedy. Another of Clara's French friends, Madeleine Rolland, came to stay at the same time as Gabrielle. She was the sister of the well-known French musicologist and author Romain Rolland, and it was through him that Clara made the acquaintance of Madeleine. The three women travelled together on the top of an omnibus to the City and had lunch in a restaurant. Madeleine was in London as one of the delegates to the 'International Guild' which incorporated London University, the University of Paris and the Collège de France. As part of her official duties she was received by King Edward VII and Queen Alexandra, at Windsor Castle.

The following year, Gabrielle returned to England to stay with Clara, but in 1909 the pattern was broken for Gabrielle was 'dangerously' ill with typhoid fever during May and unable to travel anywhere. Her recovery was swift and by August she met up with Clara in Switzerland while she was convalescing.

The last mention of Gabrielle in Clara's diary is in December 1912 in an argument on Morley Roberts' pseudo-biography of Gissing's life. Roberts had first mentioned the idea of a biography to Clara shortly after Gissing's death, but she had not felt it wise to inform Gabrielle at that time. She had been encouraging, although anxious that Roberts should protect Gabrielle and Gissing's family from any bad publicity. Unlike Wells, Roberts had fond feelings for Gabrielle, believing that she had made Gissing's last years happy. Gabrielle and Clara had become good friends with Roberts over the ensuing years. On the first anniversary of Gissing's death, when the three of them had met in St Jean-de-Luz, Clara discovered that her friend was not keen on a biography being written, so she informed Roberts of her antipathy to the project at that time. While not discouraging him from writing a biography altogether, she simply requested that he delay its publication for a few years. He was being pressurised by publishers to produce a book about his friend but agreed to wait. Clara continued to try to persuade him to wait saying that once Walter was of age he would be able to release Gissing's diary for Roberts' use, thus ensuring a fuller, more rounded work. He realised that Clara had made up her mind and that to try to act against her wishes was folly. He wrote to her on 21 April 1905 submitting to her demands:

> After reading your last letter I made up my mind to proceed no further with my book about George. I should only make trouble for myself and get myself disliked, after all. I certainly shall do nothing for 12 years ahead.[16]

By 1912 Roberts' need to write the biography of Gissing had become more urgent. This was because a young novelist, Frank Swinnerton, was planning a study of Gissing's works and had contacted Roberts for information. Roberts decided that he wished to use his knowledge himself rather than pass it to another author and refused to help Swinnerton. He began his own work which he decided to disguise as fiction with the spurious aim of protecting those likely to be damaged if a formal biography was produced. Clara agreed to show him her correspondence from Gissing, although she had reservations as to the effect on Gabrielle, still believing it to be too soon to publish his biography. Roberts asked Gabrielle if he might visit her in Paris in order to discuss the book prior to publication. She had become suspicious about the scheme, had lost her trust in Roberts and refused him the meeting. She felt as though both of Gissing's male friends had betrayed him. Clara Collet was the only one who had remained loyal and continued to fight to protect and uphold his name.

She did agree that Roberts could examine her letters from Gissing but she was not happy about his plans. Her primary concern, as always, was in ensuring that nothing untoward should be written to harm his reputation or that of Gabrielle and his family. She wrote to Roberts:

> If I seem to be lacking in cordiality in this matter don't attribute it to any want of sympathy with you. It is the consciousness of pain which any record however finely and unselfishly written, must cause to his sons and sisters...I am not attempting to deter you. George Gissing was sent into hell for the purpose of saving souls. Perhaps it is a necessary thing that his story should be written by all sorts of people from their different points of view. But I am responsible to his sons, not to society, and I feel as though I were walking on smashing glass.[17]

Despite the opposition, Roberts' book was published in December of that year under the title, *The Private Life of Henry Maitland*. The names were altered but the story was a blatant biography despite a few deliberate errors. The characters were transparently obvious. Clara was introduced as Miss Kingdon and given the occupation of an accountant, to hide her identity. Roberts included her antipathy towards his publication of the work within its pages:

> Miss Kingdon begged me not to do the book, or if I did it to hold it over until her responsibilities as executrix and trustee for the sons were at an end. But it is now nearly nine years since he died, and I feel that if I do not put down at once what I knew of him it never will be written, and something will be lost, something which has perhaps a little value, even though not so great as those could wish who knew and loved Henry Maitland.[18]

Despite Roberts' attempt to disguise the characters, the book was sold as a biography of Gissing with most reviewers revealing his identity. The theft at Owens College (or Moorhampton College, as Roberts named it), and the affair with the prostitute were soon matters for discussion amongst his critics, making life uncomfortable for Gabrielle and Gissing's sons. Some authors wrote in Gissing's defence believing him to have been too savagely dealt with by the College, but this only prompted others to come down heavily on the side of what they saw as moral right. The controversy raged amongst such papers as the *Sunday Times*, *The Star*, the *Daily News*, the *Pall Mall Gazette* and the *Evening Standard*. Wells launched his own attack on the biography which he believed to be of a poor literary standard. Not content with trying to destroy Gissing's literary reputation, Wells appears to have been intent on doing the same to Roberts, another friend. In Clara's own words, 'H.G. Wells has betrayed everyone who has ever been friendly with him and yet the man had remarkable insight into the good as well as the evil in character.'[19] The lack of loyalty by Roberts towards Gissing after his death seems difficult to understand. Not only had he exposed Gissing's early life while it could still adversely affect his two young sons and his common-law wife, but it could also harm Edith, locked in the asylum. 'Unfortunate in his life, it seems as if Gissing were destined to be unfortunate also in his death', so wrote an American critic in the New York *Nation*.

Despite Clara's support for Roberts to write the biography at a later date, she had not expected the work to have been an emotive roman à clef, but rather a serious literary work. She had not wished it to be published at this point and she found it, 'quite horrible; full of vindictive jealousy of G in relation to her and unspeakably hypocritical'.[20] She was furious with Roberts and ended her previous cordial relations immediately, never effecting a reconciliation. Despite Gabrielle's expectations, none of her relations ostracised her. Her mother had died a couple of years earlier, having ironically lived several years longer than Gissing. Gabrielle did not enter into adverse correspondence with Roberts and in Clara's words, 'She suffers but expects me to fight the battles on George's behalf and never will have any personal encounter with any of them.'[21]

Clara not only remained Gissing's most loyal friend after his death, she never forgot her pledge to help his sons should he die before her. On Gissing's death at the end of 1903, Walter, his eldest son, was 12 years old. He was at Holt Grammar School in Norfolk, where he remained until 1908, having finally settled down into a happy school life after his inauspicious beginning. As promised, Clara kept in touch with him. She visited him on 20 June 1907 and was of the opinion that his house master, Mr Eccles, was a good influence. Walter was allowed to be himself without being afraid of the consequences. Living with his mother, as a small child, must have been a harsh experience as it is clear that, whereas she maltreated both her sons, she especially despised Walter. Life cannot have been easy under the later supervision of two prim, religious, spinster school teachers whose expectations for him appear to have been impossibly high.

Under Mr Eccles, Walter was able to relax and develop his full potential. By 1907, as Clara noted, Walter's school reports were excellent. He had decided that he wished to train as an architect and Mr Eccles encouraged him, writing to his architect cousin in Liverpool and securing a position there for him when he left school the following year. Clara, however, had other plans for Walter's architectural career. She wrote to Ernest Gimson with whom she had remained in contact.

Ernest was by this time an eminent architect. After his start with Barradale's in Leicester he decided to further his career in London. As related earlier the opportunity arose for him to work for the respected architect, John Sedding, with the help of an introduction given him by William Morris after his talk at the Leicester Secular Society. Gimson worked for Sedding for two years during which time he met with Ernest Barnsley, a fellow employee, and through him with Ernest's brother Sydney, who worked for another firm of architects who also worked in the Morris style. Sedding's offices were next door to Morris' Oxford Street showrooms and his 'Arts and Crafts Movement' exerted an influence on the three young architects. After a period abroad, developing an interest in decorative plasterwork and becoming involved with Morris and Burne-Jones, Ernest Gimson decided to set up business in partnership with Ernest Barnsley and William Lethaby. They took a 'shop in Bloomsbury for the sale of furniture of our own design and make, besides other things such as plaster friezes, leadwork, needlework etc'.[22] The company was named Kenton and Co. Towards the end of 1892 Gimson and Barnsley moved their business into the Cotswolds. They set up in Pinbury and also began keeping goats, horses, dogs and chickens and growing their own food. Their speciality was furniture-making and their architectural interests were subsidiary. They did execute several commissions on small-scale domestic constructions and it was to assist in this work that Gimson decided to employ assistants. The firm had by this time moved to the Cotswold town of Sapperton. Clara contacted Gimson to see if he would be interested in employing Walter as an assistant.

Walter began work with Gimson in about 1908. Mary Comino, Gimson's biographer, suggests it was 1910, but in her diary Clara comments that Gimson offered to take Walter as one of his assistants in 1907 commencing the following year. Comino notes that Norman Jewson was the most important of Gimson's assistants and stayed with him for many years. The other two assistants, including Walter, acted as site superintendents for Gimson's architectural work. His best-known work consisted in supervising the construction of the cottage at Kelmscott for May Morris, William Morris' daughter. She had helped with the maintenance of her father's business after his death in 1896. Gimson's assistants did not become much involved in the furniture-making side of the business.

After the completion of his initial training, there was uncertainty amongst the Gissing family as to what Walter should do next. Mr Townsend, Clara's solicitor, had a cousin working in London who agreed to take him, but when Gimson was informed about the arrangement he was of the opinion that Walter would be better remaining in the country. He wanted Walter to stay in his employ, but the religious Ellen Gissing was not happy about this, as she felt that Gimson, with his secular ideas, would be a bad influence. He came up with a compromise as he was acquainted with a man involved in church restoration for the Society for the Protection of Ancient Buildings, another project begun by Morris. This man agreed to employ Walter in church restoration which met with his family's approval. He was very pleased with this solution as it meant he did not have to move to London which he did not wish to do.

By the outbreak of the First World War, he was engaged to be married. He wrote to Clara until he left for France. A letter to his aunt Ellen is extant, written in November 1914 from her home at 4, Vernon Chambers where he had been staying awaiting his orders. He was sent across to the trenches.

Walter had the same hatred of army discipline as his father. In a letter to his brother written while stationed in Winchester before crossing to France he wrote,

> Of course I am still waiting for a commission for the front. Some think the Draft will not go out now till after Easter, owing to an outbreak of measles in camp, but we have no confirmation at present: at all events I want some change, being very fed up with this life; not a quiet moment to think or write any sense!! I hope you find your job more congenial. It certainly sounds more interesting & I think you have not the same inveterate hatred of the army discipline that I have.

On 1 July 1916, Walter, along with so many other young soldiers, was killed at Gommecourt. His body was so badly mutilated that it was never identified. An ironic reminder of his father's earlier prophecies and wishes for his son.

Alfred fared somewhat better. After his mother had been committed to the asylum, Alfred went to live with a farmer and his wife in Mabe, Cornwall. Miss Orme's sister had found the accommodation. The family were good to Alfred and remained in contact at least until 1916 at which time they were still sending affectionate letters. Alfred was almost 8 years old at the time of his father's death. Clara remained in contact with Alfred as she had been with his brother. Gabrielle never involved herself in the lives of either of Gissing's sons.

Clara went to Exeter in March 1908 to visit Alfred, who was at school in the City. This was at 20, St Leonard's Road. Mr and Mrs Walters were the proprietors of the school and although Mr Walters passed her scrutiny, she was not so sure about his overweight wife who only seemed, 'all right in the main'.[23] Alfred, she found to be 'a most loveable little boy'. She took him to the cathedral, the Albert Museum and then to tea at Dillons. In a shop she saw a paint box and asked Alfred if he had one:

> He said no. When I was looking at them in the shop I asked him if he would like to buy one or would prefer something else. He said he

would like a paint box & when I chose a 2/6 one I saw that he had got out his purse and was expecting to pay for it <u>himself</u>. I believe he is going to be more like George than Walter is.[24]

She followed up her visit to Alfred with a letter to Algernon suggesting that both Walter and Alfred should spend their summer holidays with Mr and Mrs Walters, who would be at Exmoor. By the 17 May, she was able to make the exultant entry in her diary that, 'The really important event to note is that arrangements were made for Walter to spend his holidays with Alfred. He came here from Holt on the 9th and stayed the night & on the 10th in the afternoon went to Exeter with Mr Walters.' This was one of the rare occasions that the two were reunited. The boys' welfare was often in her thoughts.

Alfred left Exeter to follow his brother at Gresham School, Holt, which he attended from 1910–14, by which time he was a House Prefect. During the war he served in India and while there heard of his brother's death. The more military-minded boy ended the war as a lieutenant and remained in the army, being based in various Middle Eastern locations including Baghdad and Kufah. In 1919 he began working for the Interallied Press Censorship Committee.

Alfred lived with Margaret and Ellen Gissing in Leeds from 1920–24 and then moved to Richmond, where he lived for the next three years. He inherited the same inability to settle in one place for long from his father and for the next few years lived in Yorkshire, Herefordshire and Westmoreland. He travelled to Scotland and Italy with his aunt Ellen or Margaret. Much of his income was from sales of his father's manuscripts and books. He wrote a biography of his father and one of William Holman Hunt and gave his occupation as a writer when, in 1938 at the age of 42, he married a young widow. After the war he and his family moved to Valais in Switzerland, where he ran a UNESCO school for displaced children. In 1951 the family moved to Les Marcottes where he finally settled as a hotel-keeper. He lived there for 25 years, dying in 1975.

The pledge that Clara had made to Gissing to help with his sons until they grew up had been fulfilled. She, above all his other so-called friends, remained loyal, fought to uphold his reputation, arranged the posthumous reissue of many of his works, and above all became the best friend of his partner, Gabrielle Fleury, whom she loved as Gissing once predicted she would.

George Gissing had been the most important person in Clara's life.

NOTES

1. Mattheisen *et al.* (eds), *Letters of George Gissing*, Vol. 9, p. 308.
2. H.G. Wells, 'George Gissing: An Impression', *Monthly Review* (1904), pp. 160–72.
3. Letter to H.G. Wells, 3 March 1904 (University of Illinois).
4. Roberts, *Henry Maitland*, p. 232.
5. Ibid., p. 240.
6. Ibid., p. 105.
7. Pierre Coustillas, 'The Stormy Publication of Gissing's *Veranilda*', *Bulletin of the New York Public Library*, November 1968.
8. MSS diary, 1 August 1904.
9. Ibid.
10. Ibid., 3 June 1904.
11. Mattheisen *et al.* (eds), *Letters of George Gissing*, Vol. 7, p. 288.
12. MSS diary, 14 November 1908.
13. Ibid., 1 July 1905.
14. Ibid., 24 September 1905.
15. Ibid., Sunday 11 June 1905.
16. Pierre Coustillas, 'The Publication of *The Private Life of Henry Maitland*', *Twilight of Dawn: Studies in English Literature in Transition*, O.M. Brack Jr (ed.) (Tucson, AZ: The University of Arizona Press, 1987), p. 141.
17. Ibid., p. 142.
18. Roberts, *Henry Maitland*, p. 20.
19. MSS diary, 28 December 1912.
20. Ibid., 11 August 1912.
21. Ibid., 28 December 1912.
22. Comino, *Gimson and the Barnsleys*, p. 50.
23. MSS diary, 1 March 1908.
24. Ibid.

Part V

An Educated Working Woman and Beyond 1903–48

1

A Successful Life

During the years that Clara enjoyed her friendship with Gissing and the tumultuous aftermath, she was at the same time furthering her career. She had been employed in the newly formed Labour Department. The head of this department or ' "Commissioner for Labour" had under him three Labour Correspondents, one of whom was Miss Collet, who was to be specially concerned with women's industrial relations'.[1] A new monthly paper was founded with the aim of publishing the statistical facts thus discovered. This was the *Labour Gazette*, to which Clara was a contributor, albeit often anonymously. Her work was also discussed within its pages. The scope of women's work was expanding during this period of rapid social change and quite soon Clara was allocated her own assistant investigator.

One of the first major pieces of work she undertook for the Board of Trade was an 87-page report entitled 'Statistics of Employment of Women and Girls' which was presented to the Houses of Parliament in 1894. This report recorded the results of research conducted on lines similar to the research she had undertaken as an Assistant Commissioner the previous year. Statistics were lifted from the 1891 Census and from those already collected by the Labour Department. There is a large section on the employment of married and widowed women which she researched herself. Her conclusions, as with so many of her investigations, dispelled myths common at the time. She disagreed that more women were being employed. She said this was true for middle-class women but not for women in general. It was common for working-class women, once their husbands earned a large enough wage, to cease working altogether. For middle-class women, on the other hand, 'a high standard of comfort, a smaller field for domestic usefulness, a diminished probability of marriage, apprehension with regard to the future, have all combined to encourage the entrance into the labour market of middle-class girls'.[2] Women from very poor backgrounds were also more likely to be working than in previous decades.

Married women were less likely to be working than previously.

Overall the numbers of working women had increased but not to the extent that was generally believed. Men often spoke out against what they perceived as the increase in working women taking away their jobs and Clara was able to show them that this was not the case, thus dispelling their fear. In the near future, this in turn gave women less opposition from men, as they were less likely to believe that they would lose their livelihood as a result of women's infiltration into the marketplace. Clara Collet was not afraid to allow her statistics to speak for themselves, even when they contradicted commonly held ideas. This confidence pervaded all her relations from this point on.

Where had she found this confidence? Her good education culminating in her MA helped. Teaching enabled her to develop her talents especially those of presenting her ideas to challenging audiences. Her committee work provided access to many eminent persons, allowing her to see their vulnerabilities and revealing her own ability, which added to her self-esteem. Finally, her work for both Booth and the Royal Commissions gave her the knowledge and skills that she needed, and her hard work and confidence led to her promotion. In 1903 she was made Senior Investigator at the same time as Llewellyn Smith became Comptroller General.

She had not forgotten the person who had been responsible for giving her her first opportunity and sent a letter informing Booth of her promotion, concluding that he, 'must be almost Permanent President of the Board of Trade',[3] as so many of his researchers had ended up working there. Clara remained in touch with the Booths, spending holidays at 'Gracedieu', their house in Leicester. In July 1904, the year after her promotion, Booth had a celebratory dinner to which he invited all his former assistants with the exception of Beatrice Webb. Clara made a long entry in her diary about the event:

> Mr Booth gave us a dinner at the Savoy & the opera afterwards. Present Mr & Mrs Booth, Mr Ll Smith, Mr & Mrs Aves, Mr & Mrs Arkell, Mr & Mrs Argyle, Mr & Mrs Schloss, Mr Hardy & I. George Duckworth whose engagement to Lady Mary Herbert was in *The Times* that morning had to stay behind & have dinner with Austen Chamberlain who was in the middle of the Finance Bill; he came to the opera for the last act... and had to return to the House which went on with the Finance Bill... Mr Booth at the dinner said four persons were missing viz George Duckworth, Esme Howard (for some reason which I forget), Norman Grosvenor by death and Steven Fox who was not able to be in London. We ladies each had a beautiful large orchid & the gentlemen small ones & we all wore

them at the opera where we had the first row balcony stalls. There were no speeches from anyone.[4]

No mention was made of Beatrice's absence. Booth and his wife were no longer so close to Beatrice, and as she commented:

> It would be strange if the close personal friendship between me and the husband had not ended. Mary [Booth] has been generous, thoroughly generous, but for the last year the warm affection between us has been cooling. She has discouraged me from coming to them when they are alone, and I, sensitive to the least feeling on her side, have kept away.[5]

Clara's work involved travelling around the country and many of her later diary entries relate to this. In 1904 she was collecting statistics for the 'Cost of Living' report she was compiling. She went to Sittingbourne, Sheerness, Wellingboro, Kettering, Nottingham, Preston, Burnley and Blackburn all in the course of a couple of months.

In 1905, there was a great change in British politics; a change which must have transformed her work at the Board of Trade. The reforming Liberal administration began. This period of reform did not end until the First World War. In December 1905, David Lloyd George was made President of the Board of Trade, though his appointment lasted only two years. When Campbell-Bannerman, the Prime Minister, retired through ill-health, Asquith became Prime Minister and promoted Lloyd George to Chancellor. Winston Churchill took Lloyd George's place at the Board of Trade. During his period as a Liberal, Churchill was very much in favour of social reform, wishing to introduce bills which would help in the eradication of the 'residuum'. Beatrice Webb commented saying that:

> The big thing that has happened in the last two years is that L[loyd] G[eorge] and Winston have practically taken the limelight *not* merely from their own colleagues, but from the Labour party. They stand out as the most advanced politicians. And if we get a Liberal majority and payment of members, we shall have any number of young Fabians rushing for Parliament, fully equipped for the fray – better than the Labour men – and evolving themselves behind these two Radical leaders.[6]

Thus 1905 heralded a period of unprecedented social reform. What need was there for a person to vote for the Labour Party with the Liberals providing so much in the way of reform; Clara Collet was in the midst of all this radical activity.

9. David Lloyd George, 1st Earl L-G of Dwyfor, 1908 by
   G.C. Beresford. (By courtesy of the National Portrait Gallery,
   London.)

Hubert Llewellyn Smith, now Permanent Secretary, was able to influence the introduction of the social reforms which he was so keen to see implemented. His work at Toynbee Hall and for Charles Booth ensured that he was on the side of social reform. Both Lloyd George and Churchill were lacking in knowledge when they began at the Board of Trade and consequently looked to the educated Oxford graduate for advice. Llewellyn Smith in turn went to Clara for information about women's work. Thus she was in a position of considerable power and influence.

The first major legislation introduced was an Old Age Pension Scheme. Clara does not comment on her attitude towards this, but working as she had, collecting data for Booth's work on pensions for the Royal Commission on Labour, 'Pauperism, a Picture; and the Endowment of Old Age, An Argument', published in 1893, she was sympathetic to some form of pension scheme, provided it only granted a subsistence payment and did not take the responsibility away from individuals for making their own arrangements. She can only have been pleased to see the end of the workhouse as the only option for a regular working man at the end of his productive life. Pensioners were colloquially said to be, 'On the Lloyd George', when drawing the Old Age Pension.

Alcohol had been blamed for much of the social ruin of the working classes. It was often seen that rather than social conditions causing the poor to turn to drink, it was drink that was the primary problem, turning, as it did, many a man away from his responsibilities in the home. A Temperance Bill was planned in order to introduce Licensing Laws to regulate public house opening hours. In 1907 and 1908 Clara was busy travelling to Leeds, Bradford, Sheffield, Nottinghamshire and Manchester collecting information relating to this legislation. She commented that Lloyd George was expected to give a speech in October 1907 and that the Cabinet would shortly be discussing temperance legislation. Clara conducted much background research to this subject in order that she might have more authority. In February 1908 she interviewed Mr John Rae of the National Temperance Society and the following week spoke to a specialist doctor who lent her several items on alcoholism. On the subject of temperance, Clara herself gives no comment other than mentioning that when she visited friends of hers, 'Poor Francis was disgusted with me for talking the whole time to his father about nasty public houses.'[7] She tolerated consumption of alcohol in small quantities by other people. Gissing had enjoyed the odd glass of wine or bottle of beer, but she did not indulge in alcohol herself.

In between her travels around the country Clara continued her investigations into London work, interviewing West End tailors, masters and journeymen. She wrote:

> I have also got an interesting but far from pleasing job in interviewing West End Tailors...One outworker, a Mr Paul told me he was publishing a volume of poems. The Swedes, Danes, Dutch and Jews behave like gentlemen but the English outworker tailor is much less intelligent and less polite.[8]

In the Edwardian world where foreigners were viewed with suspicion and Jews especially were often blamed for the ills of the City, her outlook could be refreshingly candid. That she had talked intimately with an outworker about his interest in poetry illustrates her ability to communicate with the working classes and gain their trust by her open, friendly and inquisitive attitude about their lives in general other than the merely statistical angle of her work. It was this genuine interest in people which made her such a good social investigator.

In June 1907, while giving evidence for two hours to the Select Committee on Home Work, she could sense that several of the interviewers were not happy with her replies. She had spoken the truth as she saw it rather than saying what they wanted to hear. The interviewers were not used to a woman giving evidence and especially not a strong-willed woman, prepared to challenge their views and biases and totally unruffled by their questioning.

Despite being a Liberal herself, the politician Clara had the most personal relationship with was the Labour MP James Ramsay MacDonald. He had been elected, in 1900, as Secretary to the Independent Labour Party. MacDonald had been an MP for a year when Clara first met him in 1907. She may have come to know him through her friendship with his wife Margaret who, like Clara, had been working for the Charity Organisation Society during the 1890s. Margaret had been 'visiting' for the COS in Hoxton in the East End and was also a school manager and Secretary of the District Nursing Association. Although she was not working in the same area, she was based at nearby St Pancras. Both women had been involved in COS Committee work bringing them into contact with regions other than those in which they were based. In addition the two were both members of the British Association for the Advancement of Science and worked together on 'The Committee on the Economic Effect of Legislation Regulating Women's Labour' which sat during 1901 and where their friendship developed.

Clara's association with the Ramsay MacDonalds was of mutual benefit. On 14 August 1907 Margaret MacDonald telephoned Clara to ask if she would be prepared to meet with her husband at the House of Commons. She was pleased to be asked to help her friend. Her diary entries are rather brief but the casual way she commented upon this request implies it was not a unique event. Ramsay MacDonald and Clara had tea on the Commons Terrace whilst they discussed the Wages Board Bill. She reported back to Mr Llewellyn Smith on her return telling him all that had been said.

It was not only for business reasons that she met with the Ramsay MacDonalds. On 16 January 1908, she invited them to lunch with her and Professor Foxwell at the 'Villa Villa' restaurant in Gertrand Street, her favourite restaurant at which she often dined with her friends.

On 28 May 1908 she gave evidence to the 'Fair Wages Committee'. She had regularly experienced difficulties with Mr McLeod, one of her colleagues, who appears to have had problems dealing with her as a woman. Several months previously she had been asked to give evidence for this committee and had prepared for the occasion well in advance in order that she would be able to answer any questions posed. In this connection she needed to obtain the Cotton Wages tables for 1906 to illustrate women's position in that industry compared with the others. She was told by a colleague that these figures were almost ready and he would obtain them for her. When he came back he told her that Mr McLeod knew nothing about her giving evidence and had refused to let her have the figures, 'which of course I am entitled to have without [his] permission'.[9] She sent a note to McLeod informing him that she was giving evidence. He returned it immediately with a comment 'appended asking whether I was going in my private capacity, "If so the matter did not concern him." It is very characteristic of him. I shall take no notice of it and do without the information.'[10]

One of the main reforms planned by the Liberal government was to introduce unemployment insurance. Prior to being able to set this plan in motion it was necessary to introduce legislation on sweated labour; to introduce Trade Boards for regulation of minimum rates of pay, and most importantly of all, to set up Labour Exchanges which would be necessary to regulate the implementation of the insurance and to inform workers about availability of work without them having to trudge halfway across London every day or to move around the country in search of work. Clara was a part of all of these developments.

Another confrontation with McLeod resulted over her contribution to the 'Sweated Industries Bill'. On 23 February 1908 'Mr McLeod whistled up to me that a Cabinet Council was going to be held that afternoon & Mr Ll Smith wished me to hold myself in readiness for questions.'[11] She sent down for relevant information and discovered that McLeod had, several days previously, sent for this himself proving that he had deliberately withheld it from her until the last minute before the Cabinet Council would be held in order to make her look incompetent. She was against the bill and Mr Llewellyn Smith was surprised to discover that McLeod had not told her earlier to enable her to prepare her opposition to it. Instead he asked her to write her reservations that he might be made aware of her opinions. She dropped a report directly to Llewellyn Smith's office, as she believed she, 'never can feel sure that Mr McLeod will transmit anything in the shape I send it – or even transmit it at all'.[12] Was his opposition due to her gender or was there simply a personality clash between the two? As she was determined that her opposition should not be seen as 'merely destructive', she 'sketched out a scheme for the formation of Dressmaking Councils of employers and assistants'. She still preferred solutions to working conditions to be based on voluntary organisation rather than conditions imposed by government. Over the same issue Clara received a note from Margaret MacDonald:

> asking if I could suggest any lines on which her husband could usefully work against the bill. They especially wanted to know if the Cabinet were giving in after taking advice. I sent her a note saying I was sending up a memo by request and that I had invented a new scheme; on Friday I received a note asking if they might know what my scheme was & I sketched out a rough outline and sent it to her.[13]

She was, as a result of her Cabinet contacts, able to directly influence social legislation being discussed in the House of Commons.

In May 1908, Winston Churchill was elected President of the Board of Trade. Clara commented in her diary the following February that she needed to, 'put on record at once the complete changes in my official work. On Friday morning I was told that I was to attend a conference in the President's room at 5pm on Wages Boards.' Others present were to be Sidney Webb, Hubert Llewellyn Smith and of course, Churchill himself. The meeting had been called to consider the possibility of producing a Wages Board Bill in light of the fact that the Home Office was opposed to such a measure. Clara's involvement with this bill continued throughout the year and into the next. By 14 July 1909 she was present at the meeting proposing amendments to the bill. Winston Churchill, Mr Tennant, Sir Hubert Llewellyn Smith (as he was by this time) and Mr Askwith were also present. Clara almost encountered a problem in attending this meeting as it was, 'held in Sir Edward Grey's room at the House of Commons. It is the first time I have gone there. The police were rather nervous about me but took my word for being authorised to go in.'[14] Once admitted to the building, she found the occasion very instructive and useful:

> Mr Churchill told the committee at the end of the meeting that he hoped the Clause would pass but that he thought the bill a good one even without it and that if they could not see their way to accept it with it in, in order not to take up more than his share of time & also to leave time for another Board of Trade Bill he would drop the clause; but he hoped they would think better of it. I have sent in a memorandum answering their arguments.

Later she commented in her diary about Churchill:

> I don't think the Board of Trade loves Mr Churchill; but I confess that he interests me as a human being whatever his faults may be. It is partly because I only know 'intellectuals' or 'thoughtful men' that this type of person governing them appeals to a side of me which might belong to a respectable Bohemian...Of course Lord Robert Cecil appeals to me even more. I wonder if he will come to the Board of Trade ever.[15]

With regard to Churchill's attitude towards Clara as a woman she commented that:

> Churchill 'damned that fellow Carlisle' and then apologised to me for doing so. It is very amusing to contrast the different ways in which they treat me. Mr Askwith aims at treating me like a man with no more respect than a man in the same place; all the others treat me with a little more consideration because I am a woman but quite rightly don't put themselves out for me & treat me as a colleague.[16]

Over the introduction of the Labour Exchanges, Clara tendered her resignation. The reason she gave was that she wished to be released from her job that she might be able to speak, 'freely about the way in which the women's side of the Labour Exchanges is being organised; capable women being subordinated to men who know nothing and care nothing about women's interests'.[17] As with all her work, above all else, women's perspective was of

10. Sir Winston Spencer Churchill by Ambrose McEvoy.
(By courtesy of the National Portrait Gallery, London.)

paramount importance. Over much legislation and on many committees, her contribution changed the bias, improving the outcome in favour of women.

She believed that there was nothing left in the Civil Service for her to stay for. Coming just a month before her fiftieth birthday she may have been suffering a crisis due to her age. She must have realised by now, although there are still a few entries in her diary about men she found attractive, that it was unlikely that she would ever marry.

The last real relationship Clara mentions in her diary dated back to the previous year. In February 1909 an entry was made concerning Mr Ibry. She had met him through a mutual friend and commented that she, 'Liked his expression', and that when she met him for the second time she invited him to her house for dinner. For the next five months the two saw each other on either a Friday or a Saturday evening. Ibry was an interesting man with a property to sell in Russia, which he was intending to do in July, but when he returned he planned to take rooms in the West End or Hampstead so, 'I shall not see so much of him then. I shall be sorry...He is evidently now looking to meet his ideal and marry. I hope he will.'[18] Maybe he was younger than her, and she may no longer have considered herself as marriageable. She was sad at the ending of this friendship.

Over the issue of Labour Exchanges and her proposed resignation, Clara Collet had several interviews with Mr Askwith, the Comptroller General of the Commercial, Labour and Statistical Department at the Board of Trade. Initially it seemed as though Askwith tried to dissuade her from going but later she felt that he wanted her to so she wrote to him intimating that there was

> therefore, no need to prolong the discussion. He wrote that I was quite wrong. I replied that no doubt I had transferred to his mind the criticisms I had passed on myself & that as I had already said in my letter of resignation I had no shadow of complaint to make with regard to his treatment of me.[19]

She tried to obtain a good redundancy deal for herself in order to set a precedent for women in a similar position. There had been a Pension Act passed the previous year relating to men's pensions in the Civil Service. Under this, men were to receive a pension of one-eightieth of salary for each year of service, plus a lump sum of one-thirtieth of salary for each year of service. At this time the Civil Servants' Women's Associations asked to be allowed to remain under the existing legislation of 1859 which gave them a pension of one-sixtieth of salary for each year of service, subject to a maximum of forty-sixtieths. They chose this course as women's salaries were, in general, so low that they could not afford any reduction of the rates of pensions calculated on the basis of their salaries and they feared that the marriage gratuity might be abolished. Clara was earning a very good salary by this time, higher than many men in the Department. She had been earning over £300 a year as her starting salary,[20] over twice as much as Gissing had been earning at this time from his writing. Her salary had risen after her promotion in 1903 and with years served. It was not as good as men working in a comparable position, but nevertheless she was one of the highest paid women in the Civil Service. The non-acceptance for women of the 1909 pension changes would have worked against her as a high-earning woman with no interest in the marriage gratuity.[21]

She spent the following weekend with Llewellyn Smith. Although he believed her arguments made sense, he managed to persuade her to reconsider her position with regard to her retirement and on her return to London she wrote asking that she might withdraw her resignation. The request was accepted.

Several positive things had come out of the incident. First, Clara planned to give lectures on industrial questions in order to make a living but when she

> tried to imagine life without any regular daily routine [I] came to the conclusion that I should like to have a cottage at Newbury. Even now that my leaving seems a remote event, I feel that it would be wise to try & establish a country habit...I shall probably take a cottage at about £20/year in Newbury. Carrie and Edith both rather like the idea & I think the cottage might be used by them and others even if only for an occasional weekend myself.[22]

There is no evidence that she carried out this plan but it provided the embryo of an idea which led to her later retirement plans culminating in her taking her sisters and brother to live in Sidmouth.

For the present she continued living with her friend, Miss Woodgate, in Vernon Chambers, Theobald's Road, WC1.[23] Her first reaction on contemplating retirement was that this accommodation was too expensive and she ought to find somewhere cheaper. She wrote to Gabrielle to inform her of her expected reduced circumstances once she had retired and this prompted Gabrielle to find herself a smaller flat. Clara had been paying for her friend's accommodation since Gissing's death and she was becoming irritated about this arrangement, although she never complained except in her diary, 'Of course it has not been the actual payment which has been so vexatious to me but the knowledge that she was willing to let me go on year after year.'[24]

Clara decided, from this time on, to put a good part of her money into a savings plan to ensure she had extra funds for her retirement when it eventually came.

She returned to her work in the Civil Service with her old enthusiasm and vigour. The First World War made a radical change in her professional life. Her male colleagues became involved in war work, planning the continuance of production during these difficult years, or moving into other areas. Winston Churchill became First Lord of the Admiralty and she must have had great pride in knowing that she had been acquainted with him. Women took over men's jobs, both in regular industry and in the newly expanded munitions trades. She continued gathering statistical evidence of the vast changes occurring for women at the time. Although it meant an end to the reforming Liberal administration, Clara was able to take an active part in the Beveridge Reconstruction Committee working for the advancement of women on the 'Women's Employment Committee'. In this she was involved in assessing what employment women had undertaken during the war in order to plan for their smooth replacement by the soldiers on their return from abroad if it was deemed necessary. Many men had been killed at the front and some women would be able to continue in their occupations. She took this as an opportunity to analyse the part women now played, including an estimation on hours worked, wages earned, training, assessing their business capacity, and considering whether or not married women should be allowed or encouraged to work. The Committee compared the levels of remuneration with those of men performing similar tasks and the probability of the continuation of that employment after the war, either in place of men who had been thus engaged or in jobs previously carried out by women. It was agreed that no dismissals should take place until the men to be reinstated actually returned from the front. It was also decided that the returning soldiers would require re-training as technology had advanced considerably whilst they had been away and the women who had taken their places often understood the new methods whereas the men would not.

After the war she continued in the Department, being involved in the changes which took place in 1917 with the abolition of the Board of Trade and its replacement by the Ministry of Labour. 'I was there', said Clara, 'when Lloyd George created it, by telephone, one evening.'[25] She finally retired from the Civil Service in 1920, but continued working on several Trade Boards. She helped in the fixing of minimum wages for timework and piecework in the trades under their jurisdiction, implementing the Trade Boards' Act of 1906. For many years Clara had clung to the belief that ensuring people were receiving a liveable minimum wage would help prevent and cure the social problems which she had encountered.

> From that time Miss Collet's work mainly consisted in examining the statistics collected and preparing memoranda in connection with the application of the Act to different industries. The selection of appropriate industries was, in fact, largely based on her memoranda.[26]

Her attitude had, by this time, altered and she now accepted that legislation was a more realistic solution to the problem of poverty.

Interested though she was by her work, it was by no means her only pursuit. Her involvement with the Royal Statistical Society flourished and in 1892 she was elected a Fellow. She became a member of the Council of the Royal Economic Society in 1918 along with her old friends Llewellyn Smith, Henry Higgs, Professor Marshall, Professor Edgeworth and Sidney Webb, as well as John Maynard Keynes who had been elected the new editor of the *Economic Journal*. She remained a member of the British Association for the Advancement of Science (BAAS). In August 1904 she travelled to Cambridge to hear Arthur Balfour give the Presidential address to the BAAS and stayed for a couple of days at the annual conference. In 1896 she was made the first woman Fellow of University College, London, enabling her to use the college facilities at which she, thereafter, often entertained her friends as it provided a suitable place for a woman to be able to go alone. Her duties as Fellow included helping in the running of the university, mounting a campaign to protest against the London School of Economics as she disagreed with their aim to usurp University College, London, in the teaching of Economics.

Clara was elected a 'Member' of Bedford College. From 1909 the title changed to Governor, of which there were initially about 100. The role was very prestigious and separate from that of council member. Bedford College had been founded in 1849 and had been the first college of higher education for women in Britain.

In June 1905 she travelled to Sheffield to attend the Annual Congress of the Women's Co-operative Guild. This was the largest congress that the Guild had so far held and was followed by a 'great demonstration in support of Enfranchisement of women'.[27] She found the conference, 'very interesting, lunched at the Albany both days with Miss Catherine Webb'. Her support of women's suffrage was continual and can be picked up throughout her diary. She did not approve of the militant suffragettes led by the Pankhursts; her ideas were similar to those of Millicent Garrett Fawcett and her sister, Elizabeth Garrett Anderson. In November 1908 she attended another Women's Suffrage meeting at Queen's Hall, London with her friend, 'flatmate' and colleague, Miss Woodgate. This was a special meeting arranged for professional and industrial women supporters. Mrs Garrett Anderson was in the chair – Clara did not say that Mrs Garrett Anderson was the 'Chairman' but that she was in 'the Chair'.

Another outlet for her interest in women's issues was the National Union of Women Workers (NUWW). How much time she spent engaged with this organisation is rather vague. The NUWW had been formed in 1895 and its inaugural members included Beatrice Webb and Mrs Alfred Booth (Charles Booth's sister-in-law), both known to Clara. Webb made an impassioned, 'appeal for the overworked and underpaid women of the time'.[28] The objectives of this organisation were:

> The encouragement of sympathy of thought and purpose among the women of Great Britain and Ireland; the promotion of their social, civil and religious welfare; the gathering and distribution of serviceable information; the federation of women's organisations and the formation of local Councils and Unions of Workers.[29]

One aspect of the NUWW which Clara disliked was its emphasis on prayer and religion. Beatrice Webb was also unimpressed by this aspect of the Union. She attempted, in vain, to remove the religious bias and as a protest resigned from the Executive, remaining a member in order, 'to keep the Union straight on industrial questions'.[30] By 1900 there were 28 branches and by 1905 there were 40. At each annual conference a different theme was chosen for discussion. Over the years Elizabeth Garrett Anderson, Josephine Butler, Emily Davies and Clara Collet's old headmistress, Miss Buss, all made contributions. Clara may have been to more of these conferences, but the only documented attendance was for 1907. The theme chosen for that year was 'women and employment' which may have been why she felt compelled to go. Seven papers were read on subjects including, 'The Position of Women in Unskilled Work', 'The Position of Educated Women as Paid Workers' and 'How to Improve the Life and Conditions of the Worker'.

During her working years she also joined the Craft School Committee. This was founded by Toynbee Hall, and the first mention of her connection with it occurs in a letter from Gissing to her on 10 January 1902 thanking her for sending a report on the school. He agreed that it, 'must be doing admirable work, & I quite understand the pleasure of helping in its direction'. By the following April she was looking at potential new premises for the school and viewed a building she named as the 'Jews' House' with a Mr Cooke to see whether it would be suitable. The original site of the school had been 137–141, Globe Road, East. It had been established to teach practical skills to local people in order to improve their employment chances. By 1900 there were 58 students enrolled in trade classes and 71 in art classes. Funding came from the Technical Education Board. Llewellyn Smith was also involved. The equipment was, according to a report from the funders, very good, as were the teachers, yet there was concern about falling student numbers. The school taught cabinet-making, wood-carving, carpentry and joinery, plumbing, building construction and plastering. Initially the classes were intended for poor boys. By 1900 there was no mention of classes for women. A school with the purpose of educating poor adults and boys so that they might escape their poverty appealed to Clara. This was the way she had always advocated helping the poor. She had not been on the committee for long before women were included in the scheme. By 30 April 1908 she was in negotiation with Miss Durham, the London County Council Inspector of Technical Instruction Classes for Girls. They went out to dinner together and afterwards visited the Craft School. The next day she arranged dress-making classes for girls.

Despite her heavy commitments, Clara found time for a full social life. Some of it overlapped with her work and committee involvement, as she often dined or went to the theatre with her colleagues. She dined at the Lyceum with Miss Woodgate; visited the theatre with Mary Booth; had weekends away with the Llewellyn Smiths; dined at the Villa Villa. She was invited annually to her old school teacher Mrs Bryant's garden party; went on long walks around London with friends; regularly attended classical concerts and especially enjoyed the promenade concerts in the summer, favouring composers such as Beethoven, Haydn, Bach, Strauss and Tchaikovsky.

11. Stanley and Beatrice Webb, Baron and Lady Passfield in 1940.
(By courtesy of the National Portrait Gallery, London.)

About 1900 Clara moved for a couple of years to 90, Woodside, Wimbledon. Gissing complained to Gabrielle in a letter of April 1900 that, on a trip he had made from France to London, he had been unable to meet Clara at her home as Wimbledon was so far away and they had agreed to meet at the 'Writers' Club', a literary club for women in Norfolk Street WC, in central London.

It seems to have been something to do with her 'worries and griefs'[31] that Clara Collet moved again. Whatever these problems were they appear to have commenced in the spring of 1902 and continued for several months, culminating in her being forced to leave her home. 'I fear you have had grievous worries, to drive you away from your own house.' Gissing commented in one of his letters 'Well, you are not so dependent, I think, as I am upon domestic comfort; but doubtless you will settle again before long.'[32] The change solved the mysterious problem, for by 12 June he wrote, 'I gather from your letter that the worst of your troubles are over.'

Whatever the upset or reason for her enforced move, she once more established a comfortable life in central London, living at 36, Chenies Street Chambers, Bloomsbury WC. The following year she changed accommodation again to live at 4, Vernon Chambers, Theobald's Road. These central addresses made it easy for her to travel around London and enabled her to return home late at night from her evening outings.

Vernon Chambers was inhabited by other of her friends and colleagues. Professor Marshall rented a flat in the block. Although living primarily in Cambridge he sat on many London committees, several of which Clara attended. His wife, Mary Paley Marshall, was a member of the Royal Economic Society and the British Association and was also friendly with Clara. Mary wrote a review in the *Economic Journal*, 1902, on Clara's book, in which she praised the work and its author. With Miss Woodgate, Mary Paley Marshall and Professor Marshall all sporadically in residence in Vernon Chambers, the block provided her with a degree of security.

She went out most nights attending functions when in London, but she often spent time away from town. Her work continued to take her all over the country and she had many friends throughout England with whom she could stay while on these trips. She was able to take advantage of their hospitality and preferred staying with friends to staying in local hotels.

Clara enjoyed travelling. She spent most of her annual holidays abroad, making numerous trips to France and Paris, calling upon Gabrielle or Romain and Madeleine Rolland. She visited

Switzerland where she met up with Gabrielle and the Rollands, and at least twice she ventured to Norway.

On one of her journeys to Paris during the summer and autumn of 1908, she received a telegram informing her of the death of her 'Mamma'. She had died painlessly in her sleep on Thursday 24 September. Clara returned immediately to London to be with her family but she makes no comment about being upset. The family had been finding 'Mamma' increasingly difficult and demanding. There had been family problems for some years. Carrie's illness had forced her to resign from Wyggeston by 1904. This illness, about which Clara gives no details in her diary, continued it seems, from that time for several years. A woman named Miss Bolus was hired to nurse her. In January 1905 she commented that Carrie was ill and again in June that year that she had been in bed for seven weeks and had gone to St Leonards near Hastings, with Miss Bolus, in order to convalesce. The convalescence must have been unsuccessful as she spent all of July and part of August in bed but by the end of the month Clara had better news saying that she was up once more. The problem must have been chronic since in February 1912 there was mention once more that Carrie was convalescing, this time in Sidmouth, where Clara visited her. Thus began the family's long association with Sidmouth. Despite these extended periods of illness Carrie lived until 1940, by which time she was well into her eighties.

Clara's elder brother Wilfred had, like her, also gone to University College, London. As they were both nonconformists this was the most appropriate university to attend as it welcomed all regardless of their religion. On obtaining his degree in 1881 and before Clara began her MA at the university, he entered the Colonial Service and was initially sent to Fiji. After 16 years he was transferred to Cyprus. By 1905 he was appointed to British Honduras. Wilfred was the only one of the Collet children to marry. Mary, his wife, remained in England to give birth to their first child. Wilfred Robert was born the month after Wilfred's departure. Mary soon also became involved in helping with the difficult matriarch. Clara recorded:

> Yesterday, Good Friday... I went to tea and dinner at Finsbury Park [i.e. 7, Coleridge Road]. Mary is staying there with the baby in order to let Edith have a holiday. Mamma of course attributes Mary's self sacrifice to save herself the expense of board and lodgings for a time. Mamma makes everyone miserable and never for a moment entertains the idea that nothing but a sense of duty makes them endure it.

Carrie has devoted herself to obeying her wishes and Mamma never says a kind thing about her. She is actually looking to sending Florence [Bolus] away 'when Carrie dies'. Of course in a way she is not responsible for being so heartless to Carrie, she is too old to know what she is doing. But one wants to be sorry for her and it is impossible when she passes her whole time in imputing falsehood etc. to everyone who waits on her. She never asks for affection but demands obedience from everyone and she manages to make meals a torture to Carrie and Edith. Mary was very good to her but she finds it trying and says she is nearly as tyrannical as she was eighteen years ago.[33]

Clara was the only family member, other than Wilfred, not actively involved in the day-to-day management of her mother. She visited 7, Coleridge Road regularly; most weekends throughout her professional life she would visit but, presumably owing to her work and her other commitments, she was unable to devote as much time as her brothers and sisters.

Mary went to join her husband abroad. They had two more boys. Mary died from heart failure on 28 December 1912 after six days of illness following pneumonia contracted as a result of 'oedema of the larynx'. Clara appears to have been more upset over this bereavement than she had been over the death of her own mother, commenting in her diary on the fact that Mary had a 'beautiful' character. Mary did not live to see Wilfred gain his knighthood or complete his career in British Guyana. The children were left in England to be brought up by their aunts. Wilfred retired in 1923 and died in 1929 at the age of 72, the first of the siblings to do so.

Edith continued with her work as a school teacher at the North London Collegiate School until her retirement. She lived for a period with Clara at 36, Berkeley Road, Crouch End. Gissing commented how pleased he was that the two of them should be together, although he had his reservations:

Your sisters coming to live with you will necessarily make a good deal of change; all for the better, I hope. I am in favour of this drawing together of kinsfolk, whenever it can be managed. But of course, there is much to be said for the other alternative – that one should keep aloof in order to give as little trouble & pain as possible to those whose natural sympathy is awakened by all one's distresses.[34]

Of course it would be very convenient for the two sisters to live in Berkeley Road situated, as it was, so close to Coleridge Road, enabling them to assist and check on their old family home without having to live there. But for most of her life, Edith, unlike her sister, lived at 7, Coleridge Road with her parents and later together with Caroline and Harold, before they sold it and moved to 13, South Hill Park Gardens, Hampstead when they had all retired.

After years of living in central London, Clara relocated once more out into the suburbs. She followed her brother and sisters to Hampstead where they had settled shortly before. She wished to maintain her independence and thus chose to live at 81, South Hill Park Gardens. She was still there by 1919 just before her retirement from the Civil Service. It seems something of Gissing's restlessness had rubbed off on her for she then changed addresses again, albeit not far. She purchased a new property at 61, Swains Lane, Highgate, with a rather macabre perspective, looking as it does into the cemetery where Karl Marx is buried. According to the obituary written by Charles Trevelyan for the *Royal Statistical Journal* in 1948, 'The garden of the little house she had for a time at Highgate was a riot of anything that liked to grow there – mostly St John's Wort, as it happened – and the result seemed to her just as it should be.'

Clara's diary ends in February 1914, so the last years of her life have to be pieced together using her published work and her retirement projects, along with the testimonials from two Sidmouth residents who remember the family in their final home together.

Aside from her Trade Board employment in her early retirement she teamed up once again with Hubert Llewellyn Smith to assist him in his follow up to Charles Booth's *Life and Labour*. Entitled *The New Survey of London Life and Labour* it was undertaken from 1930–35. Her contribution was relatively small but she was, by 1930, 70 years old. She wrote a 40-page chapter on 'Domestic Service' using census material as her source. Llewellyn Smith's work was not considered as important as the original carried out by Charles Booth, but nonetheless fulfilled a useful comparative role, highlighting the changes which had occurred during the ensuing 30-odd years.

Her old friends remained important to Clara. Appointments and lunches with Ramsay MacDonald continued. She corresponded with Gabrielle and commented on the death of Gabrielle's little dog, Bijou. Ellen Gissing came to stay for over a month in 1909. She did not mention the reason for the visit in her diary, although it may have been to discuss Walter's future; however, the length of stay suggests more a holiday than purely a business trip.

Once she had retired, she took up several new pastimes. Apart from her association with the Trade Boards she developed her interest in Indian affairs. Aunt Sophie, her father's sister, had close ties with the Brahmo Samaj sect of Hinduism, developing links between them and the Unitarians. She had published a Year Book of their events and wrote a history of one of their most prominent leaders, Rammohun Roy, published in 1900. Clara's association with India was influenced by her aunt's relationship with the country and by her own ancestry. She learnt Hindustani and wrote an article for the *Economic Journal* in 1924 reviewing 'Labour in Indian Industries, by Dr G. M. Broughton', in which the author had highlighted the atrocious conditions prevailing in that country's factory and mining industries. Clara believed that the study by Dr Broughton 'cannot but be painful reading to anyone conscious of responsibility for the welfare of India... There is a great awakening to a sense of the need for Government action.'[35] This was in contrast to views held by many at the time that India was there to be exploited for the good of Britain and it did not matter how that was achieved. She had added the issue of racism to her agenda.

Clara Collet acquired many Indian friends including Professor P.C. Mahalanobis whom she first met in 1913, while he was studying in England. He wrote that there was 'close contact between the leaders of the Brahmo-Samaj and the Collet family; I myself belong to the Brahmo-Samaj, and was introduced to Miss Collet by a friend'.[36] She was, he says, still working for the Civil Service at that time and would invite a number of friends around to her small flat in Holborn, and the evening would be spent drinking coffee and engaging in intellectual conversation. Clara 'would constantly make penetrating observations and witty remarks with a twinkle in her eyes.'[37] Other Indian students would join these evening soirées. She was responsible for changing the direction of Mahalanobis' life. Her enthusiasm for statistics was transferred to him, altering the course of his studies from mathematics and physics to statistics. He returned to India in 1915, writing regularly to his friend. On a trip to England in 1926 he and his wife visited her in Highgate, and said: 'We were both deeply touched by the kind way in which she received us.' She was overjoyed to find that Mahalanobis was deeply involved in working with statistics. She introduced him to the Royal Statistical Society, which led to his becoming a Fellow. This must have been a first for the Society; a woman introducing an Indian man. Professor Mahalanobis' contribution to the RSS continued long after Clara had left the Society. In 1946 he presented a long paper entitled,

'Recent Experiments in Statistical Sampling in the Indian Statistical Institute'. In introducing the Professor, the Chair commented that it gave him pleasure to be able to hear:

> an account of the notable progress achieved in India under the direction of Professor Mahalanobis and that he had been the guiding spirit of the Indian Statistical Institute. Not only had he personally done good work, but he had had the capacity of selecting and encouraging other men of ability, of organising team-work in the highest sense of that rather dubious expression. The result was that they now had in India one of the foremost statistical research institutions in the world, and they knew to whom that achievement was primarily due.[38]

What they probably did not know was that it was Clara who was responsible for Mahalanobis' conversion to statistics in the first place, at her little flat in Holburn. Mahalanobis believed that Clara had 'a brilliant mind, and a charming personality; and always looked on the brighter side of things'. He said he always, 'consider[ed him]self fortunate in having close contact with her when I was young, and I recognize her formative influence on my life in many ways'.[39]

The other area in which she interested herself in her later years was in her own family genealogy. In collaboration with Henry Haines Collett, a distant relative from another family line, a four-volume *History of the Collett Family* was compiled which included all the different branches of her family, some of whom altered the original spelling of the name to add a further 't' to the end. She claimed that, 'To the Antiquary the question of spelling is of no consequence. Exact spelling is a modern fancy.'[40] This hand-produced work must have taken up much time. The second volume deals with her own family tree and gives a detailed account of her ancestry.[41]

This work continued and in 1933 she published *The Private Letter Books of Joseph Collet* in which she collected together Joseph Collet's correspondence written while he was working for the East India Company and wrote an extensive introduction to the book. She continued compiling family history throughout her final years. The last work appeared posthumously, and was another collection of family correspondence, *The Letters of John to Eliza, a Four Years' Correspondence Course in the Education of Women, 1806–1810*.

Although she wrote regular articles for the journals of both the Royal Statistical Society and the Royal Economic Society, these consisted mainly of reviews of other people's work and more depressingly of obituaries of many of her friends. In 1923 she wrote one of Sir Charles Loch for the *Economic Journal* in which she defended his position and that of the COS, which had been largely discredited by the time of his death and was viewed as an old-fashioned institution. Socialism had by the 1920s superseded individual philanthropy as the means to improvement of the conditions of the working classes. Although Clara herself had moved on from her original position by 1923, she remained loyal to her old friend, who had devoted his life to the charity.

In 1936 she wrote an obituary of her University College teacher, mentor and friend, Professor Herbert Somerton Foxwell. In this document Clara describes the establishment of her Junior Economic Club. It met from 1890 until 1920 at University College when it changed its headquarters to the Clare Market, LSE, under the presidency of Sir William Beveridge. His ideas and inspiration for the welfare state may have come to fruition during the stimulating discussions at Clara's club.

In 1940 she wrote an obituary for her lifelong friend Henry Higgs. She compared him with her theatrical idol, Henry Irving, commenting that they had many common physical characteristics and mannerisms. She gave a brief outline of his life, the pinnacle of which was his becoming Campbell-Bannerman's Private Secretary in 1905. Although extremely deaf in his old age he remained involved with many committees, but

> quite unable to hear the comments of others present, in which indeed he seemed to take no interest, his argument would continue as an entirely solo performance, frequently on some other item of the agenda than that under discussion; the only Chairman, in my experience, who was able to make him desist until his oration was really finished, being Edwin Cannan, who used to take him almost by the throat, shouting down his ear that we were not discussing that matter, and putting his hand over his mouth until he gave up.[42]

In 1945, aged 85, Clara wrote an obituary for her friend and colleague, Hubert Llewellyn Smith, in which she not only gave details of his life, but added a little about his time with her and Charles Booth during their work together collecting information for *Life and Labour*.

By 1936 Clara had become ill herself, contracting breast cancer which necessitated the removal of one of her breasts, a pioneering operation at that time and one which would not usually result in much of an expectation of prolongation of life. Clara, like her sister

12. William Henry Beveridge, 1st Baron Beveridge by Muspratt, 1938. (By courtesy of the National Portrait Gallery, London.)

Carrie, convalesced in Sidmouth. Most people, at the age of 76 and having been diagnosed and operated on for cancer, would expect their lives to be over, put their feet up and wait for the end to come. In her usual convention-defying manner Clara decided that Sidmouth was a pleasant area and that she and her two sisters and brother should sell their houses and all move permanently to the seaside. Considering her precarious state of health, her age, and that of her siblings (all in their seventies and eighties), this was an extraordinary decision for her to make and for her family to agree to. Thus began the final chapter of her life.

NOTES

1. Martindale, *Women Servants of the State*, p. 47.
2. *Report by Miss Collet on the Statistics of Employment of Women and Girls*, (C-7564), Printed for HMSO 1894.
3. University of London, Senate House, letter to Booth from Collet, 23 October 1903, (I/4803 MS 797).
4. MSS diary, 19 July 1904.
5. MacKenzie and MacKenzie (eds), *Diary of Beatrice Webb*, p. 272.
6. Randolph S. Churchill, *Winston S. Churchill: Young Statesman 1901–1914* (London: Heinemann, 1967), p. 315 quoted from Webb's diary, 30 November 1910.
7. MSS diary, 21 October 1907.
8. Ibid., 2 February 1908.
9. Ibid., 28 May 1908.
10. Ibid.
11. Ibid., 23 February 1908.
12. Ibid.
13. Ibid.
14. Ibid., 14 July 1909.
15. Ibid.
16. Ibid.
17. Ibid., 10 August 1910.
18. Ibid., February 1909.
19. Ibid., 10 August 1910.
20. Mattheisen *et al.* (eds), *Letters of George Gissing*, 19 November 1893 to Ellen Gissing.
21. Martindale, *Women Servants of the State*, chapter 7 gives more detail on the subject, pp. 159–75.
22. MSS diary, 10 August 1910.
23. This property was bombed during the Second World War.
24. MSS diary, 10 August 1910.
25. P.C. Mahalanobis, 'Obituary: Clara Elizabeth Collet', pp. 252–4.
26. Ibid.
27. *Women's Co-operative Guild Report 1903–1914*, Coll. Misc. 657/3 British Library

of Political and Economic Science, London School of Economics.

28. Kathleen Freeman, *National Council of Women: The First Sixty Years: 1895–1955* (London, June 1955).

29. Daphne Glick, *The National Council of Women of Great Britain: The First One Hundred Years – 1895–1994* (London: National Council of Women, 1995), p. 6.

30. Ibid., p. 10.

31. Mattheisen *et al.* (eds), *Letters of George Gissing*, 16 April 1902 to Collet.

32. Ibid., 3 June 1902 to Collet.

33. MSS diary, 14 April 1906.

34. Mattheisen *et al.* (eds), *Letters of George Gissing*, 19 March 1897 to Collet.

35. Clara E. Collet, 'Broughton: Labour in Indian Industries', *Economic Journal* Vol. 34 (September 1924), pp. 457–9.

36. Mahalanobis, 'Obituary: Clara E Collet', p. 254.

37. Ibid.

38. 'Proceedings of a Meeting of the Royal Statistical Society', *Journal of the Royal Statistical Society*, Vol. 111, Pt. IV (1946), p. 325.

39. Mahalanobis, 'Obituary: Clara E. Collet'.

40. Collet and Collett, 'The History of the Collett Family: The Family', Vol. 1.

41. See Appendix 1 for more on Collet's ancestry.

42. John Maynard Keynes, 'Obituary: Henry Higgs', *Economic Journal* (December 1940), p. 557.

2

The Final Chapter

Carrie, Harold and Edith moved from their comfortable Victorian home in South Hill Park Gardens, Hampstead, with Clara to a large wooden bungalow clad in galvanised iron, painted in red oxide and with an asbestos roof. It had a deep wooden veranda facing the sea. Inside there was a long corridor with rooms off both sides rather reminiscent of an army barracks. The building was perched high up on the cliff edge overlooking Sidmouth and the sea, although it was set back a couple of hundred feet from the cliff face. The address was 'Clifton', Cliff Road, Sidmouth. There were no fitted carpets and only a few rugs. The aura of the place was austere, frugal and utilitarian.[1] The only remarkable item in the bungalow was the grand piano placed in the annexe, which was played by Robert Collet, Wilfred's son, when he visited his aunts and uncle and who had inherited Collet Dobson Collet's flair for music. Elizabeth Nash became Clara's companion during her last years, and her daughter, Connie, can remember standing unobserved on the veranda listening transfixed as Robert Collet played the piano.[2]

The other luxury was Clara's large collection of books which she allowed acquaintances to borrow. A friend of Mrs Nash was studying at Balliol College, Oxford, and when Clara came to hear of this she offered her entire collection of books for his use during his studies.

Despite her long working life spent amongst the rich and famous, she was still able and keen to befriend 'ordinary' folk. She discovered that the young apprentice water inspector, Gerald Counter, who regularly had to inspect the property, had an interest in politics. Like her, and unlike the majority of other residents in Sidmouth at the time, his politics were left-wing. They struck up a friendship and she lent him books. She gave him one by William Morris and suggested he should read *The Town Labourer*, and *The Village Labourer* by John Hammond and his wife Barbara, as they revealed the harshness of English social conditions. Hammond was a liberal who turned towards socialism as he became older. In the general election after the Second World War, Clara, in common with so many other former Liberals, voted Labour for the first time, to ensure the setting up of the welfare state by her old friend and colleague William Beveridge.

The family reflected the state of their house; austere and frugal in their behaviour and utilitarian in their dress. They were all of small stature. Harold was a short man who usually wore a trilby hat.[3] Carrie wore her white hair plaited at night. She dressed in black silk and had her pince-nez clipped to her belt during the day. Edith had become a little eccentric in her dress. Clara wore sensible navy costumes teamed up with grey stockings, no doubt to keep her warm in the chilly exposed clifftop bungalow. How the family managed to communicate with the rest of Sidmouth is a mystery, for to reach the bungalow necessitated a half-mile walk up an almost perpendicular road or alternatively a climb up hundreds of steps which a fit 15-year-old would find exerting. The clifftop position was rather an impractical choice as a final abode for a family of elderly people with no car. Possibly the station cabs were brought into use on a regular basis.

Carrie, whose health had always seemed so precarious, was over 80 when she moved to Sidmouth. She died a couple of years later. Harold had to be taken into Lustways nursing home at some stage during the Second World War and was nursed in his final illness by Elizabeth Nash. He subsequently died on 7 January 1945, aged 87, leaving his estate to be shared by Edith and Clara.

Edith died in the bungalow on 21 November 1946. She left her sister the sum of £2,293. Clara was now alone. Elizabeth Nash remained in contact with her after the death of her brother and during all her remaining years, becoming her full-time companion. Her daughter Connie remembers her as small and thin, with a liking for black coffee and oat cake made from Quaker oats. She would never take a large slice as she ate very little. Most of her time was spent in her continued study of genealogy and she even had the fancy that Elizabeth Nash (née Wilkinson) was in some way distantly related to the Collett family. This was most probably wishful thinking born out of affection for her companion and although the name Wilkinson does appear once in her collection of Joseph Collet's letters, it appears to be describing a friend rather than a relative.

She continued to keep busy until the very end of her life. She had *The Times* delivered daily and borrowed two books a day from the mobile library.

At some point during her retirement she began a study of pre-Victorian novels in which she looked at them from a statistical viewpoint to attempt to uncover the lifestyles of the characters and thereby discover more about the times in which their authors were living. She set out to conduct a historical or sociological survey. In this Clara was influenced by her knowledge of the way in which Gissing wrote and how 'realistic' his novels were. He was familiar with the lives of the people about whom he wrote, through first-hand observation and research. He experienced the problem of being an educated man living amongst the lower classes and his work reflected this disparity. Clara knew this and believed that many other authors worked in a similar way. She wrote that she agreed with Sir Walter Scott's definition of a novel as, 'fictitious narrative...[in which] the events are accommodated to the ordinary train of human events, and the modern state of society'.[4] She differentiated between the 'Romance' and the novel claiming that the definition for the former was, 'a fictitious narrative in prose or verse, the interest of which turns upon marvellous and uncommon incidents'. She excluded 'romances' from her survey and included only what would today be classed as 'social realism' – exactly the type of work at which Gissing excelled. She understood that 'The so-called historical novel generally throws light on the period during which it was written',[5] and was useless when it came to looking at the historical period in which it was set. In order to prove her point that much can be learnt about historical periods through literature, she quoted Charlotte Brontë who wrote that, 'The first duty of an author is, I conceive, a faithful allegiance to Truth and Nature; his second, such a conscientious study of Art as shall enable him to interpret eloquently and effectively the oracles delivered by those two great deities.'[6] Having defined her terms and described what she was setting out to achieve, that is, a study of historical and sociological conditions, Clara Collet went on to list the authors she was planning to study. There were 54 authors on the list of whom 24 were women. There then followed an author by author survey in which she outlined the characters to illustrate the differing social conditions in which they lived. In line with all of her statistical work, this quirky study is liberally interspersed with tables breaking down the class structures, and occupations of the various people who appear in the novels. It does not seem that any use was ever made of this work.

In her old age, Clara had become quite a formidable presence. She returned her daughter-in-law's letters with all the spelling mistakes marked in red and returned Christmas presents as she did not believe them to be necessary. She had written in her diary, as a young woman, that she had the ability to upset anyone and every-

13. Clara Collet in her seventies. (By kind permission of Jane Miller.)

one, and this trait appears to have remained with her throughout her life. Her companion, however, thought her a 'dear old lady' of whom she was extremely fond. Although there are photographs of her in her early retirement portraying her as a rather plump woman with a double chin, towards the end of her life Elizabeth Nash and Gerald Counter both remember her as thin. This was an outward sign of the illness which was to finally kill her.

Two years after Edith's death, on a showery August day in 1948, Clara Collet died. The breast cancer, contracted 12 years previously, had insidiously spread to her intestines and colon. She had been in pain for some time and knew that death was on its way. Her companion prepared her a small dish of stewed apples which she thought would be easy for her sick patient to digest. Clara ate this and then in the presence of Elizabeth Nash and her nephew Robert Collet she died. A white lace handkerchief was laid over her face and she was left for the living to pay their last respects. Mrs Nash hurried home to tell her daughter Connie the sad news and together the two returned to 'Clifton'. Connie was only a young woman at the time and was reluctant to enter the bedroom where Aunt Collet, as Connie called her, lay. Her mother insisted she must go in and the two women entered together. The elder woman went over to her dear friend, raised the handkerchief so that Connie could see the peaceful face, then she took hold of Clara's hand which she lifted and stroked. Connie found herself stroking her own hand in sympathy and the whole ritual was very moving as she had loved the 'dear old lady' herself.

Clara was as unconventional in death as she had been in life. Her religious beliefs had lapsed although she had in her latter years become interested in the Liberal Jewish movement. Thus a normal Christian burial or cremation was not her chosen option. Instead, on 5 August, two days after her death, Potbury's, the local Sidmouth undertakers, arranged for her body to be taken by train to Waterloo station in London, from where it was transported to University College Hospital to be used for medical research – her final wish. A burial certificate was issued on 22 April 1950 but it is not known where the body was finally laid. It must have been either Battersea or Morden Cemetery but records for that time have not been kept. Her body was used for anatomical study and teaching for the benefit of medical students at the hospital which remains a teaching centre to this day.

Clara's obituaries ranged from five-page-long epitaphs in the *Royal Statistical Society Journal* and the *Royal Economic Journal*, to shorter ones in the local papers, *The Times*, *The Telegraph* and the

Journal of Education. There can have been few mourners. Apart from her nephew Robert Collet, Clara had outlived most of her immediate family and friends. She left an estate worth £7,768 3s 3d. This puts paid to any idea that her frugality during her last years was a result of any financial difficulties.

Clara bequeathed a copy of *The Private Letters of Joseph Collet* as well as her travelling clock to Elizabeth Nash and left her an annuity of £70 in order that she might be able to visit Connie, who was shortly leaving for South Africa with her husband. In the event apartheid was introduced and the couple stayed in Sidmouth where they remain to this day, but the gesture was one which was not lost to the family.

NOTES

1. I thank Mr Gerald Counter for the description of the bungalow. He was the local water inspector and regularly visited Clara Collet.
2. The bungalow and its annexe were demolished in the 1960s.
3. Mr Counter gave me this description of the Collets.
4. Cited in Clara E. Collet, 'A Statistical Survey of Pre-Victorian Novels', unpublished, p. 2. Warwick University, Modern Records Centre, MSS 29/3/13/1/3.
5. Ibid., p. 2.
6. Ibid., p. 3.

Epilogue

What must Clara Collet have thought in those last lonely months spent high on the cliff looking out to sea; all her brothers and sisters dead and just the occasional visit from her nephew and his family with Robert Collet's music to brighten up her quiet existence from time to time? Did she evaluate that long life of hers in order to ascertain the changes which she had helped to bring about? Did she ever think about how much the status of women had changed over the last 87 years? Surely she must have done and she had already made assessments of the changes wrought over various periods in her life.

In an article written in 1900, she used an extract from Charlotte Brontë's novel, *Shirley* in order to illustrate the situation in 1849, 50 years earlier:

> I believe single women should have more to do – better chances of interesting and profitable occupation than they possess now... Look at the numerous families of girls in this neighbourhood – the Armitages, the Birtwhistles, the Sykes. The brothers of these girls are every one in business or in professions; they have something to do; their sisters have no earthly employment but household work and sewing; no earthly pleasure but an unprofitable visiting; and no hope, in all their life to come, of anything better. This stagnant state of things makes them decline in health: they are never well; and their minds and views shrink to wondrous narrowness. The great wish – the sole aim – of every one of them is to be married, but the majority will never marry; they will die as they now live. They scheme, they plot, they dress to ensnare husbands... Men of England! Look at your poor girls, many of them fading around you, dropping off in consumption or decline; or, what is worse, degenerating to sour old maids – envious, backbiting, wretched because life is a desert to them... Fathers! cannot you alter these things? Perhaps not all at once... You would wish to be proud of your daughters and not to blush for them – then seek for them an interest and an occupation which shall raise them above the flirt, the manoeuvrer, the mischief-making tale-bearer. Keep your girls' minds narrow and fettered – they will still be a plague and a care, sometimes a disgrace to you. Cultivate them, give them scope and

work – they will be your gayest companions in health, your tenderest nurses in sickness, your most faithful prop in age.[1]

This Clara claimed, had been the situation in 1849. Middle-class women had nothing to do but get married, sew and make a household for their menfolk. Woe betide those women who were unable to find a suitable husband. There were few options for them. If they came from a middle-class family with little money they would probably be condemned to becoming a companion to a rich old woman or, like Clara, teach. By 1900, the situation had changed. Clara saw it thus:

> We may safely assert that no middle-class woman of average intelligence, educated in the high schools established during the last twenty-five years, is unable to earn a living if she chooses to do so. And one very important change has taken place. Whereas thirty years ago it was the rule for many parents, although with little hope of bequeathing an income to their daughters, to support them at home in expectation of their marriage, this lack of foresight is becoming rare... There is now the least excuse for the woman who marries merely to obtain a livelihood. The economic advance has at least been sufficient to enable women to preserve their self-respect. Next, it must be admitted that the work which educated women are paid to do is in the main useful and satisfying work. They no longer think of supporting themselves by acting as useful companions to useless women; nor do they have to spend their time in imperfectly imparting valueless facts in the schoolroom. The teaching and nursing professions, which include more educated women in their ranks than any other, have made great advances.[2]

Many of these changes had been implemented by Clara. In countless papers, in her book and in her many talks her message was the importance of education and the necessity of providing more varied occupations for educated women. Her years as a teacher in a progressive girls' school with a wide curriculum providing examinable academic subjects helped to impart her attitudes on an individual level, and her constant campaigning in the public sphere after she entered the Civil Service and joined the many and various committees in which she had influence, changed opinions, resulting in the introduction of the necessary legislation on the wider level. In addition her work as a Fellow of University College, London, and as Governor of Bedford College played their part in bringing about better educational opportunities for women.

As early as 1902, she was aware of the possible pitfalls which might occur as a result of these changes in women's status which she had helped to introduce.

> Our pioneers were full of enthusiasm in their journey to the promised land where sex barriers should be removed and sex prejudices die away. Those of us who passed through the gates which they opened for us were...often unpopular among those we left behind and were delighted with the novelty of the country before us. The next generation are coming into the field under new conditions. To begin with, it is realised that work is work...The glamour of economic independence has faded, although the necessity for it is greater than ever.[3]

When in her seventy-fifth year, Clara gave a talk at the Adam Smith Club.[4] It was entitled, 'The Present Position of Women in Industry'. In this she gave an update of the situation she now saw. She began by describing the position as it was when she was a child:

> Those days of the sixties and seventies [when] it seemed to be an almost everyday item of news that some working woman, kicked nearly to death by her husband had implored the magistrates on his behalf not to punish him by imprisonment...In 1870, however, an Act was passed giving married women the legal right to their own earnings as wage workers. This legal emancipation of women was of far greater importance, potentially affecting as it did quite 98% of married women, than the Married Women's Property Act of 1882, which...gave the propertied wife full ownership. But the great majority of women were illiterate, and it took at least forty years for them and their children to realize their legal status, and they were still not owners of their own persons. If a wife left her husband and earned wages to support herself and children, he could no longer legally draw her wages and pocket her savings, but he had other powers to make her separate existence impossible, and she worked in the labour market at great disadvantage. Many men never knew that they had lost their 'right' to their wives' earnings, but many who did felt an increasing reluctance to let them become wage-earners; the wife was to stay at home, and the daughter could go out to work. The father's right to his children's earnings was untouched. Compulsory education and factory and workshop Acts gradually raising the limit for leaving school and entering wage service, steadily...worked for the protection of children from 1878 onwards.[5]

She continued by discussing the situation of working-class women in the sweated trades and how low their pay was at this time:

large numbers of needle-workers entered the market as casual workers for the sake of pocket money... The living-in system, which had prevailed in businesses giving full employment to unmarried women and girls, gradually became hateful to the workers and unprofitable to employers when restrictions on hours of work put an end to their unregulated overtime.[6]

In Clara's opinion, the legislation against married men had probably been the single most important change wrought in the position of women for this was most usually, the

predominating influence of the position of men and women in marriage. This position has been vitally affected by laws prescribing the terms in which marriage must be entered...The economic emancipation of married women in England dates from 1870; their political emancipation from 1918. Not till 1939 will free-born women voters appear on the register.[7]

Many changes in the status of women had been encountered by Clara over her 60 years of work, but which changes had she actually influenced by her own efforts? A.L. Bowley, in his obituary of Clara, claimed that,

Her subject had special importance at a time when much attention was given to the 'sweated industries', and the sequel at a later date was the establishment of Trade Boards and minimum wages in industries where wages were exceptionally low.[8]

Her aim had been to improve social conditions and her statistical work for the Board of Trade and before had drawn attention to the appalling levels of pay and conditions in many industries, especially in the sweated trades. Her report on 'Women's Work' for Charles Booth, the part she played in the Royal Commission on the Employment of Women, the research on 'The Status of Employment of Women and Girls', her report on the 'Money Wages of Indoor Domestic Servants', and the report on the 'Earnings and Hours Enquiry', all contributed towards highlighting how poor wages were, which led to the passing of the Trade Boards Act of 1906:

And from that time Miss Collet's work mainly consisted in examining the statistics collected and preparing memoranda in connection with the application of the Act to different industries. The selection of appropriate industries was, in fact, largely based on her memoranda in the period before the 1914 war.[9]

Clara was in part responsible for ending the bad conditions of the 'Sweated Trades'. One of her early ambitions had been to see a raising of wages for the poor and she played a role in imparting those increases by the implementation of the Trade Boards on which she sat for many years of her working life and in which she continued to be involved for the first 11 years of her active retirement.

Although her personal contribution to the women's rights movement was small, the impact she made was large. She stood as an exemplar. She did not chain herself to railings or throw herself in front of horses, instead she worked alongside men in high political positions whose attitudes with regard to women's ability were changed by her achievements. How could Lloyd George, Churchill and Ramsay MacDonald not have been impressed by her? She could improve the case for women's rights directly through her work and the legislations she helped to introduce and indirectly through the example she set. Her work for Beveridge emphasised the work women had been engaged upon during the war influencing the situation for them after the war had ended. Attitudes had changed for ever. No longer could women be seen as incapable of doing equal work to men when they had been engaged in working in ammunition factories and other factory work, producing food, and generally doing all the work men had done prior to their exodus to war.

Clara must have been satisfied at the changes she had seen taking place during her life. When she had been born, women were not allowed to take a university degree or enter the Civil Service. A husband had a legal right to beat his wife with a stick and keep any money that she earnt. By the time Clara died, women were able to enter many professions, had a legal right to their own money and property, could vote, and could take their husbands to court should they beat them. She played a part in this change in women's status as a result of her years collecting statistics, illustrating the plight of the 'sweated trades'; or the likelihood that a woman would have to turn to prostitution as her only course of action when a husband habitually took her wage packet even after they had separated.

By her death in 1948, the position for the 'odd women' like herself, who either chose not to marry or were unable to do so, had changed beyond all recognition from when she started her career in the late 1870s. For the uneducated woman in the 'sweated trades' regulations had improved conditions and raised wages. By 1948, a single woman living in the East End while still not well off by today's standards, at least would be able, provided she put in a good day's work, to earn a living wage. She could do this without working a 16-hour day. This was in part due to Clara's efforts in the Trade Boards and the regulations with regard to hours of work and wages she spent so much of her own working life trying to get adopted.

A middle-class woman, like herself, was no longer condemned to work as a teacher or companion as the only 'respectable' work available. By 1948 the Civil Service employed women in all departments. They were not confined to locked and guarded rooms as the first women were forced to be. Women doctors, career nurses, paid social workers, business women, clerical workers, secretaries, were no longer unusual but commonplace. Women were able, with enough determination, to find employment in most professions. 'Manufacturers and business men', were by this time beginning, as Clara had long ago wished, to, 'train their daughters as they train their sons'.[10] Her vision for women as laid down in *Educated Working Women* in 1902, had mostly been realised by the time of her death. She was able to die a satisfied woman.

NOTES

1. Cited in Clara E. Collet, 'Through Fifty Years: The Economic Progress of Women', in Collet, *Educated Working Women*, pp. 135–7.
2. Ibid., pp. 137–9.
3. Ibid., pp. 142–3.
4. 12 January 1935, published in 1942 in the *Royal Statistical Journal*.
5. Clara E. Collet, 'The Present Position of Women in Industry', pp. 122–4.
6. Ibid.
7. Ibid.
8. A.L. Bowley, 'Obituary: Clara E. Collet', pp. 408–10.
9. C.T. (Charles Trevelyan), 'Obituary: Clara E. Collet', pp. 252–3.
10. Collet, 'The Prospects of Marriage for Women', p. 63.

THE COLLET FAMILY TREE

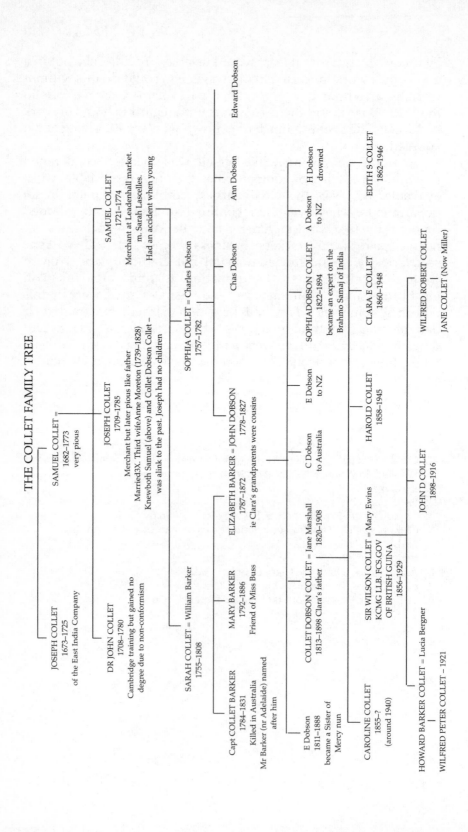

JOSEPH COLLET
1673–1725
of the East India Company

SAMUEL COLLET =
1682–1773
very pious

DR JOHN COLLET
1708–1780
Cambridge training but gained no
degree due to non-conformism

JOSEPH COLLET
1709–1785
Merchant but later pious like father
Married3X. Third wifeAnne Moreton (1739–1828)
Knewboth Samuel (above) and Collet Dobson Collet –
was alink to the past. Joseph had no children

SAMUEL COLLET
1721–1774
Merchant at Leadenhall market.
m. Sarah Lascelles.
Had an accident when young

SARAH COLLET = William Barker
1755–1808

SOPHIA COLLET = Charles Dobson
1757–1782

Chas Dobson   Ann Dobson   Edward Dobson

Capt COLLET BARKER
1784–1831
Killed in Australia
Mr Barker (nr Adelaide) named
after him

MARY BARKER
1792–1886
Friend of Miss Buss

ELIZABETH BARKER = JOHN DOBSON
1787–1872   1778–1827
ie Clara's grandparents were cousins

C Dobson
to Australia

E Dobson
to NZ

SOPHIADOBSON COLLET
1822–1894
became an expert on the
Brahmo Samaj of India

A Dobson
to NZ

H Dobson
drowned

E Dobson
1811–1888
became a Sister of
Mercy nun

COLLET DOBSON COLLET = Jane Marshall
1813–1898 Clara's father   1820–1908

HAROLD COLLET
1858–1945

CLARA E COLLET
1860–1948

EDITH S COLLET
1862–1946

CAROLINE COLLET
1855–?
(around 1940)

SIR WILSON COLLET = Mary Ewins
KCMG LL.B. FCS.GOV
OF BRITISH GUINA
1856–1929

JOHN D COLLET
1898–1916

WILFRED ROBERT COLLET

JANE COLLET (Now Miller)

HOWARD BARKER COLLET = Lucia Bergner

WILFRED PETER COLLET – 1921

Appendix 1

Genealogy of the Collet Family

The Collets originated from Rouen in the time of Edward the Confessor and during the successive centuries Clara's ancestors were, for the most part, merchants. In the Middle Ages they traded in wool and wine and in the fifteenth century added sugar, tobacco and spices. Collet Dobson Collet's great-grand-uncle John had been a doctor who had trained at Cambridge but had been refused a degree due to his nonconformist religion. His other great-grand-uncle Joseph learnt the trade of a merchant in Sweden and later worked in London where, although he married three times, produced no children. His third wife was very young and he a septuagenarian when they married. Consequently she outlived him by 40 years and was still alive when Collet Dobson Collet was a child, providing a link to the past. She was able to remember her husband's father, Samuel, (1682–1773) and through him learnt directly of the great Joseph Collet, the family's star, who was Samuel's brother. Clara exhibited many of the characteristics which had made Joseph great.

Joseph had been born in 1673 into a Baptist family that had earned their living through trade. His religion encouraged honesty and unlike many other merchants, he was not interested in elevating his social status by becoming a land-owning squire. Joseph Collet was not afraid to speak his mind even when it was unwise to do so. Free speaking, especially on matters of religion, was a dangerous pastime in the seventeenth century when heretics were still sometimes condemned to death. Joseph, as the eldest son, inherited his father's business in 1698. He married, had one son and four daughters and then, tragically, his wife died. Shortly afterwards he became bankrupt as a result of the war with France. That his bankruptcy was not his fault is illustrated by the offers of help made by his friends. They were prepared to lend him money or give him references.[1] Joseph Collet was a proud man and would not accept gifts from his friends. He owed £3,000 to his creditors, which although not legally bound to do so, he was determined to pay back. From the recommendations of his friends, Joseph was offered the post of Deputy Governor of York Fort in Sumatra for four years under the East India Company. This post must have been accepted with reservation on Joseph's part, for Sumatra was in political turmoil and difficult to access. There was great danger as each boat had to pass through huge surf to reach the island. That was after a five weeks' sea voyage from India which could only be undertaken during four months of the year. Once there the climate with its damp and heat killed many of the white people who had no immunity to the local diseases and no drugs to treat them.

Joseph Collet was prepared to take the risk as he had been told that in addition to the salary of £300 per year, there would be the opportunity of doing trade with the locals thus increasing this income considerably. Unfortunately his bad luck continued. His ship was seized by the French in Rio de Janeiro on his way to Sumatra and he was forced to leave his son John and another man as surety for the payment of the ransom money he was required to hand over to be allowed to continue his journey.

Once in Sumatra, Joseph used his excellent administrative skills coupled with fairness and honesty to instil political stability into the land. To improve his chances of avoiding disease he moved the Deputy Governor's residency from Fort York to a new location which he named Fort Marlborough. Fort York had been too near to a swamp. These measures proved successful or else he was just lucky as Joseph survived his four-year assignment and by 1716, when he was due to leave Sumatra, he had the satisfaction of knowing that he was leaving it more prosperous and stable than when he had arrived. He had also been able to dispatch the money to pay his creditors before he left the settlement for India.

On arrival in Madras, Joseph discovered with some surprise that on taking up his post in Sumatra, his name had been put down for the Madras Council. As a result of deaths and departures his name was second from the top of the list by the time he was back in India. A year later the President departed, leaving Collet to take his place. It was a position with influence and responsibility as well as opportunities to make money. Rumours abounded that the Governor could make as much as £10,000 a year; a fortune in those days. Joseph's son was finally able to join him at this time, having been released from South America. Shortly after his arrival he contracted a fatal illness. Joseph Collet barely mentioned this tragedy in his letters. He seemed as stoical as he had been when his wife had died. He was a man who did not like to share his hardships with others. Joseph may have felt pain less than other men or just become hardened as a result of previous tragedies. He may simply have been exhibiting the English 'stiff upper lip' and refused to allow others to see his anguish.

His great-great-great-grand-niece Clara Collet was the same. Hardly a word of complaint about anything appears in her diary or letters, unlike Beatrice Webb whose diary is full of self-pity. When Clara had problems she worked harder. She was lucky in having a good constitution enabling her, like Joseph before her, to be able to work hard without collapsing under the strain as many less fortunate people do. Beatrice Webb regularly fell victim to her weak nervous system as did Clara's friend Eleanor Marx. Both these women suffered periodically with poor nerves and depression leading to sleep and eating problems causing weight loss in the case of Beatrice and ultimately led to Eleanor's suicide. Clara mentions nothing more than a single cold and one other minor period of upset in the whole of her diary which covered over 30 years of her life.

That Joseph immersed himself in work on his return to Madras is self-evident. He was busier and more successful than he had been in Sumatra, trading, purchasing ships on which he gave employment to many, and, in one letter to his brother-in-law he reports that he had bought goods worth £12,000. Joseph did not keep his wealth for himself. He sent money to pay for the education and support of his daughters back in England. Despite his increased wealth Joseph warned his daughters against marrying for money but to marry 'sober, honest men of good estate',[2] as he believed this to be the way to happiness.

On his eventual return to England, Joseph planned an exciting new career in politics. He was pleased that the Stuarts had been ousted from their rule and even considered feigning conformity for the sake of his venture. His politics had become more radical during his time abroad. His outspokenness on matters of religion in his letters back home, and his views prefigure the later Unitarian beliefs of his descendants. He wrote 'a paper attacking the Christian doctrine of the Trinity'.[3] His attitudes show an independence of spirit and an ability to speak up against issues with which he disagreed. This was another trait that his great-great-great-grand-niece inherited from him. Clara was never afraid to voice her concerns about various issues whatever the cost. This characteristic resulted in some people finding it difficult to feel close to or love her, but it did, as it had for Joseph before her, result in her gaining people's trust and respect. The Indian influence also permeated down to her and her contemporaries. Her aunt Sophia became heavily involved with the Brahma Samaj movement and later Clara made many Indian friends and felt a great deal of personal and national responsibility for the Indian colony,[4] believing that it was Britain's obligation to alleviate the bad working conditions in Indian factories rather than being interested only in financial gain.

After living so many years abroad, Joseph, on his return to England in 1720, was unable after all to pursue politics, as his health had begun to decline, so he settled down in Hertford Castle, where he died five years later and was buried in the nonconformists' graveyard at Bunhill Fields.

Of Joseph's brother Samuel's three sons, only Samuel Junior produced heirs, and both were women. Samuel Junior followed the family tradition of trading as a merchant but he remained closer to home, basing himself at Leadenhall in London. At the age of 39 he suffered a serious accident resulting in his becoming an invalid. He died only a year after his father in 1774. His daughters both married and hence the family name was lost. Sarah Collet, the eldest, married William Barker who had little business sense and although 'a well intentioned and loveable man', after the death of his wife 'he seems to have abandoned the attempt to earn a living'.[5] Sophia Collet, the younger daughter, married Charles Dobson, 'an entirely irresponsible'[6] man who deserted his children when his wife died. They were brought up by Anne (Moreton) Collet, their great-aunt. Thus the wealth was lost.

In Sarah and Sophia's offspring, the Collet spirit of adventure surfaced once again. Captain Collet Barker emigrated to Australia where he was killed by aborigines whilst leading a party exploring areas hitherto unknown to white people. The mountain he discovered was named after him – Mount Barker, which is situated near Adelaide. A monument of Captain Barker was erected in St James' Church in Sydney. Charles Collet Dobson ventured to South America, his business was unsuccessful and he never married.

Elizabeth Barker and John Dobson were less adventurous. They did not even look far for marriage partners and the cousins were married in 1810. John Dobson worked looking after the estate of a cousin. He died young having contracted typhus fever in the course of his work but not before he sired seven children – Collet's aunts, uncles and of course, her own father. Of these seven, one went to Australia, two to New Zealand, one became an Anglican 'Sister of Mercy', the youngest son drowned in adolescence.

Clara's aunt Sophia and her father, Collet Dobson, both officially took back the family name lost as a result of the matrilineal descent of their grandparents. Sophia fervently pursued her Indian interests, writing *The Brahmo Year Book, Indian Theism and its Relation to Christianity* and a partly completed biography of Rammohun Roy, the instigator of the Brahmo Samaj religion. She did not marry because of, 'complicated physical troubles, of which she was a most patient and cheerful victim throughout life'.[7] She moved in literary circles being acquainted with Emerson, the American Unitarian poet and essayist, and Louisa M. Alcott, the author of *Little Women*. Maybe Sophia's love for literature rubbed off on her niece for Clara Collet was an avid reader all her life.

NOTES

1. H.H. Dodwell (ed.), *The Private Letter Books of Joseph Collet*, with an introduction and appendix to her family history by Clara E. Collet (London: Longmans, 1933), pp. xii, 238.
2. Ibid., p. pxxi.
3. Ibid., p. pxxiii.
4. Clara E. Collet, 'Labour in Indian Industries', A review of a book by Dr Broughton, *Economic Journal* (September 1924) pp. 457–9.
5. Collet and Collett, 'History of the Collett Family', p. 19.
6. Ibid., p. 21.
7. Ibid., p. 23.

Appendix 2

Chronology of Clara's Life and Historical Events

1860   Clara Collet born 10 September to Jane (1820–1908) and Collet Dobson Collet (1813–1898). Lived in Hornsey Lane, Islington.

1865   Cambridge Local Examinations (like GCSEs) opened to girls.

1866   Barbara Bodichon, *Reasons for the Enfranchisement of Women*.
       Emily Davies, *The Higher Education of Women*.

1869   Girton College, Cambridge founded.
       John Stuart Mill, *On the Subjection of Women*.
       Clara meets Eleanor Marx for the first time.

1870   Women first allowed to become Civil Servants to work in telegraph offices.
       Forster's Education Act.
       First Married Women's Property Act.

1871   Paris Commune.

1872   Clara sent to Calais to learn French.

1873   Clara begins at North London Collegiate School.

1876   Clara takes her Cambridge Local Examinations.
       The *Diplomatic Review* in financial difficulties.

1877   The Dogberry Club formed by Clara and Eleanor Marx.

1878   University College, London allows women to take its degrees.
       The Collet family now based at 7, Coleridge Road, Crouch End.
       Clara begins work as a teacher at Wyggeston Girls' School, Leicester.

1879   Clara passes her first BA degree.

1880   Clara passes her final BA degree.

1881   Ernest Gimson apprenticed to Barradale's Architects.

1882   Married Women's Property Act.
       Social Democratic Federation founded (Marxist).
       Clara attends a lecture given by Arnold Toynbee.

1883   Andrew Mearns, *The Bitter Cry of Outcast London*.
        Clara passes her Teacher's Diploma.
        EW proposes to Clara.
1884   Clara elected to council of Charity Organisation Society.
        Eleanor Marx begins to live openly with Edward Aveling.
        Fabian Society formed.
        Clara attends a lecture given by William Morris.
1885   Clara moves to London to begin her MA degree in
        Political Economy.
        A rift has formed between Clara and Eleanor Marx.
1886   Ernest Gimson moves to London to work for J.D. Sedding.
        Charles Booth begins his work *Life and Labour of the People
        in London*. Beatrice Webb (née Potter) begins to work for
        Booth.
        Clara obtains MA and wins Joseph Hume scholarship. £20
        per year for three years – continues to study mathematics.
1887   Clara gives lectures to supplement studies.
1888   Jack the Ripper murders five women in the autumn.
        Clara takes up residency in the East End in autumn to
        collect statistics for Booth's chapter on 'Women's Work'.
1889   Clara engages in 'Balfour's Battersea Enquiry'.
        'Maria Edgeworth and Charity' published by *Charity
        Organisation Review (COR)*.
        'Charity and Strikes' *COR*.
1890   Elected Vice President of Toynbee Economic Club.
        Gissing meets Edith Underwood. Reads *Life and Labour*.
        Clara collects information for Booth's work on Pensions.
        Works at Ashby-de-la-Zouch workhouse.
        'Foreign Competition' published in *COR*.
        'The Economic Position of Educated Working Women'
        read to South Place Ethical Society.
        'Women Working in Large Cities' in *COR*.
        'Salaries of Women Teachers' written for *Journal of
        Education*.
1891   'George Gissing's Novels: A First Impression' for *COR*.
        'Women's Work at Leeds' in *Economic Journal*.
        'Charity Organisation' for *COR*.
        'The Occupations of our Mothers and Grandmothers' for
        meeting of Toynbee Economic Club.
        Wrote 'Undercurrents' and 'Over the Way' around this
        time under pseudonym 'Clover King'.
1892   'The Novels of George Gissing' lecture delivered at the
        Ethical Society.

Gissing comments in his diary that he has heard that someone has given a lecture on his work.

'Prospect of Marriage for Women' published.

Made a Fellow of the Royal Statistical Society.

Carries out work as Assistant Commissioner for the Royal Commission on Labour.

1893   Begins employment as Labour Correspondent for the Civil Service in the Board of Trade.

18 July meets George Gissing for the first time – on the River Thames at Richmond.

October – to Paris on holiday.

1894   'Three Ideal COS Secretaries' read at Denison Club and published for *COR*.

Visits Switzerland in December.

1895   Married women prevented from continuing in employment in the Civil Service.

'Statistics of Employment of Women and Girls' published in *RSS Journal*.

Moves to 36, Berkeley Road, Crouch End.

1896   Gissing takes Walter to live in Wakefield.

Gissing meets H.G. Wells for first time.

Clara stops in Wakefield to visit Walter on her way home from a work trip. Edith has major breakdown.

1897   Gissing separates from Edith – travels to Italy.

Clara visits Ireland.

Clara visits Charles Booth at Gracedieu Manor, his home in Leicester.

1898   'The Expenditure of Middle-Class Working Women' first published.

'The Collection and Utilisation of Official Statistics bearing on the Extent and Effects of the Industrial Employment of Women' published in RSS Journal.

Gissing in Italy until spring. Clara sends him a portion of her diary in February. He meets Rosy Williams (Beatrice Webb's sister) and has a relationship with her in March. He returns to England in April. Clara destroys Gissing's letters to her from 10 February 1898 until 22 July 1899. She destroys her diary for almost the whole period of her relationship with Gissing – from 1891 – December 1898, when she makes entries in October and December and then no more until June 1904, six months after Gissing's death.

Gissing meets Gabrielle Fleury in July.

Clara's father dies in December.

1899   'The Age Limit for Women' published.

'Money Wages of Indoor Servants' report discussed in *Labour Gazette*.

Clara promises to be Fleury's friend.

Gissing and Fleury live together.

Clara visits Gissing and Fleury in Paris in October.

1900   Clara moves to 90, Woodside, Wimbledon.

Writes 'Mrs Stetson's Economic Ideal' published in 1902 in *Educated Working Women*.

Writes 'Through 50 Years – The Economic Progress of Women'.

Ernest Gimson marries Emily Thompson.

Clara goes on holiday to Norway.

1901   Working for the British Association for the Advancement of Science on the 'Committee on the Economic Effect of Legislation Affecting Women's Work'.

1902   *Educated Working Women* published incorporating six previously published essays.

Clara begins an appeal for funds to increase the number of staff teaching economics and statistics at University College, London.

Clara involved with the Craft School.

Edith Gissing committed to an asylum. Alfred Gissing moves to foster parents in Cornwall.

1903   Clara promoted to Senior Investigator at the Labour Department.

Writes review on *The Strength of the People* by Helen Bosanquet, in *Economic Review*.

28 December George Gissing dies at Ispoure in South West France.

1904   Begins year of dispute between H.G. Wells and Algernon Gissing and Clara re *Veranilda*.

Gabrielle comes to stay with Clara in May.

Clara attends Booth's celebratory dinner at the Savoy followed by the opera.

Living at 4, Vernon Chambers, Theobald's Road.

1905   Lloyd George President of the Board of Trade.

Clara Secretary of Economic Club.

1906   Wrote 'Motives for Saving' in COS review.

Wrote report to the Earnings and Hours Enquiry.

1907   Arranges for Walter Gissing to work for Ernest Gimson.

Attends National Union of Women Workers conference on

Women's Work.

1908   Sweated Industry Bill – dealings with James Ramsay MacDonald.

Clara gives evidence to the Fair Wages Committee.

Clara's mother dies.

Churchill the new President of the Board of Trade.

Clara visits Alfred Gissing in Exeter.

1909   Has dinner most Fridays or Saturdays with Mr Ibry with whom she has become friendly.

1909   Labour Exchange Act.

Trade Boards Act – Clara gives evidence – results in improved wages for 'sweated workers'.

1910   Resigns from Civil Service because of disagreement over implementation of the Labour Exchange Act. Withdraws her resignation after talk with Llewellyn Smith.

1912   *The Private Life of Henry Maitland* by Morley Roberts is published.

Wilfred Collet (Clara's brother) made Governor of Honduras.

Clara meets Professor Mahalanobis.

Mary Collet (Clara's sister-in-law) dies. Note: her diary says 1912 but genealogy of Collet family says 1910.

1914   'The Professional Employment of Women' published in *Economic Journal.*

1915   Walter writes to Alfred from Clara's address where he is staying prior to going to war.

1916   Walter Gissing killed at Gommecourt – body never identified.

1917   Joins the Beveridge Reconstruction Committee.

Labour Department of Board of Trade becomes the Ministry of Labour. Clara was 'there when [Lloyd George] created it'.

1918   Women over the age of 30 given the right to vote.

On Council for Royal Statistical Society.

1919   Is living at 81, South Hill Park, Hampstead.

1920   Retires from Civil Service but continues on various Trade Boards.

1923   'Obituary: Sir Charles Loch' by Collet in *Economic Review.*

1926   Goes to Ministry, to sit on Trade Board, by hearse as no transport running due to General Strike.

1927   'Some Recollections of Charles Booth', published in *Social Services Review.*

Wilfred Collet dies.

1930	Works again for Hubert Llewellyn Smith collecting information and writes a chapter for his work *New Survey of London Life and Labour*.
1935	Compiles *The History of the Collett Family* with Henry Haines Collett. 'The Present Position of Women in Industry' – read at the Adam Smith Club. Published in *RSS Journal* in 1945.
1936	Has a breast removed and convalesces in Sidmouth. Moves Harold, Caroline, Edith (her brother and sisters in their late seventies and early eighties) to live on a cliff top in Sidmouth.
1940	'Obituary: Henry Higgs' published in *Economic Journal*.
1942	Has the early years of her diary typed and makes additional comments.
1945	'Charles Booth, The Denison Club and H. Llewellyn Smith' published in *RSS Journal*.
1948	Clara died 3 August 1948. Body sent to London for medical research.
1949	*The Letters of John to Eliza* published.

Select Bibliography

Manuscript Collections

Arts and Crafts Archives, Cheltenham Art Gallery and Museum
Gimson Correspondence
British Library
The History of the Collet Family
British Library of Political and Economic Science, London School
of Economics
Beveridge Collection
Booth Collection
New Survey of London MSS
Passfield Papers
Bromley Library
H.G. Wells collection
London Metropolitan Archives
Toynbee Hall Minute Books and Correspondence
The Marshall Library of Economics, University of Cambridge
Collet document 1/2
North London Collegiate School, Edgware, Middlesex
NLCS Archives
Regent College, Regent Road, Leicester
Wyggeston Archives
University of London Library, Senate House
Booth Correspondence MS 797 I/XXXX
University of Warwick, Modern Records Office
Collet MSS

Books and Articles

Adams, Ruth, 'George Gissing and Clara Collet', *Nineteenth-Century Fiction* (June 1956), pp. 72–7.
Barwell, Claire, *Europa Biographical Dictionary of British Women* (1983), entry on Clara Collet.
Besant, Walter, *All Sorts and Conditions of Men – An Impossible Story*

(London: Chatto & Windus, 1882).

Black, Clementina, *Married Women's Work* (London: Virago, 1983).

Booth, C., *Life and Labour of the People in London*, 10 Vols (London: Macmillan, 1892–97).

Bowley, A.L., 'Obituary: Clara E. Collet', *Economic Journal* (June 1950), pp. 408–10.

British Parliamentary Papers, Industrial Relations, Vol. 27, Labour Commission, Session 1892, (Shannon, Ireland: Irish University Press, 1970), pp. 8909–61 and 8845–908 (Booth's evidence on the chapter of his *Life and Labour of the People in London* on 'Women's Work', compiled by Clara E. Collet), pp. 489–92.

British Parliamentary Papers, Industrial Relations, Vol. 43, Labour Commission, Session 1893–94, (Shannon, Ireland: Irish University Press, 1970), Appendix 86 (Summary of 'Pauperism, a Picture; and the Endowment of Old Age, An Argument by Mr Charles Booth', Ch. 5, evidence collected by Clara Collet on 'Pauperism at Ashby-de-la-Zouch'), pp. 988–97.

British Parliamentary Papers, Industrial Relations, Vol. 30, Factories, Session 1894, (Shannon, Ireland: Irish University Press, 1970), ('Statistics of Employment of Women and Girls in England and Wales', by Clara E. Collet), pp. 1–87.

British Parliamentary Papers, Minutes of Evidence Taken Before the Select Committee on Home Work, 26 June 1907, evidence given by Clara E. Collet, pp. 36–50.

British Parliamentary Papers, Minutes of Evidence, Fair Wages Committee, 28 May 1908, evidence given by Clara E. Collet, pp. 284–90 and pp. 311–12.

Churchill, Randolph S., *Winston Churchill: Young Statesman, 1901–1914*, Vol. 2, (London: Heinemann, 1967).

Coats, A.W., 'The Appointment of Pigou as Marshall's Successor: Comment', *Journal of Law and Economics*, Vol. 15, (1972), pp. 487–95.

Collet, C.D., *Diplomatic Review* (Published and printed by C.D. Collet, 1866–77), British Library, Newspaper Library, Colindale, London.

Collet, Clara, E., Letters from Gabrielle Fleury, Collet MSS Warwick University Modern Records Office. Collet 29.

Collet, Clara E., Manuscript diary, Collet MSS Warwick University Modern Records Office. Collet 29/8/1 (1–146).

Collet, Clara E., Ministry of Labour and Board of Trade Official Papers, Collet MSS Warwick University Modern Records Office.

Collet, Clara E., Papers of Collet, Collet MSS Warwick University

Modern Records Office.

Collet, Clara E., Typed diary, 'Diary of a Young Assistant Mistress 1878–85', Collet MSS Warwick University Modern Records Office, MSS29/8/2 (1–81).

Collet, Clara E., 'Undercurrents', (short story written under the pseudonym of Clover King and reprinted by Bouwe Postmus in *The Gissing Journal*), Collet MSS Warwick University Modern Records Office, MSS 29/3/13/4 (1–41).

Collet, Clara E., 'Socialism', *Wyggeston Girls' Gazette* (April 1887), pp. 131–4.

Collet, Clara E., 'The Economics of Shopping', *Wyggeston Girls' Gazette* (July 1887), pp. 151–7.

Collet, Clara E., 'Women's Trade Unions', *Wyggeston Girls' Gazette* (April 1888), pp. 202–4.

Collet, Clara E., 'Extracts from Notes of a Visit to Sheffield', *Wyggeston Girls' Gazette* (July 1888), pp. 227–30.

Collet, Clara E., 'Charity and Strikes', *Charity Organisation Review*, Vol. 5, (1889), pp. 472–3.

Collet, Clara E., 'London Children, (2) Girls (Secondary Education)', *Life and Labour of the People in London*, in Charles Booth, First Series, Poverty III, Blocks of Buildings, Schools, (1889), pp. 290–306.

Collet, Clara E., 'Maria Edgeworth & Charity', *Charity Organisation Review*, Vol. 5, (1889), pp. 418–24.

Collet, Clara E., 'West End Tailoring – Women's Work', *Life and Labour of the People in London*, First Series, Poverty IV, (1889), pp. 149–56.

Collet, Clara E., 'Women's Work', in Charles Booth, *Life and Labour of the People in London*, First Series, Poverty IV, The Trades of East London connected with Poverty. Ch. 9. (London: Macmillan, 1889), pp. 256–327.

Collet, Clara E., 'Working Women in Large Cities', *Charity Organisation Review*, Vol. 6, (1890), pp. 60–5.

Collet, Clara E., 'The Wicked Consumer', *Charity Organisation Review*, Vol. 6, pp. 114–15.

Collet, Clara E., 'Educated Working Women' (Extracts from a lecture delivered by Collet), *Wyggeston Girls' Gazette* (April 1890), pp. 340–4.

Collet, Clara E., 'Looking Backward' (a review of a book by Edward Bellamy), *Wyggeston Girls' Gazette* (July 1890), pp. 6–8.

Collet, Clara E., 'Foreign Competition', *Charity Organisation Review*, Vol. 6, (May 1890), pp. 185–8, (continued July 1890), pp. 285–9.

Collet, Clara, E., 'Salaries of Women Teachers', *Journal of Education*

(1 August 1890) (read and discussed at a meeting of the University Association of Women Teachers), pp. 412–16.

Collet, Clara E., 'Women's Work in Leeds', *Economic Journal*, Vol. 1, Part III, (1891), pp. 460–73.

Collet, Clara E., 'The Occupations of our Mothers and Grandmothers', paper presented at the Toynbee Economic Club (1891). Not known if still available.

Collet, Clara E., 'Strikes and Lockouts, 1889', *Charity Organisation Review*, Vol. 7, (February 1891), pp. 74–81.

Collet, Clara E., 'Wages and the Standard of Living', *Quarterly Journal of Economics*, Vol. 5, (April 1891), pp. 365–8.

Collet, Clara E., 'Charity Organisation', *Charity Organisation Review*, Vol. 7, (May 1891), pp. 210–16.

Collet, Clara E., (as Clover King), 'Over the Way', *Home Chimes* (May 1891), pp. 298–307.

Collet, Clara E., 'Reports of the Massachusetts Bureau of Statistics of Labour on Working Women', *Economic Journal*, Vol. 1, (June 1891), pp. 398–405.

Collet, Clara E., 'Prospects of Marriage for Women', *The Nineteenth Century*, Vol. 31, (June 1891), pp. 537–52.

Collet, Clara E., 'Tutwork and Tribute in West Barbary', *Charity Organisation Review*, Vol. 7, (August 1891), pp. 323–4.

Collet, Clara E., 'George Gissing's Novels: A First Impression', *Charity Organisation Review* (October 1891), pp. 375–80.

Collet, Clara E., 'Three Ideal COS Secretaries', reprinted in *The Gissing Journal*, Vol. 28, No. 2, (April 1892) (under the title 'A Great Deal of Brain to the Square Inch: A Forgotten Essay by Clara Collet', Pierre Coustillas (ed.)).

Collet, Clara E., 'Report by Miss Clara E. Collet (Lady Assistant Commissioner) on the Conditions of Work in London', *Royal Commission on Labour: The Employment of Women*, Parliamentary Paper C–6894 (23) (London: HMSO, 1893), pp. 1–26.

Collet, Clara, E., 'Report by Miss Clara E. Collet (Lady Assistant Commissioner) on the Conditions of Work in Luton and Bristol', *Royal Commission on Labour: The Employment of Women*, Parliamentary Paper C–6894 (23) (London: HMSO, 1893), pp. 27–43.

Collet, Clara, E., 'Report by Miss Clara E. Collet (Lady Assistant Commissioner) on the Conditions of Work in Birmingham, Walsall, Dudley and the Staffordshire Potteries', *Royal Commission on Labour: The Employment of Women*, Paper C–6894 (London, HMSO, 1893), pp. 45–63.

Collet, Clara E., 'Report by Miss Clara E. Collet (Lady Assistant

Commissioner) on the Conditions of Work in Liverpool and Manchester', *Royal Commission on Labour: The Employment of Women*, Parliamentary Paper C–6894 (London: HMSO, 1893), pp. 65–82.

Collet, Clara E., 'Report by Miss Clara E. Collet (Lady Assistant Commissioner) on the Conditions of Employment of Shop Assistants, Milliners, Dressmakers and Mantlemakers in Provincial Towns and of Workers in Certain Miscellaneous Trades in London', *Royal Commission on Labour: The Employment of Women*, Parliamentary Paper C–6894 (London: HMSO, 1893), pp. 83–96.

Collet, Clara E., 'Employment of Women', *Wyggeston Girls' Gazette* (July 1895), pp. 12–17.

Collet, Clara E., 'Statistics of Employment of Women and Girls in Industrial Centres', Parliamentary Paper, *Journal of the Royal Statistical Society*,Vol. 58, (September 1895), pp. 518–28.

Collet, Clara E., 'The Philosophy of Thrift', *Charity Organisation Review* (October 1895), pp. 410–19.

Collet, Clara E., *Family Budgets* (London: P.S. King, 1896).

Collet, Clara E., '(Review of) *Family Budgets*', *Economic Journal*, Vol. 6, (December 1896), pp. 570–3.

Collet, Clara E., 'Report by Miss Collet on changes in the Employment of Women and Girls in Industrial Centres', Parliamentary Paper C–8794 (London: HMSO, 1898).

Collet, Clara E., 'The Collection and Utilisation of Official Statistics Bearing on the Extent and Effects of the Industrial Employment of Women', *Journal of the Royal Statistical Society*, Vol. 61, (June 1898), pp. 219–60.

Collet, Clara E., 'The Expenditure of Middle-class Working Women', *Economic Journal*, Vol. 8, (December 1898), pp. 543–53.

Collet, Clara E., 'Report by Miss Collet on the Money Wages of Indoor Servants', Parliamentary Paper C–9346 (London: HMSO, 1899).

Collet, Clara E., 'Standards of Living and Ideals of Life', *Charity Organisation Review*, Vol. 5, (February 1899) (new series), pp. 75–80.

Collet, Clara, E., 'The Age Limit for Women', *Contemporary Review*, Vol. 76, (December 1899), pp. 868–77.

Collet, Clara, E., 'Through Fifty Years: The Economic Progress of Women', in Eleanor M. Hill and Sophie Bryant (eds), *Frances Mary Buss Schools' Jubilee Record* (London: NLCS, Jubilee Magazine, 1900), pp. 156–60.

Collet, Clara E., 'Mrs Stetson's Economic Ideal', *Charity*

Organisation Review, Vol. 7, (March 1900) (new series), pp. 156–60.

Collet, Clara E., 'Notes and Memoranda: Wages Boards in Victoria', *Economic Journal*, Vol. 9, (December 1901), pp. 557–65.

Collet, Clara E., *Educated Working Women: Essays on the Economic Position of Women Workers in the Middle-Classes* (London: P.S. King, 1902).

Collet, Clara E., 'Review of H. Bosanquet, *The Strength of the People'*, *Economic Review*, Vol. 13, No. 49, (March 1903), pp. 81–4.

Collet, Clara E., 'Motives for Saving', *Charity Organisation Review*, Vol. 19, (June 1906) (new series), pp. 297–305.

Collet, Clara E., 'The Social Status of Women Occupiers', *Economic Journal*, Vol. 71, (September 1908), pp. 513–15.

Collet, Clara E., 'Women in Industry', *Tracts Relating To Women: 1–2* (London: Women's Printing Society, 1911), pp. 3–30.

Collet, Clara E., 'Changes in Wages and Hours of Labour of Women and Girls in Dressmaking Industry in 1906 compared to 1863 – West End' (1912), Modern Records Office, Warwick University. MSS 29/4/1/1–13.

Collet, Clara E., 'Changes in Wages and Hours of Labour of Women and Girls in the Ready-Made Tailoring Trade in 1906 compared to 1863' (1912), MRO, Warwick University. MSS 29/4/2/19–31.

Collet, Clara E., 'Changes in Wages and Hours of Labour in the Dressmaking Industry in 1906 Compared to 1863 – Rest of United Kingdom' (1912), MRO, Warwick University. MSS 29/4/1/32–49.

Collet, Clara E., 'Changes in Wages and Hours of Labour of Women in the Sewing Machine Trades in 1906 Compared to 1863' (1912), MRO, Warwick University, MSS 29/4/2/1–18.

Collet, Clara. E., 'The Professional Employment of Women', *Economic Journal*, Vol. 25, (December 1915), pp. 627–30.

Collet, Clara E., 'Cost of Food for an Adult Woman', *Journal of the Royal Statistical Society*, Vol. 79, (June 1916), pp. 300–3.

Collet, Clara E., Various Minutes and papers relating to her work with the Board of Trade, contained in the 'Beveridge Collection – Reconstruction' (1917), and 'Coll Misc', unpublished (1917–19), British Library of Political and Economic Science (BLPES).

Collet, Clara E., Collet was a signatory to: *Ministry of Reconstruction. Report of the Women's Employment Committee*, Parliamentary Paper (Cd. 9239) (London: HMSO, 1919).

Collet, Clara E., 'Obituary: Sir Charles Loch', *Economic Journal*, Vol.

33, (March 1923), pp. 123–6.

Collet, Clara E., 'Review of F.D. Watson, *The Charity Organisation Movement in the United States*', *Economic Review*, Vol. 33, (September 1923), pp. 410–13.

Collet, Clara E., 'Labour in Indian Industries', A review of a book by Dr Broughton, *Economic Journal*, Vol. 34, (September 1924), pp. 457–9.

Collet, Clara E., 'The Development of Ruskin's Views on Interest', *Economic History*, Vol. 1, (January 1926), pp. 23–33.

Collet, Clara E., 'Some Recollections of Charles Booth', *Social Services Review* (1927), pp. 384–9.

Collet, Clara E., 'Domestic Service', in Hubert Llewellyn Smith (ed.), *New Survey of London Life and Labour*, Vol. 2, (London: P.S. King, 1931), Ch. 8.

Collet, Clara E., 'Herbert Somerton Foxwell: Obituary', *Economic Journal* (December 1936).

Collet, Clara E., 'Colet's Inn at Dublin', *Genealogist Magazine* (September 1938), pp. 143–5.

Collet, Clara E., 'Review of H. Martindale, *Women Servants of the State, 1870–1938*', *Economic Journal*, Vol. 49, (March, 1939), pp. 124–5.

Collet, Clara E., 'Obituary: Henry Higgs', *Economic Journal* (December 1940), pp. 546–61.

Collet, Clara E., 'The Present Position of Women in Industry', *Journal of the Royal Statistical Society*, Part II (June 1942), pp. 122–4.

Collet, Clara E., 'Obituary: Charles Booth, The Denison Club and H. Llewellyn Smith', *Journal of the Royal Statistical Society*, Pts III–IV, (1945), pp. 482–5.

Collet, Clara E. (ed.), *The Letters of John to Eliza: A Four Years' Correspondence Course in the Education of Women* (Privately published, c. 1949).

Collet, Clara E., 'Statistical Survey of Pre-Victorian Novels', n.d. Modern Records Office, Warwick University, MSS 29/3/13/1/2–36. Unpublished, Circa 1945–8.

Collet, Clara E. and Collet, Caroline M., 'Amusements for Evenings at Home', *Wyggeston Girls' Gazette* (December 1885), pp. 46–7.

Collet, Clara E., and Collett H.H., 'The History of the Collett Family' (1935) (Unpublished MS held in British Library).

Collet, Clara E. and Sanger, Dorothy, *Changes in Wages & Conditions of Domestic Servants in Private Families & Institutions in the County of London* (October 1930).

Collet, Sophia Dobson, *The Life and Letters of Raja Rammohan Roy*

(Privately published, 1900).

Comino, Mary, *Gimson and the Barnsleys: Wonderful Furniture of a Commonplace Kind* (London: Evans Brothers, 1980).

Comyn, Marian, 'My Recollections of Karl Marx', *The Nineteenth Century and After*, Vol. 91, (1922), pp. 161–9.

Coustillas, Pierre, 'The Stormy Publication of Gissing's *Veranilda*', *Bulletin of the New York Public Library*, Vol. 72, No. 9, (November 1968), pp. 588–610.

Coustillas, Pierre (ed.), *London and the Life of Literature in Late Victorian England: The Diary of George Gissing, Novelist* (Brighton: Harvester Press, 1978).

Coustillas, Pierre, The Publication of 'The Private Life of Henry Maitland', *Twilight of Dawn: Studies in English Literature in Transition*, O.M. Brack, Jr. (ed.) copyright 1987 The Arizona Board of Regents. Reprinted by permission of the University of Arizona Press.

Coustillas, Pierre, 'Walter Leonard Gissing (1891–1916): An Anniversary', *The Gissing Journal*, Vol. 32, No. 3, (July 1996), pp. 13–23.

Dimand, Mary Ann, Dimand, Robert W. and Forget, Evelyn L. (eds), *Women of Value: Feminist Essays on the History of Women in Economics* (Aldershot: Edward Elgar, 1995).

Dodwell, Professor H.H. (ed.), *The Private Letters and Books of Joseph Collet* (with an introduction and appendix of her family history by Clara E. Collet) (London: Longmans, 1933).

Evans, Dorothy, *Women and the Civil Service* (London: Pitman, 1934).

Frances Mary Buss Schools, *Jubilee Magazine* (1900).

Freeman, Kathleen, *National Council of Women: The First Sixty Years: 1895–1955* (London, June 1955).

Gimson, Sydney, 'Part 1', *Random Recollections of the Leicester Secular Society* (Leicester: Leicestershire Records Office, 1932).

Gissing, George, *Workers in the Dawn* (3 Vols. London: Remington, 1880).

Gissing, George, *The Unclassed* (3 Vols. London: Chapman & Hall, 1884).

Gissing, George, *The Nether World* (3 Vols. London: Smith, Elder, 1889).

Gissing, George, *New Grub Street* (3 Vols. London: Smith, Elder, 1891).

Gissing, George, *Born in Exile* (3 Vols. London: A &C Black, 1892).

Gissing, George, *The Odd Women* (3 Vols. London: Lawrence & Bullen, 1893).

Gissing, George, *The Private Papers of Henry Ryecoft* (London: Constable, 1923).

Gissing, George, *Veranilda* (London: Constable, 1904).

Gissing, George, *Will Warburton* (London: Constable, 1904).

Gissing, George, 'A Lodger in Maze Pond', *The House of Cobwebs* (London: Constable, 1906).

Gissing, George, and Wells, H.G., *A Record of their Friendship and Correspondence* (London: Rupert Hart-Davis, 1961).

Glick, Daphne, *The National Council of Women of Great Britain: The First One Hundred Years – 1895–1994* (London: National Council of Women, 1994).

Goring, Rosemary and Goring, Jeremy, *The Unitarians* (Exeter: Religious and Moral Education Press, An Imprint of Arnold-Wheaton, 1984).

Gould, F.J. *History of the Leicester Secular Society* (Leicester: Leicester Secular Society, 1900).

Greenslade, William, 'Walter Gissing: A Further Note', *The Gissing Journal*, Vol. 34, No. 1, (January 1998), pp. 17–19.

Halperin, John, *Gissing: A Life in Books* (Oxford: Oxford University Press, 1982).

Jones, Gareth Stedman, *Outcast London: A Study in the Relationship between Classes in Victorian Society* (first published 1971; London: Penguin, 1984).

Kapp, Yvonne, *Eleanor Marx, The Crowded Years, 1884–1898*, Vol. 2, (London: Lawrence & Wishart, 1976).

Kapp, Yvonne, *Eleanor Marx, Family Life: 1855–1883*, Vol. 1, (London: Virago, 1979).

Keynes, John Maynard, 'Obituary: Henry Higgs', *Economic Journal* (December 1940), pp. 546–61.

Korg, Jacob, *George Gissing: A Critical Biography* (Seattle, WA: University of Washington Press, 1963).

MacKenzie, Norman and MacKenzie, Jeanne (eds), *The Diary of Beatrice Webb*, Vol. 1, *Glitter Around and Darkness Within* (London: Virago & LSE 1982–86).

Mahalanobis, P.C., 'Obituary: Clara Elizabeth Collet', *Journal of the Royal Statistical Society*, Series A, Vol. III, Part III, 1948, p. 254.

Marshall, Mary P., 'Review of Clara E. Collet, *Educated Working Women*', *Economic Journal*, Vol. 12, (June 1902), pp. 252–7.

Martindale, Hilda, *Women Servants of the State, 1870–1938. A History of Women in the Civil Service* (London: George Allen & Unwin, 1938).

Mattheisen, Paul F., Young, Arthur and Coustillas, Pierre (eds), *The Collected Letters of George Gissing*, Vols. 5, 6, 7, 8 and 9, (Athens,

OH: Ohio University Press, 1994–97).

Mearns, Andrew, *The Bitter Cry of Outcast London* (London: James Clarke, 1883).

Miller, Jane, *Seductions: Studies in Reading and Culture* (London: Virago Press, 1990).

Miller, Jane, *School for Women* (London: Virago Press, 1996).

Mowat, Charles Loch, *The Charity Organisation Society: 1869–1913: Its Ideas and Work* (London: Methuen, 1961).

Nicolaievsky, Boris and Maenchen-Helfen, Otto, *Karl Marx* (London, 1936).

O'Day, Rosemary and Englander, David (eds), *Retrieved Riches: Social Investigation in Britain 1840–1914* (Aldershot: Scolar Press, 1995).

Our Magazine (North London Collegiate School magazine) various entries about Collet from 1878–98.

Parker, Julia, *Women and Welfare: Ten Victorian Women in Public Social Service* (1989).

Pearson, Karl, *Grammar of Science* (London: Walter Scott, 1892).

Picht, Werner, Dr, *Toynbee Hall and the English University Settlement Movement* (trans. Lilian A. Cowell) (London: G. Bell & Sons, 1914).

Postmus, Bouwe, 'Clara Collet's Clairvoyance', *The Gissing Journal*, Vol. 31, No. 4, (October 1995), pp. 1–32.

Prochaska, F.K., *Women and Philanthropy in 19th Century England* (Oxford: Clarendon Press, 1980).

Rawlinson, Barbara, 'Devil's Advocate: George Gissing's Approach to the Woman Question', *The Gissing Journal*, Vol. 33, No. 2, (April 1997), pp. 1–14.

Richards, G. A., *The History and Aims of the Association*, MRO Warwick University, unpublished MSS 59/7/14.

Ridley, Annie E., *Francis Mary Buss and Her Work for Education* (London: Longmans, Green, 1895).

Roberts, J.M., *A History of Europe* (Oxford: Helicon Publishing, 1976).

Roberts, Morley, *The Private Life of Henry Maitland* (London: Eveleigh Nash, 1912).

Robertson, Mary, 'Notes on Books', *Our Magazine* (North London Collegiate School, March 1894), pp. 14–15.

Rumbelow, Donald, *The Complete Jack the Ripper* (London: Guild Publishing, 1987).

Samuels, Warren J., 'Economics as a Science and Its Relation to Policy: The Example of Free Trade', *Journal of Economic Issues*, Vol. 14, No. 1, (March 1980), pp. 163–85.

Sastri, Sivaneth, *The History of the Brahmo Samaj* (Calcutta: Sadharin Brahmo Samaj).

Schulz, William F., *The Unitarian Universalist Pocket Guide* (Boston, MA: Skinner House Books, 1993).

Scrimgeour, R.M., *The North London Collegiate School – 1850–1950: A Hundred Years of Girls' Education*, (Oxford: Oxford University Press, 1950).

Seymour-Jones, Carole, *Beatrice Webb: Woman of Conflict* (London: Allison & Busby, 1992).

Smith, Hubert Llewellyn, *The Board of Trade* (London & New York: G.P. Putnam's & Sons, 1928).

Smith, Hubert Llewellyn, *New Survey of London Life and Labour*, 2 Vols, (London: P.S. King, 1931).

Tomalin, Claire, *The Life and Death of Mary Wollstonecraft* (London: Penguin, 1974 (repr. 1985)), pp. 44–63.

C.T. (Trevelyan, Charles), 'Obituary: Clara Elizabeth Collet', *Journal of the Royal Statistical Society*, Series A, Vol. III, Part III, (1948), pp. 252–3.

Tsuzuki, Chushichi, *The Life of Eleanor Marx, 1855–1898 – A Socialist Tragedy* (Oxford: Clarendon Press, 1967). Reprinted by permission of Oxford University Press.

Vicinus, M., *Independent Women: Work and Community for Single Women, 1850–1920* (London: Virago, 1985).

Webb, Beatrice, *My Apprenticeship* (London: Penguin, 1971).

Webb, Beatrice, *The Diary of Beatrice Webb; Volume One – 1873–1892 – Glitter Around and Darkness Within* (London: Virago, 1982), pp. 87–8.

Wells, H.G., 'George Gissing: An Impression', *Monthly Review* (August 1904), pp. 160–72.

Wells, H.G., 'The Truth About Gissing', *Rhythm, Literary Supplement* (December 1912).

Wells, H.G., Experiment in Autobiography, Vol. 2, (London: Victor Gollancz & Cresset Press, 1934).

Whitbread, Hilary and Zanker, Kathryn (eds), *Wyggeston Girls' Centenary: 1878–1978* (Rushden: Regent College, 1978).

Women's Co-operative Guild Report 1903–1914 Coll. Misc. 657/3 British Library of Political and Economic Science, London School of Economics.

Zimmeck, Meta, 'Strategies & Stratagems for the Employment of Women in the British Civil Service 1919–1939', *Historical Journal*, Vol. 27, No. 4, (1984), pp. 901–24.

Index

1. Most references are to Clara Collet and the influences on her life.
2. CC is used as an abbreviation for Clara Elizabeth Collet.
3. Page numbers in italics refer to portraits or illustrations.